COPEAU

Texts on Theatre

Berthold Mahn 1920

Jacques Copeau lisant "Saül" à André Gide

Frontispiece Jacques Copeau giving a public reading of *Saul*
by André Gide; drawing by Berthold Mahn.

COPEAU

Texts on Theatre

*Edited and translated by John Rudlin
and Norman H. Paul*

London and New York

First published 1990
by Routledge
11 New Fetter Lane, London EC4P 4EE

Simultaneously published in the USA and Canada
by Routledge
a division of Routledge, Chapman and Hall, Inc.
29 West 35th Street, New York, NY 10001

Typeset in 10/12pt Garamond by
Ponting–Green Publishing Services, London
Printed and bound in Great Britain by
T. J. Press (Padstow) Ltd Padstow, Cornwall

British Library Cataloguing in Publication Data
Copeau, Jacques, *1879–1949*
Copeau: Texts on theatre.
1. Theatre. Directing
I. Title   II. Rudin, John III.   Paul, Norman H.
792.0233

Library of Congress Cataloging in Publication Data
Copeau, Jacques, *1879–1949*
Copeau: Texts on theatre.
p.   cm.
Includes bibliographical references.
1. Theater audiences.   2. Criticism.   I. Title.
PN1590.A9B48   1990   89-10955
792'.01–dc20

ISBN 0-415-05253-X

CONTENTS

v

Part II   The theatre

FIGURES

Frontispiece Jacques Copeau giving a public reading of *Saul* by André Gide; drawing by Berthold Mahn.

INTRODUCTION

In his *Journal* for 20 December 1943, Jacques Copeau wrote:

I shall be sixty-five on 4 February 1944. It is time I get started; just like that, without knowing where I am going. The chief thing is to get down to the task and try to see it through to the end. For a long time now, I have been burning with the need, not to narrate my life-story nor to write my memoirs in well-ordered chapters, but to throw pell-mell into a series of volumes everything I have done and not done, learned and thought about, imagined, composed, failed at, succeeded in; that is, to confess completely to myself and to God, for posterity if it preserves this jumble or, lacking that, for my friends and family; the whole thing under the title of *Registres*.[1]

This project goes back to the first years of the Vieux Colombier, that is about thirty years ago. I had understood at that time that, being engaged in active life to the limit and often beyond my capabilities, simultaneously director and actor, poet and technician, failed writer determined not to be one (failed, that is), creator of images and dreamer of ideas, critic and adventurer (as Péguy used to call me), I should never have time to write books. Yet, it seemed to me that I had something to say and that posterity would not refuse to listen to it, that it might perhaps even be interested. Especially, I was not resigned, and am not still, to having produced only perishable, ephemeral things, remembered only by a few of my contemporaries through the distortions, failings or exaggerations of their own memory. [...] I have spoken often of this project to those about me, and it has constantly been put off over the last five years.

That is why I am plunging into it now, refusing to reflect any longer, and why I am writing this Preface...

Copeau intended to include in his book a 'little of everything from all periods of my life, from my earliest memories and writings to my most recent achievements'. In a letter to Roger Martin du Gard he referred to it as 'a great, sprawling volume'. But, due to a chronic illness, undiagnosable at the time, such concerted use of his faculties was beyond his powers in the last years: when he died five years later, Copeau's *Registres* were still in the project stage. The work on his papers was later taken up by his nephew Michel Saint-Denis, only to be interrupted by his own death in 1971. It has since been continued by Copeau's daughter, Marie-Hélène Dasté and his niece and secretary, Suzanne Maistre Saint-Denis, with the assistance of several scholars.[2] In her Preface to *Registres I* the former quotes her father recounting a dream:

> I was seated opposite a painter's easel and, with each brush-stroke, he was drawing the falsest image of me. I started by laughing at it, and then I became alarmed, but too late. The finished portrait had already been titled. I understood that henceforth, in order to be recognised in the world, I would have to model my traits on those of this grotesque face.

Four volumes of *Registres* have so far been published with the intention of preventing that dream from becoming a prophecy. Marie-Hélène's Preface continues:

> Jacques Copeau's work, which continues to live unrecognised by most and in particular by the young, has been partially disfigured through the years, and the very influence that it exerted has often obscured or travestied his thinking.
>
> By the publication of his *Registres*, we wish to retrace the itinerary of his impassioned search, to survey its passage through his work, to rediscover his ideas in their original freshness and energy, to show that he unceasingly sought to create a new dramaturgy based on the stage and the actor, to restore the dramatic poet to his rightful position, and the theatre to its proper existence independent of literature.
>
> We shall seek to bring out this 'profound intuition' which led him to open up so many paths towards the birth of that 'drama of modern times' which he constantly called for.

We cannot claim to give these *Registres* either the form or the density they would have had if Copeau had edited them himself [...], but we can attempt to present them in a spirit close to that which he has indicated to us.

The present anthology in English draws on the extensive materials made available through those first four volumes of *Registres* and also the final two, currently in preparation, as well as on other published and unpublished sources. The editors wish to thank Marie-Hélène Dasté for her generous assistance and permission to quote from the material in her private collection at Pernand-Vergelesses, as well as from the documents deposited in the Fonds Copeau at the Département des Arts du Spectacle of the Bibliothèque de l'Arsenal in Paris. Since Copeau's thinking remained remarkably consistent throughout his career, a thematic rather than a chronological approach has been adopted. The bulk of what has hitherto been published about Copeau, particularly in English, has concerned his work as a theatre director. Since he himself always regarded having begun with the founding of a theatre rather than its school as a necessary expedient, we have allowed ourselves the luxury he could not afford of having his writings on the education of the actor as an exordium.

Part One, 'The School', shows that when Copeau was able to experiment in the setting up of such an education, it was not to provide for the theatre of the present, but to prepare for a future art of performance which, despite the subsequent efforts of directors such as Grotowski, Barba and Mnouchkine and the influence of Schools such as that of Jacques Lecoq, does not yet obtain in the present. Part Two, 'The Theatre', concerns the manner in which Copeau brought to his Vieux Colombier enterprise his own austere literary tastes, high artistic standards and the principle that staging should be subordinate to the play itself. Part Three, 'Past and Future Forms', reveals how, since he had an almost religious conception of drama as the most difficult and highest form of a collective art, his search for artistic perfection led him to abandon the exploitation of any isolated innovation (which might have led to sterile repetition for the sake of material success), in order to pursue his higher ideal of 'the renewal of man in the theatre'. It was a question, he believed, of recovering the idea of the Chorus, in the antique meaning of the word: 'A technical pre-occupation of a fundamental kind brought us straight back to the source of inspiration: the Chorus is the mother-cell of all dramatic poetry, and it was from poetry that we had gone astray.'[3] This view necessitated a development of a complete education for the actor (as opposed to a 'dramatic training'). 'For the purposes of Art', he wrote in the 1921 brochure for the Vieux Colombier School,[4] 'education is a more important factor than vocation. And this is as true for theatrical art as it is for any other.'

Note on translation: 'réalisation' has normally been rendered as 'production', 'mise en scène' left as *mise en scène*, but 'metteur en scène' given as 'director'. The Fonds Copeau in the Bibliothèque de l'Arsenal in Paris is abbreviated FC, and the Marie-Hélène Dasté collection at Pernand-Vergelesses, as M-H D. The *Nouvelle Revue Française* is commonly referred to as the *NRF*, the *Cahiers Renaud-Barrault* as *CRB*. All publications Paris unless otherwise indicated, all text by Copeau unless italicised. An attribution 'from' indicates that less than the whole original work has been quoted and lacunae during an extract are indicated '[...]'.

Every attempt has been made to trace the ownership of copyright of quotations made from works other than those by Copeau.

CHRONOLOGY

1879	(4 February) Jacques Copeau born in Paris.
[1887	André Antoine founds the Théâtre-Libre]
[1888	Constantin Stanislavsky founds Society of Art and Literature in Moscow]
[1889	Otto Brahm founds the Freie Bühne in Berlin]
1889–97	Copeau studies at the Lycée Condorcet, often attending the Théâtre-Libre, the Comédie-Française and the Châtelet; sees Sarah Bernhardt and Mounet-Sully; writes short naturalistic plays; fails oral examination, repeats final year.
[1891	Paul Fort founds the Symbolist Théâtre d'Art. J. T. Grein founds the Independent Theatre in London]
[1893	Lugné-Poë founds the Théâtre de l'Oeuvre]
1897	Performance of Copeau three-act drama, *Brouillard du Matin*, by Condorcet students receives enthusiastic review from Sarcey, reigning critic of *Le Temps*, who hails him as the new Dumas *fils*.
1897–9	Copeau enrolled at Sorbonne, fails written examination; continues to write plays and attend the theatre; on a visit to London with his father, sees Forbes-Robertson and Mrs Patrick Campbell in *Hamlet*.
[1898	Stanislavsky and Nemirovich-Danchenko found Moscow Art Theatre]
[1899	Publication of Adolphe Appia's *Die Musik und die Inscenierung*]
1901	Copeau begins *La Maison Natale*, an autobiographical drama; publishes his first theatre reviews.
1902	Elopes to Copenhagen to marry Agnès Thomsen; birth of Marie-Hélène.

Moscow. The Washington Square Players founded in
New York]

1915   Copeau visits Craig in Florence, Dalcroze, Appia, Igor
Stravinsky and Georges Pitoëff in Geneva; corresponds
with Jouvet on plans for a new stage; opens first tentative
drama school with Suzanne Bing; begins plans for new
form of improvised comedy.

1916   Lectures and directs plays in Geneva; visits Dalcroze
School; accepts government proposal for propaganda
tour of Vieux Colombier in America, but unable to
obtain release of actors from service, decides on lecture
tour.

1917   Six-month lecture tour: in New York, Columbia, Little
Theatre, Drama League, Washington Square Players,
Yale, G. P. Baker's '47 Workshop at Harvard; Otto Kahn
offers to finance company tour; summer spent in Paris
reorganising company, preparing repertoire, supervising
(by correspondence) the reconstruction of the Garrick
Theatre in New York; season opens in New York in
November.

1918   Kahn accepts financing of second season, offers country
house in New Jersey for summer lodging and rehearsals
for entire company; first season ends with two-week
tour of Washington and Philadelphia; second season
opens in October.

1919   Copeau dismisses Dullin from the company; lectures at
Cleveland Playhouse, Smith College, Chicago Drama
League. Season ends in April, succeeded at Garrick by
the newly formed Theatre Guild; returns to France to
plan re-opening in Paris; translates Shakespeare's *Winter's
Tale* for opening.

1920   Vieux Colombier re-opens in February; two-month
summer tour of forty-two cities; new season in October;
Copeau receives government subsidy; School opens; publication of first *Cahier du Vieux Colombier*, 'Les Amis
du Vieux Colombier'. [Piscator founds the Volksbühne
in Berlin, Meyerhold directs the Free Theatre Company
in Moscow, Firmin Gémier founds the Théâtre National
Populaire]

1921   Lectures in Holland and Belgium on work of Vieux
Colombier; Kenneth MacGowan visits; Pitoëff invited

by Copeau to produce *Uncle Vanya*; two-week summer tour of French Occupation Zone in Germany; season begins October; Jules Romains appointed director of School; publication of second *Cahier*, 'L'Ecole du Vieux Colombier'. [Gaston Baty founds La Chimère, Dullin founds l'Atelier]

1922   Lectures in France, Belgium and at the International Theatre Exhibition in Amsterdam; Dullin invited to present first productions of his Atelier at the Vieux Colombier; receptions for Eleonora Duse and Stanislavsky at Vieux Colombier; two-month summer tour of France, Germany and Switzerland; Jouvet leaves company to direct the Comédie des Champs-Elysées; Vieux Colombier season begins October; second company created for provincial tours.

1923   Copeau gives dramatic readings and lectures at the School; takes over direction after dismissal of Romains; second company on tour in Belgium, Holland and French provinces; Brussels Théâtre du Marais invited to Vieux Colombier; one-month summer tour of Switzerland and provinces; season begins end October; première of Copeau's *La Maison Natale*; publication of his selected reviews, *Critiques d'un autre temps*.

1924   Dramatic readings at School; pupils give first presentation for Friends of the Vieux Colombier – a Japanese Noh, attended by Gide and Granville Barker; Copeau announces closure of School in May; two-week summer tour of provinces; transfers company to Jouvet; death of Copeau's mother and brother-in-law; retires to Morteuil (Burgundy), with several pupils and a few members of Vieux Colombier company to pursue research.

1925   Dramatic readings and lectures to help finance 'Les Copiaus'; first performance in Burgundy villages; Copeau assumes direction from Michel Saint-Denis, moves to Pernand-Vergelesses, organises training curriculum.

1926   Dramatic readings and lectures: first tour of 'Les Copiaus' in Switzerland, première of Copeau's *L'Illusion*; begins preparation of Molière edition (10 vols, 1929); accepts invitation of Theatre Guild to direct *Karamazov* in New York.

1927 Lectures to American Laboratory Theatre and Theatre Guild; resumes dramatic reading in France, Switzerland, Denmark, Belgium and England; acts in mystery play in Chartres; two-month tour of 'Les Copiaus' in France, Belgium, Holland and Switzerland. [Formation of Cartel of directors by Jouvet, Pitoëff, Dullin and Baty. Artaud founds the Théâtre Alfred Jarry]

1928 Marriage of Marie-Hélène and Jean Dasté; Copeau begins monthly series of articles for *La Nación*, Buenos Aires (to 1941); 'Les Copiaus' on tour in Belgium, Switzerland and England.

1929 Dramatic readings in Holland, Belgium and France; 'Les Copiaus' on tour in France and Switzerland; Copeau dissolves the company; press campaign fails to have Copeau named director of Comédie-Française; publishes preface to Diderot's *Paradoxe sur le Comédien*.

1930 Dramatic readings and lectures in Switzerland and Belgium; Saint-Denis founds the 'Compagnie des Quinze'. [Léon Chancerel founds the 'Compagnie des Comédiens Routiers']

1931 Publication of *Souvenirs du Vieux Colombier*; dramatic readings and lectures in Belgium and France; failure of plan for union of avant-garde theatres; publishes Prefaces to Musset's plays and Shakespeare's *The Tempest*. [Foundation of Group Theatre in New York]

1932 Dramatic readings and lectures in France, Belgium, Holland; named professor at Brussels Conservatory; directs *Jeanne*, by H. Duvernois, in Paris.

1933 Dramatic readings and lectures in Belgium, Switzerland, Italy, France, Algeria, Tunisia and Morocco; directs *Miracle of Saint Uliva* at Maggio Fiorentino; leaves Brussels Conservatory; begins weekly reviews for *Nouvelles Littéraires* (to 1935).

1934 Dramatic readings and lectures in France, Switzerland and Italy; directs Gide's *Persephone* at Paris Opera, *As You Like It* at Dullin's Atelier Theatre; publishes Preface to Stanislavsky's *My Life in Art*.

1935 Directs *Savonarola* at Maggio Fiorentino; unsuccessful project for a repertory theatre in Paris.

1936 Directs *Much Ado About Nothing* in Paris; acts in films for first time; named co-director of Comédie-Française with Baty, Dullin and Jouvet; directs *Le Misanthrope* at the Comédie-Française.

1937   Directs *Trompeur de Seville*, by André Obey; Racine's *Bajazet* at the Comédie-Française; readings and lectures on a cruise to Athens; directs François Mauriac's *Asmodée* at the Comédie-Française. [Jean Dasté and André Barsacq found the 'Compagnie des Quatre Saisons']

1938   Readings and lectures; directs Italian translation of *As You Like It* at Maggio Fiorentino; named examiner at Paris Conservatory; conflict with Claudel ends in abandoning production of *l'Annonce faite à Marie* at Comédie-Française; directs Roger Martin du Gard's *Testament du Père Leleu* at Comédie-Française. [Artaud publishes *Le Théâtre et son Double*]

1939   Trip to Madagascar to visit daughter Edi in convent; publication of translation of Shakespeare's tragedies (five volumes); begins monthly articles for *Le Figaro* (to 1940).

1940   Readings and lectures in Belgium, Holland, Greece, Bulgaria, Romania and Turkey; named interim director of Comédie-Française; directs *Le Misanthrope, Un Caprice, Le Carosse du Saint-Sacrement, Le Pacquebot Tenacity, Twelfth Night*, and engages Jean-Louis Barrault for *Le Cid*.

1941   German occupation authorities discharge Copeau from Comédie-Française for anti-Nazi sympathies; publication of *Le Théâtre Populaire*; begins writing *Le Petit Pauvre* and translating Shakespeare's Comedies.

1942   Finishes *Le Petit Pauvre*; begins work on his *Registres*; directs diction classes at radio school in Beaune.

1943   Directs *Le Miracle du Pain Doré* for 500th anniversary of Hospices de Beaune; begins play on Mary, Queen of Scots for Marie-Hélène.

1944   Lecture to theatre students in Paris.

1945   Records readings and memoirs for radio.

1946   Publication of *Le Petit Pauvre*; readings and lectures in Belgium; André Barsacq revives *Les Frères Karamazov* at the Atelier. [French government creates subsidies for provincial theatre centres in an effort to decentralise productions; as an outcome, Jean Dasté directs the Centre Dramatique in Saint-Etienne. In Paris, the Renaud-Barrault company opens at the Théâtre Marigny]

[1947 First Edinburgh Festival. Jean Vilar founds the Festival d'Avignon. Piccolo Teatro founded in Milan. Actors Studio in New York. Michel Saint-Denis sets up the Old Vic Theatre centre and the Young Vic in London]

1949 French theatre figures celebrate Copeau's 70th birthday; Copeau dies in Beaune, 20 October; Dullin dies in Paris, 11 December.

Part I
THE SCHOOL

1

THE CHILD AT PLAY

In 1913 when Jacques Copeau wrote his manifesto announcing the opening of the Vieux Colombier Theatre, 'An Attempt at Dramatic Renovation',[1] formal actor training was virtually unknown in France, or indeed anywhere else in Europe. In France it was practically limited to the 'Conservatoire National de Musique et de Déclamation', founded in 1795, principally to teach actors the elocution techniques necessary for entry into the Comédie-Française. André Antoine, director of the Théâtre Libre (1887–94) and subsequently of the Théâtre Antoine, had already severely criticised the Conservatoire's methods:

> *Each student received only about ten hours of personal attention a year. [...] Then again the teaching is limited to a small number of scenes from classic plays and roles are assigned indifferently to all temperaments. It is possible for a student to work on a single part for three years, and on the strength of that, win the grand prix, and be elected to the troupe of the Comédie-Française.[2]*

Furthermore, students were not admitted on merit, but through influence, as Antoine himself had discovered when he tried to gain entrance.

Copeau now stated his belief that there could be little hope of the theatre of the future again becoming a vital socio-cultural force unless it were provided with (and indeed provided by) actors who were not only properly trained exponents of their medium, but had also been educated for the expression of it from an early age. With the model of Stanislavsky's Moscow Art Theatre School in mind, he declared in his manifesto:

3

Our intention is to open an acting school at the same time as the theatre, alongside it, and on the same principles.

But it was only through the public work of the new theatre that those principles could be made known, and the need for a teaching laboratory in which to develop them become manifest. Regretfully, he continued,

It is to be feared that the pressure of work at the beginning of our enterprise will prevent us from perfecting the project of the school. As soon as we can, we will give it our full attention. At that time we will reveal our plans in a subsequent article.[3]

Thus, as a temporary expedient, the Theatre had to precede the School which, in an ideal world, would have furnished the actors for its first company. The opening season of productions at the Vieux Colombier Theatre lasted for eight months, from October 1913 to May 1914, culminating in the enormous success of the production of Twelfth Night. *The 1914/15 season was in preparation when war broke out. Copeau contended that his first attempt at 'dramatic renovation' had been justified by its success, but – as he had already announced in the 1913 manifesto – the work was only provisional, waiting for its full expression on the new methods which would emerge from the Vieux Colombier School. That School, when fully operational, would be*

free of charge, and we will assemble there very young people, even children, and some men and women who have a love and instinct for the theatre, but who will not yet have compromised that instinct by the defective methods and habits of the profession. Such a contingent of new forces will later make up the substance of our company.

The ideal would be to start with the children: they might sometimes work alongside the apprentice actors, but they would also receive, ab initio, a dramatic education for which their own untutored play would be the inspiration, as Copeau's own childhood imaginings had been for his adult conception of theatre. It is, therefore, appropriate to begin this anthology with an amalgam of his own early reminiscences and the dramatic significance which he later considered them to have contained.

A SACRED ORIGIN

What can I bring you? A testimony, that's all.

I have been through all the experiences of a man whose very life has been identified with the theatre, whose every thought had the theatre for its object. I am justified in thinking that the daydreams of my childhood were as full of dramatic forms as the night-long hours of insomnia of my adulthood. I cannot tell whence came this first, irresistible attraction that I felt for the theatre. It was evident in all the tastes and habits of my childhood. Since then, I have often thought about the essence of the dramatic sensibility, of the nature of that irresistible movement which makes us, as Nietzsche puts it, 'live through souls and bodies other than our own'.[4] The primitive tribesman who throws himself down before the rising sun or accompanies the last rays of the day with a mournful chant, the child who, in sheer bodily delight, jumps and shouts for joy on a spring morning: that is where to find the origin of exultation. Whatever may have been, as one century followed another, the forms that dramatic inspiration and play have assumed, let us not forget that they have a sacred origin deep in the heart of man.

[From the first of three lectures (in English) to the American Laboratory Theatre,[5] New York, 9, 16, 26 January 1927, M-H D]

THE CHILDHOOD HOME

The windows of the house where I was born, on the Faubourg Saint-Denis, Paris, opened on one side upon some low roofs, absolutely flat and uniformly grey. To the child I was at the time, this level surface presented a vast field, limited only at the far end by a high, narrow wall with a single opening, rather like Mélisande's tower, or a sketch by Gustave Doré, or again like a Gordon Craig set. To the left, the field was open to the breezes, clouds and sounds, with a little tree that was dark coloured in winter and light in the spring. It would have been completely bare, like a desert sunrise or a stage after the performance, if there were not, to the right just below my window, a small building, dark and sordid, festooned with dirty linen, which attracted my curiosity. Through its clouded window I could hear voices, which were almost always raised in anger, and sometimes I could see in the dusk the bare arm of a woman, slowly twisting her hair with her hand.

On the other side of my house, the other slope of my kingdom, was a sunken courtyard filled with boxes and barrels. From morning till night, I could see a man bent over, wrapping and unwrapping dishes with a clear, regular clinking, amid a pile of straw and multi-coloured papers. For me the whole apartment was like a theatre. In my leisure hours of solitude and boredom, I sought long and carefully the discovery of I don't know what secret.

I remember a secluded corner where a sombre tapestry conjuring up a forest in autumn hung on one wall, and by the other stood a sideboard impregnated with the odours of wax and various foods. There the child would crouch, as if in a fireplace, sending up the dense smoke of his dreams.

The living room, which was almost always dark, solemn and unfathomable, harboured for me pleasures of the imagination that were even more mysterious. Large chairs under grey covers slept on the edges of the carpet like monsters on the sea-shore. There were golden reflections and, way at the back, on a dark cabinet, there was a piece of blue crystal which sparkled like an underwater plant.

The mind of the child wanders amid such semblances. He links his own fairyland to the bits of reality that he observes with a relentless eye and absorbs with a bold heart. This is the way we compose our first dramas, which we try out in our games and mull over in silence. The original crucible where we forge the creative power which stays with us all our lives, though often diminished, is to be found in the impregnable silence of the child, his sad reveries, his faculty for furnishing a refuge for his anticipations under a table or in a cupboard. From our twentieth or twenty-fifth year on, we no longer invent anything. We cease to control our life; it controls us! Even then, if it were only life that controls us! But it's our career, our *métier*. We expend the treasures we accumulated under the protection of our youthful guisings. We reveal one by one all the secrets of our childhood and adolescence. [...]

Then I'd lean out of the window. From that height the slightest movement of people or the displacement of objects distorted their appearance with a strangeness that filled me with expectation and wonder. Before I ever became aware of the ferocity of the Shake-spearean world, I used to gaze at the big cats in the well of a courtyard as they fought with a regal fury over scraps of offal...

Then, in the spring, the curtains would open onto the windows of the neighbouring house. The singing of several canaries seemed a real signal of the season's arrival. Neatly arranged in columns, one above the other like figures to be totalled, one could take in at a glance five vestibules, five living-rooms, all alike. One could hear the doorbells ring. One saw the doors open, the errand-boy from the *Bon Marché* store delivering his little packages, the children returning from school, the master of the house taking off his alpaca coat before sitting down to lunch, and the lady of the house busying herself at various tasks, in her morning dress or her flannel-ette house-coat, hair up in curl-papers. When everyone had gone out, around the middle of the afternoon, sometimes the housemaids would come to the window, loosening their blouses, to take the air.

It was in this way that my childhood curiosity was bathed in a reality of gestures, little events and actions that taught me about life, or at least helped me to imagine it. I never tired of these spectacles, however unimportant or unremarkable they might be. They filled my mind with those minute details, indications and life-like nuances through which dramatic characters allow themselves to have sub-stance and through which their emotions are revealed.

Alone, I would try to reproduce certain attitudes exactly, making myself give them the inner feelings that I supposed they required. One day, when a friend arrived unannounced while my mother was in the middle of sewing, I observed from a secluded corner the two women exchanging confidences in low voices. With a sorrowful expression, my mother lowered her head and, murmuring some-thing in a mournful voice, continued to cut some material into thin strips with a mechanical movement of her right hand. This regular, vacant gesture, and the light sound of the scissors in the material, seemed undoubtedly to me to be an irreplaceable accompaniment to the melancholy expression that had moved me. The next day, seeking to re-enact it, I succeeded in putting myself into that situation only by using a pair of nail-scissors with which I proceeded to cut up a few inches of my suit into little pieces. Ask actors. They will tell you that, very often, the right prop contributes better than any effort of the imagination to the induction of that internal attitude which we refer to as our emotional sincerity...

I spent my holidays in the countryside, where the dried bed of a brook seemed altogether ideal for the recitation of episodes from the *Iliad*, brandishing small rocks and branches the while. The tops of rows of linden trees served as a leafy bower where I would imprison my little playmate in order to tell her stories or secrets.... I also recall the attic where we would go to listen to the patter of a rainstorm on the roof-tiles; the empty stable where we conversed secretly like animals tethered to the crib; the darkened laundry room where I would light fireworks at the risk of setting the house on fire.

In these and thousands of other theatres, I would seek the stirring of a secret fibre, the exaltation of something resembling flesh, the love of human beings and of nature, with the urge to escape, to become transformed, or to be consumed, or to sacrifice oneself. I was transforming life. I would put everything into every action and seek out partners. Everything that rose up in my imagination, everything that had troubled my heart, or my mind, everything that I had learned, felt, invented, I had to act out immediately; to the end, whatever the risk. Not that I lacked accomplices to join me in my fantasies, but that they would not follow me long or far enough. They would stop playing either from fatigue, lack of conviction and concentration, or from fear, for I wanted to plunge into the fiction so deeply and so far as to be able to lose myself, to the point where it was difficult to return...

I never had need of a lot of artificial preparation or complicated scenery in order to summon up drama or comedy. The form of a piece of furniture or the colour of a curtain created the stage characters for me, already determining their situation and even outlining their character. The corner of a garden path would make me envisage a meeting. An aroma, a strain of music, often opened up the spatial possibilities of a drama for me.

It is because of these games which filled my childhood and the leisure times of my youth, games which mixed reality and poetry, that I believe I had to rediscover and pursue them, that, smitten by the theatre at the same time as by life, I approached it rather late and asked of it perhaps more than it can give. And, undoubtedly, it was so that nothing impure, gross or brutal could offend these fantasies I used to dream up, that I wanted to undo and reconstruct the instrument of the theatre, as a child takes apart a toy as a diversion, one might say, from its original purpose, its accepted use, and to force it to become something approaching a higher fancy of the mind.

[A composite of selections from lectures given to the Theatre Guild, New York, 23 January 1927 (unpublished) and to the Société des Annales, Paris, 3 February 1933 (published in *Conferencia*, Apr. 1, 1933); first published and reprinted in this form in *Registres I*, pp. 35–40]

DRAMATIC ASPIRATION

Encourage children in their play, the creative activity of free and happy children in a new world every hour of their imaginative existence. Understand, stimulate, develop in them the need for diversion which is really a dramatic aspiration. Such is the very simple attitude we take, thereby following the best of modern educational methods.[6] It is a question of encouraging simultaneously and harmoniously certain faculties which no amount of specialisation later will be able to warp. Gymnastics, dancing, singing, painting and drawing, architecture, a taste for costume, poetry, improvisation, are among those pastimes which can easily become part of a child's activity without any representation or ambition for a diploma, but solely for their own sakes, through inner need or exuberance. When these are added to the study of languages, of geometry, of history, of weaving, of clay modelling, of the other sciences and crafts, the child's education is well planned. Acquaintance with, love and respect for the great dramatic masterpieces, these come before any fancy for interpretation. The need for self-expression when there is an outlet, springs from the very soul of the child, unfolds according to his imaginative processes, and later becomes mingled, when he is attentive, with the memories of his reading and the stories told to him, of the figures of history, of romance and legend, of the characters of his own dreams and those which he has seen about him which he transforms and parodies. All this is within him, lives within him. It is his heritage. Never will he find himself, later in life, face to face with a literary work as an object of interpretation. No. All works are *within* him. He does not have to change towards them. He continues to be himself, he does not cease to exist the moment that the fiction takes possession of his gestures, of his thought, and of all his reactions. ...

I have beside me three children[7] whose unconscious genius amazes me. I have seen them create without effort, forms, colours, objects, costumes and disguises, invent actions, plots, people and characters, in a word transfigure everything that came near them. I have seen their taste form itself with perfect surety without having the least effect on their *naïveté*. I have seen their example inspire other children of their own age to mingle with their play, and rejuvenate adults who came to take part in their entertainments which they celebrated with an antique candour.

That is why I believe that without scientific pedantry, without

9

scholastic theories, merely with good sense, sound faith and love, we may gradually be able to form in future days a miniature college of beautiful, innocent and robust children, capable of creating a pure tradition and endowing the art of theatre with a religious dignity.

[From 'Children and the Future Art of Theatre', *The Modern School*, New York, October 1918, pp. 294–5]

TOWARDS A NEW CONCEPT OF THEATRICAL INTERPRETATION
(Ideas for the founding of a Vieux Colombier School)

Our own children. We have our eyes on them. We should take them right now and devote all our care to them, if we want to see the dawn of a dramatic renaissance. For I predict that when they go up on the stage, we shall see things that we have never seen before...

So let us welcome our pupils from the ages of 10–12.

From all social strata, children from the working class, the middle class or from artistic parents. City, provinces, countryside.

Someone objects: What! Without waiting for a sense of vocation to develop?

Precisely in order to prevent such a sense developing.

What is called 'vocation' for the theatre, nine times out of ten, does not warrant being encouraged. Such a vocation is already a deformation. [...] I knew, once, a stupid young lady, unable to recognise 'a doublet from a pair of breeches' who wrote Comedy with a 'K' and Conservatoire with a double 'S'. She had a penchant for 'declaiming'. She took medication to acquire a tragic pallor and her vocation began with her make-up.

This is the kind of candidate we have for the theatre. Rotten to the core.

We are intervening in the children's lives in order to prevent them becoming like that.

Once registered in the Vieux Colombier School we would take complete charge of them.

You object: But how can you be sure that, from a twelve-year old child, a dramatic vocation will develop?

I answer: The school's atmosphere will propitiate such a development.

It will not be a school for actors, but for theatre artists: dancers, musicians, mimes, stage managers, scene-painters, costume designers, carpenters, stage-hands, etc.

There will inevitably be drop-outs.

Objection: Even supposing that I can make use of my pupils' natures, through the influence of education and atmosphere, this will reduce the part played by individual talent to a minimum.

Answer: The great actor of the future will not come from this school. I am not looking for *the great personality*, the *great individualist*.

There is only one great personality, one great individual who has the right to dominate the stage: that is the poet;[8] and through him the dramatic work itself.

My aim is to propitiate, to exalt the work, and for that purpose to form a brotherhood of artists who will be its servants.

I care little for the great actor. If pressed I should say that in every age the great actor was the enemy of dramatic art. For great dramatic art what is needed is not a great actor, but *a new conception of dramatic interpretation*.

Do not suppose that I am going to give them a technical education, hypnotise them with the fact that they are being called on to become actors. On the contrary.

Preserve them from theatricality.

Keep them normal.

Give them an all-round upbringing.

And draw them towards the great art of theatre without their suspecting it, so to speak.

General education. Not a special branch of teaching more arid than the others. Class hours mixed with play-time, manual work and games. [...] From the diversity of teaching will come amusement, emulation, joy. All instruction to be like a big game, where one feels more and more carried away by the development of one's faculties.

Let it not smack of pedagogy.

Play should remain as free as possible.

The entire experience of the child comes from playing.

He chooses a game according to his inclination, his personality.

He is sincere and true to himself.

The more a child is tutored, the richer his imagination, the more musical he becomes and the more he imagines things plastically, the more he is able to make things with his hands, and, in addition, the more his body becomes supple, trained, rich in responses, the more his play will be rich in adventures, inventions, and the more it will be varied and *dramatic*.

Few pupils.

So as not to have to direct them from too great a distance.

Rather like a family.

While looking at my own children.

Playing.

Children teach us authentic inventiveness.

Enhance their games, excite them without joining in too much.

Help them.

If their imagination slackens for lack of an accessory, suggest a prop they might use.

Edi's sword.[9] No patience to make a beautiful one. I help her make it. She sees my patience, my care. I let her wait a long time for it.

Dreams will grow around the sword. From the love she has for it is born the character of the Knight.

We observe the children at play. They teach us. Learn everything from children. Impose nothing on them. Take nothing away from them. Help them in their development without their being aware of it...

All this is difficult to describe, because it is still in a state of experimentation, nothing dogmatic. Inspired from life and human contact. Full of promise. Labour of patience. Already begun.[10]

Aim for nothing less than making the actor, not only the medium, but the source of all dramatic inspiration.

[From Copeau's notes for the third lecture (given in French) at the Little Theatre, New York, 'L'Ecole du Vieux Colombier', 19 March 1917, reprinted in *Registres IV*, pp. 507–13]

2

IDEAS IN COMMON: EDWARD GORDON CRAIG

Copeau drew together ideas from many sources in his vision of a School of Dramatic Art as the ultimate, necessary source of dramatic renovation (which was in itself only intended to be a training ground for the dramatic renaissance to follow). Some of these ideas were formed as a result of encounters, often deliberately sought, with other teachers, practitioners and theoreticians. Indeed, he was at times accused of unoriginality: at worst plagiarism, at best offering nothing new. In March 1918 he defended himself against his American critics in a lecture to the New York Drama League:

I have been reproached here by some who say my ideas on *mise en scène* and acting are not appreciably different from those of Gordon Craig, Max Reinhardt and Granville Barker. To this list could be added: Appia, Meyerhold and Stanislavsky, and a few others. How could one not be delighted by this meeting of minds and common approach? Here are seven or eight different individuals, independent, who share a common idea. Admitting that it be true, it is encouraging, the beginning of something, a basis for understanding and collaboration.[1]

In 1915, after being refused military service on account of a lung condition, and with the Vieux Colombier Theatre seemingly closed for the duration, Copeau had made use of his time in developing the conceptual side of his quest, travelling to Italy to meet Edward Gordon Craig at his school at the Goldoni Arena in Florence and then to Switzerland to study the teaching methods of Emile Jaques-Dalcroze. Dalcroze also introduced him to Adolphe Appia, many of whose concepts Copeau later adopted into the permanent staging at the Vieux Colombier. What practical use to make of his encounter with Craig proved more of a puzzle, one worth working at even if

13

no immediate solution were to be found. On 3 June 1917, at the end of his visit to America, he said, in an interview with Djuna Barnes, then of the New York Morning Telegraph:

> I do not always succeed in following [Craig] because he is so far ahead of me at this time. I hope one day to see what he sees, understand what he understands. Until then, I cannot say whether his dreams are true or false. Perhaps he is divinely right. I know he is a master in his way and that this way is not for ordinary mortals. You see, he goes far back to seek his inspiration, to the Greeks and the Egyptians. He has some Egyptian masks that are among the most beautiful that I have ever seen. Yes... maybe he is on the right road.

A DEBT ACKNOWLEDGED

There has not been a single artist of the theatre during the last twenty-five years who is not indebted to a greater or lesser extent to Gordon Craig. For my own part, I cannot but recognise, and gladly, how much I am indebted to him. Thanks to him the ceiling of the playhouse has been burst open and we can now see the sky. He was the great initiator, the first inspiration. He has pointed out to us the road upon which we have not, as yet, taken but a few hesitating steps. He has placed way ahead of us a difficult ideal, which we are still far from reaching. I confess that I did not always understand him well during the first two months I spent in daily contact with him. It took me some time before I could discern the horizon that his genius-like presentiment had discovered. Incomplete as his doctrine may be, it is an essential one. He goes deep down into the heart of all fundamental problems.

When I left him I was keenly aware that something in me was changed, that new germs were only waiting an opportunity to develop.

[From the first lecture to the American Laboratory Theatre, (given in English) New York, 9 January 1927, op. cit.]

FIRST ENCOUNTER:
Florence, September – October 1915

In August 1915 I wrote to Edward Gordon Craig for the first time, asking him for his authorisation to have his book, *On the Art of the Theatre*, translated and published in French. He answered by inviting me to meet him in Florence. I joined him there on Tuesday, 14 September, and stayed with him until Sunday, 17 October.

It was in Florence, in 1908, that Craig founded his quarterly review *The Mask*, and in March 1913, backed by a wealthy Englishman, he opened his School for the Art of the Theatre in the Goldoni Arena.

In the magazine, which I shall edit after the war,[2] I shall study and discuss Gordon Craig's influence and ideas as found in his writings, engravings, productions and the numerous conversations we had together. There exists more than one point on which we differ. But we have too many ideas in common, too many shared aspirations and hatreds, for our work and our actions not to be inevitably linked in the future. [...]

Tuesday, 14 September 1915

I have lunch at Craig's. A painful mental tension from communicating in a foreign language (Craig does not speak a word of French), with a man I do not know, whom I feel has nothing in common with me except a great love of theatre. What is more, the nature of our knowledge is not the same. After an hour's conversation he says: 'Well. You have much of a literary man. You are not *of the theatre*.'[3] Indeed, I come to the theatre via literature; I started my theatrical career through a disgust for base theatrical productions and values, prompted by a literary morality. I have been in the theatre for only one year. Having once come into contact with it, I realised that everything must be changed, remodelled, and that is one of the reasons I wanted to meet 'such a craftsman as Craig is'. Son of Ellen Terry and an architect, Craig was born into the theatre. He knows everything about theatre through heredity, experience, erudition and meditation. I have everything to learn from him, he has nothing to learn from me. I feel that I have nothing of interest to say to him, for fear of disappointing and boring him completely; the more so as his natural enthusiasm had brought him to expect so much from our meeting. I let him talk, my throat dry and my eyes wide open. He talks in snatches, shows me his books, his engravings, and makes me aware of my ignorance. He is continually 'in high spirits', and I am 'rather depressed'. [...]

15

A perfect cosmopolitan. Very English for all that ('half English, half Irish', he says), with his need for neatness and order in his affairs, at once very positive and very chimerical. At various moments, two distinct men appear clearly in him. A tall young man with clear eyes,[4] a smiling face, open, radiant, impulsive, witty and sarcastic, quick to show enthusiasm and involvement, which he expresses with the conciseness of genius, grimaces, leaps and the shaking of his mane of grey hair. Then, when he comes up against an objection or a difficulty, when he is contradicted, his face becomes pinched, dried up, loses all its charm and radiance, he becomes incisive, hard and his weaknesses are revealed. He takes his head in his hands convulsively and utters a kind of little moan. But it passes quickly. His gracious vivacity takes over: 'You know I am such a stupid fellow... I may catch some things at a glimpse, but I can't learn anything. I am like a big potato with sproutings here and there... But I think I am a little bit of an artist. That's all.' [...]

First visit to the Goldoni Arena. One enters into an old, de-consecrated church, full of books, portfolios, engravings, models, glass cabinets containing masks, marionettes, bits of costumes, etc. On a shelf is the mirror before which Tomasso Salvini made up all his life and which he gave to G. C. Next to it, Henry Irving's. From there one passes on to the stage, decorated with greenery and furnished with a small, one-storey, wooden house that G. C. had built himself and where he often spent the night. Hammock, easy chairs, table. A whole cluster of clay hand-bells hangs on a string. And before us is the open-air 'arena' with its circular brick gradins. A young catalpa tree grows in the centre. In various corners and rooms are the library, various studios, the workshops for the property makers, electricians and carpenters, and numerous stage models on which Craig is working. I take them all in at a glance. Whether I do not show enough enthusiasm or whether he does not care to show me everything in detail, Craig lets fall the canvas coverings saying each time: 'unfinished'. [...]

Wednesday, 15 September

Lunch with Craig. [...] I let Craig talk. In his discourses on theatre, on the future of theatre, it is never a question of anything completely definitive. Or, at least, he seems to be interested only in an internal, technical renovation of the conditions of dramatic production as produced entirely by theatre people, by a genius who is not necessarily a dramatist. He shows me some very pretty engravings of ancient ceremonies in the great squares of Florence. He says: 'That is theatre, that is what I should like to do – let the cities give me full freedom to organise beautiful outdoor spectacles like that. It seems so stupid to me to unlock the doors of an enclosed space in order to enter at a certain hour.' For him the actor is not an artist. Nothing artistic can be done with the human face. When I ask him whether he does not wish to give any performances in the Goldoni Arena, he answers: 'Oh! no, I won't spoil it. That's a good place to work in you know'. In his remarks on dramatic works, there is no question but that he will complain that they are encumbered by words. He says ,'No doubt, no doubt... there will always be such a thing as conversational theatre, social theatre... "Yes, very charming". But it is not theatre.' And later: 'You see, it would be good, from time to time, to make some completely nonsensical attempts. It makes no difference whether they succeed or not. It would be good to try. Shakespeare, for example. I'll tell you how. It would be a completely terrifying method.... A quarter of the text would not be spoken. Because, you understand, today, the great dramatic works are a little like the prayers in a Catholic mass. When an actor starts "To be or not to be"... and so on, and so on, it's as if he were saying: 'Our Father which art in heaven' and so on.... We know what it is all about. No, enough of that...' Here we have the need for novelty at any price, the spirit which is not free, for, as Chesterton says, 'The only true free-thinker is he whose intellect is as much free from the future as from the past.'[5] There is always something in what Craig says, often some precious truths. But he goes first this way then that, criticising, prophetising. One never gets anywhere with him. One cannot see his goal. He says: 'It is sad to think that I have worked so long and know so little.' One never knows anything if one does not know where one is going. That is why his science, his experience, his erudition, often seem to me to be so useless and almost puerile.

Nothing tires me in conversation so much as these unsifted inspirations which light up the horizon, sometimes in the west, sometimes in the south, misleading all who approach. I need solid ground under my feet, a meeting point, an orientation.

I end by saying to Craig:

'Listen. There is something in all this that I do not understand. As I hear you speak, a question comes up constantly which you must answer first so that what you say makes sense to me.... You speak of the "art of the theatre", "the European theatre", "the future of the theatre", and you say that you are on the way "towards a new theatre". But, in the end, what will this new theatre be like? Is it going to be born out of your desire? You deny wanting to improve what exists and you declare that it is a question of having something new. For all that, it will not come to life out of nowhere. What indication is there of it? Where is the work in which it is germinating? For it must involve dramatic works. You say readily that you do not care about contemporary works, that they have nothing in common with the theatre of the future. You own to having broken with contemporary dramatic production. You will have no part of it. You disown it. You deny it. At what moment will the new dramatist come into contact with this new theatre which you are prophesying?... In short, what are the proofs of the need, the expectation from which the new theatre will come? It cannot correspond solely to the need or expectation of one artist. What would become of it when that artist passed on? Finally, do you think that a movement for the renewal of dramatic art which is not accompanied or necessitated by the production of new work, is realistic, living, necessary?'

My question obviously embarrasses him. He frowns, and begins: 'Will you also say that in order for painting to exist one first needs pictures? That for musical art...' But he stops, sensing that his argument does not stick. He pauses and starts again:

'Indeed, it is possible. Therefore, I have no idea what I am, to what I correspond.... All I can say to you is that I have never yet encountered, strictly speaking, a dramatic work in the sense that I mean' (in what sense is what he still does not explain and I cannot figure out. No doubt that is because the means to fulfil himself have never been given him.) 'Shakespeare? – No. Shakespeare is a poet. In my eyes, he does not belong to dramatic art.... As for contemporary production, I confess that I should admit quite willingly that it stop completely for a great number of years.'

These are intellectual views, having nothing to do with reality. Yet G. C. claims to deal in realities. I like him better when he criticises. His criticisms are almost always excellent.

He is inexhaustible in his praise for Irving and for Ellen Terry, his mother. He says, laughingly, that he holds the 'old acting' in highest esteem. His admiration for the Italians is almost limitless. His great man is Giovannni Grasso, the Sicilian. He says: 'The

Italians begin acting like that' (and he does a wordless imitation of a running conversation). 'Then, suddenly, the big thing appears, the passion, the genius. The English are completely opposite, from the start' (and he takes on the pleasant air of a lead actor, weighed down by thought). 'But they do not go any further.'

He tells me about his work with Stanislavsky and Danchenko in Moscow for the production of *Hamlet* at the Art Theatre. It lasted six months and ended, after much discord, with a performance that did not satisfy Craig at all and misrepresented his thoughts on more than one point. The history of almost all such enterprises is moreover the history of as many errors and failures.

He speaks about *Hamlet* very well, and gets carried away. Notably about the scene with the actors, of Hamlet's joy in seeing them arrive, of the young actors running towards him, leaning forward to blow him kisses, loaded down with their theatrical props, flying about 'like birds in a storm of feathers'. It is a magnificent expression; I think it shall henceforth influence my vision of that scene. Like migratory birds, wandering, free.... G. C. shows me some very graceful designs of these actors in *Hamlet*. They are indeed 'birds', with wings and feathers. The *metaphore* is imperturbably worked through for the stage. It is now that I think I see the point where Craig's thought tends to become forced. In my thinking, it is the actor, through his gracefulness, his air, his acting and delivery, who should make the spectator say: 'like birds in a storm of feathers'.

Craig says he is tired, at the moment, of working with texts. His ambition is to have constructed in America, financed by a group of American bankers, an enormous stage on which he will produce 'The most big thing ever seen in America', a performance of Bach's *Passion according to Saint Matthew*! That is the very thing which would repel and horrify me the most. I decline to give an opinion. Craig rejects Europe, where everything is done and seen in a small way. He speaks only of colossal undertakings and of millions to produce them.

He says: 'My interests are neither in London, in Paris, nor in Berlin; they are in Florence... and in America.'

To tell the truth, I believe they are nowhere. G. C. is not attached to any country, nor any public. His action has no soul. It is not imperatively wanted or effectively demanded by anyone. His friends are at the far ends of the earth. My conviction is that there is infinitely more soul and a more fertile seed-bed in my little theatre, which exists and lives with all of its poverty and imperfections. This takes nothing away, however, from his importance as an innovator and an initiator.

CRAIG'S SCHOOL

[*A few months later, back at home in Le Limon, Copeau re-reads his notes and tries to clarify his impressions of Craig's School*]

During my stay in Florence, I spent several days in the Goldoni Arena and I felt its exhilarating atmosphere. I visited the little museum, examined the models, leafed through the portfolios of designs and engravings, went into the library, the print-shop, the workshops [...] but all was empty, deserted, lifeless. I did not see the School in action. The war, in taking away all subsidies, has scattered its pupils.

The spirit of the School is excellent, such as I had seen it described.[6] It does not open up any prospect that I had not already considered before. Its programme is mine: by the diversity, the universality of research and knowledge, de-specialising and re-normalising the future actor, making him a human being, open, in harmony with life, a master-artist in his art, but with a general cultural background.

I noted the excellent method by which there is an exchange between specialists of the knowledge acquired in their work, and which makes each of them both a master and a pupil.

Also praiseworthy is a division between paying and salaried pupils – a division that I intended to establish, prompted by the *Schola Cantorum* of Vincent d'Indy.[7]

However, I do not believe that there were ever any paying pupils at the Arena. May I add that, in my view, this brochure should be considered as a programme, not a report, and that the activities and organisation it portrays, I think, existed only in Craig's imaginary theatre and not in the Goldoni Arena. I think that all the branches of teaching and experimentation described were, in reality, reduced to very little. I think that one must tone down this tableau, which is a little too grandiose and trumped up by fervour and ambition. This report is partly real and partly imagined. It does not seem to me that 'Gymnastics, Fencing, Dancing, Mimo-Drama, Improvisation', for example, ever had much place in the work of the Arena's guests. Who is this Mr Marriott? I don't know, but I have some reservations about him [...]

20

Thursday, 7 October (1915)

I had suspected that Craig was the only one, or practically so, to write in *The Mask*. I asked him discreetly, knowing how he made use of his various signatures. Finally, the other evening, I asked him: 'Who is Mr Symar?' He fell silent for a moment, then gave me a side-long glance, and with the sharp, slightly dry look he used in his conversation about personal interests, confessed: 'Well, Mr. Symar... does not exist at all... quite between you and me. He is one of my Javanese marionettes, the big old one. Poor dear Symar!' [...]

[*A few months later...*]

It is there that we touch upon a curious and distressing aspect of Gordon Craig's personality, as well as everything which surrounds him: this tendency to *force* reality, to amplify it, to surpass it, to disavow naturalness. There is a bit of the mimic in all that. Adolphe Appia, a few days later, said of Craig: 'How can one not be touched by the warmth of his feeling? But there is something of the actor in him, yes... of the fraud.' This description is so insulting that only Appia's smile could express it so delicately that I understood it. My contact with Craig in Florence was enough to dispel almost all my apprehensions. But the more I think about it now, the more I sense that taint of affectation in his feelings, thought and writings which put me on my guard in spite of loving and admiring him. Craig is not, as they say, a dreamer infatuated with vaporous ideas. He can be a meticulous realiser, though there again he goes too far, but he is a visionary, a megalomaniac, a dilettante. And when he gets down to practical realisation, his enthusiasm, instability, ambition, pride and genius make him overstep the bounds of reality. It seems to me that he belongs to a class of people that I know well, whose words, in spite of their sincerity, and whose very personality, *discredit* them...

I must not forget in all this that, in founding a school, Craig does not feel the same need as I do, does not pursue the same goal. He does not even pursue any immediate goal. He is not a theatre director. He is not trying to form a company of actors to fulfil the requirements of a repertoire. Theoretically, the actor does not interest him. [...] It is his theory of the 'Uber-Marionette'. His desire is to start from the beginning, with no thought for the future or any short-term production plan. His ambition is to create 'a new material for the theatre of the future'. He has often said to me: 'You believe in the actor. *I do not.*' The pupils who emerge from his teachings will be 'stage-managers'. But for what stage? So why then: 'Gymnastics, voice training, fencing, dancing, etc.'? There is a contradiction there that clashes, a vagueness that I cannot penetrate and that Craig himself feels enveloped by. He told me: 'I feel out of practice...' [...]

What is more, from what I know of Craig's character and from what he confessed to me in conversation, I am led to believe that he has none of the essential qualities of a leader, a director, least of all, an educator.

'You should solidly establish your school, here in Florence, devote yourself to it completely, tie it in with the best undertakings around the world, and thus become the centre of all your own endeavours.' I expressed this wish to Craig; he answered with a smile: 'I am such a bad centre. I really have too many faults to be a centre.' [...]

But what is certain is that Craig's personality is exciting. That is especially what I owe him, after a month of daily contacts: a great excitement, along with a more intense awareness of my means, an increased faith, the certainty of being on the right road, and an urgent need to produce. [...]

[From 'L'Ecole du Vieux Colombier', unpublished notebook, 205 typed pages from hand-written entries, 1915–20, M-H D, printed in part in *Registres I*, pp. 275–300]

3

EDUCATING THE ACTOR

Copeau's ideals for the Vieux Colombier School, like Craig's for the Goldoni Arena, were only partially to be achieved. His vision was of working (and playing) with children, of instilling the kind of deep respect for an inherited tradition that is fundamental to many Oriental theatre schools, for example the family-based Ryu *of the Japanese Noh. Among the volumes in Copeau's study in his house at Pernand one finds the* Transactions and Proceedings of the Japan Society, London *for 1912–13 and Fenellosa and Pound's 1916 book on the Noh, both marked up for his attention by his collaborator, Suzanne Bing.*

But the research and practical investigation of such ideals was continually interrupted by the exigencies of production work. Copeau's refusal to let the Vieux Colombier be compromised by subsidy meant that there were too many performances to give, too many new plays to rehearse, for him to offer its School the kind of personal attention he believed it required. As head of the family, he was a remote figure for many of the pupils. However, some children did grow up in and around the School, both his own and those of other members of the company, as part of an extended family, much in the manner of the commedia dell'arte *troupes of the sixteenth century, circus performers or present-day theatre groups such as Bread and Puppet in America or Footsbarn from England. But in 1913, the first priority, since the Vieux Colombier Theatre, for practical and economic reasons, had to be started before the Vieux Colombier School, was to offer some re-education to those young actors Copeau had chosen to perform in the first season:*

unselfish young enthusiasts whose ambition is to *serve* the art to which they dedicate themselves. To free the actor from

23

cabotinage,[1] to create around him an atmosphere more suited to his development as a man and as an artist; to cultivate him, to inspire conscience in him and to initiate him into the morality of his art: it is to that end we stubbornly bend our efforts. We shall always have in view the development of individual talents and their subordination to the ensemble. We shall fight against the encroachment of professional tricks, against all professional distortions, against the ossification of specialisation. In short, we shall do our best to re-normalise these men and women whose vocation is to simulate all human emotions and gestures. So far as it is possible for us, we will take them outside the theatre and into contact with nature and with life![2]

The School's first experiments in training and educating the actor were combined with the first rehearsals of the Vieux Colombier repertoire over a period of two months working, mainly in the garden, at Copeau's family home in Limon, some thirty miles from Paris. Such de-urbanisation of the actor was one of Copeau's constant pre-occupations. When he was persuaded to take a mixed company of seasoned and new performers to the United States in the latter years of the Great War, he again felt it vital to remove them from the city between seasons, from New York to the summer home of his patron, Otto Kahn,[3] in Morristown, New Jersey. But again there was the 'pis-aller' of trying to combine the work of School and Theatre, to the detriment of the former. Jessmin Howarth, a pupil of Jaques-Dalcroze employed by Copeau to conduct the physical training, recalls:

> In the early summer of 1918, Otto Kahn lent Copeau a large house in Morristown, New Jersey, and we all moved there and lived together. We could now try to make a few experiments and I must say that Copeau gave me every help and encouragement. I gave the men, the women and the children a class in (I suppose I should call it) gymnastics, every day before breakfast, and we managed to get in a few sessions of improvisation, pantomime and dance instruction. Copeau was not able to be with us all the time, but Suzanne Bing and Dullin were particularly keen, and Charles used a lot of the material we sketched out there in his courses at the 'Atelier'[4] later (which I also supervised on occasion).
>
> However, again, there was a killing winter programme to

24

prepare; stage and costume designing had to be speeded up; the company's schedule called for the mise en scène *and rehearsal of one act a day.*[5]

Small wonder, then, that on his return to post-war France, Copeau became increasingly preoccupied with the need for a private place where the demands of public performance would no longer dominate the search for an appropriate education for the actor of the theatre of the future.

A PRIVATE PLACE

No one has yet been concerned with establishing a private place where, in an atmosphere of simplicity, honesty, comradeship and firm discipline, the young Servants of Theatre will acquire the complete technique and spirit of their profession; where they will learn to consider their art, not as an easy game, a brilliant and profitable craft, but as an idea that demands hard, relentless, complex, often unrewarding work, to be achieved through great self-sacrifice – work which is done not only with the mouth, nor even with mouth and mind, but also with the body, with the whole person, all the faculties, and with the whole being...

This private place I speak of, this source of renewed inspiration for an entire epoch; it is up to the State, in a well-organised society, to assure its security and growth. But the official education at our *Conservatoire*, at least as far as dramatic art is concerned, no longer has any real life, any *raison d'être*. We have been complaining about it for a long time, and the critics have made that into a cliché. There is even talk of a re-organisation. I do not doubt that its present director [...], who is an artist and an honest man, is doing his best. But I am convinced, personally, that it is not possible to refloat this old boat, any more than our *Comédie-Française* can be re-equipped. The flood of a strong tradition seems to be still upholding these rudderless institutions; they are floating like derelicts adrift.

The National Conservatoire is no longer a School. There is no unified discipline. The teaching is without doctrine. There is no method. There can be no school where the pupils speak scornfully of its teaching; where the professors are resigned to the inefficacy of their efforts and are mostly uninterested in their job; where the teaching methods inevitably result in infecting the pupils with tricks of the trade and bad habits, little by little imposing those habits in the guise of progress, which then become encrusted on the whole person, deadening their sensibilities; where no flame burns, no freshness is preserved; where even the best intentions are wasted; where the spirit of competition and career-climbing has replaced the cult of art and respect for the profession; and finally, where the young people who should be our hope for the future reside as if in a waiting-room, a cramming shop, waiting to get out as soon as possible with a diploma in hand.

The survival of the *Conservatoire* is deadly, not only because it does not fulfil its function but also because what remains of its prestige and official approval attracts young people whose best developed gifts could flourish elsewhere. It is the emptiness of this teaching which, in many minds, unfairly discredits the very idea of a School, sets personality above education, selects extravagance as an antidote to academicism.

We are not sufficiently aware that the decrepitude of academic teaching has as its first cause the age-old divorce of properly so-called professional teaching from apprenticeship. This question of apprenticeship comes up today in all the crafts. It is the same for us in the theatre industry as in other industries. And it is towards its solution that we should be working, socially as well as professionally. That is why we should not deny, because one style of teaching has failed, the fecundity of all teaching or the legitimacy of all Schools. We do not have the right to say that we can do without teaching; it is not true. All artists seek instruction, even if it is bad. [...]

Theatre has fallen so low in France that everyone must become aware of it and at least discuss it. Current production has become so insipid that even the most paltry novelty finds an audience to welcome it as revitalising. Moreover, there are theatre people quite ready to admit that things cannot continue in this way, that in the end, 'something' must be done to come out of it. They do not even know the illness they are dying from, but are getting ready to lead a full life after it. They think that a good remedy is easy to find, ready at hand, and that it would be enough to apply it so that we can 'recover' in a few days. Indeed, they are doing 'something'... Thus, between this twofold inclination, *infatuation* on the part of the audience and *bluffing* from the professionals, there is much room for confusion, sham and all sorts of hypocrisy.

If we had critics who knew how to differentiate between what is and what is not, they would keep a close eye on such outbursts of vitality which, from time to time, seem to want to galvanise our stage, and I believe they would find, not the prelude to a renaissance, but all the evidence of that phenomenon known to medicine as the euphoria of the dying.

We cannot speak of a renaissance, nor even envisage its possibility, as long as we have not begun at the beginning, that is by the creation of a School and of a teaching which will restore its working conditions.

It is too often imagined that novelty is change.

It is certainly not change that we need (especially premature, artificial and forced change), but a serious return to principles. Such change does not depend on us. The hand of a great man is needed, or perhaps the shock of great circumstances;[6] I see no true transformation possible in the theatre except through and by a social transformation. New dramatic forms will come from new ways of living, thinking and feeling. That is why I have never dared use the word renaissance. I always believed that our 'chapel', our laboratory, our School, whatever one calls it – could not honestly be described as anything but a renewal or, even better, a preparation. Renewal of dramatic feeling through an understanding of the masterworks, and a renewed contact with the great technical traditions. Preparation of the means suitable to the play of a broader, freer and more audacious dramatic imagination. Where the soundest and most sincere efforts at renewal will take place, where the most rigorous and best oriented preparation will be pursued – it is there that a dramatic renaissance has the most chance of finding a point of departure.

I was told that, around 1910, M. Jacques Rouché invited Edward Gordon Craig to accept the technical direction of the Théâtre des Arts, and that Craig imposed the following condition: that the theatre would first be closed to the public for ten or fifteen years in order to allow him to begin his work from the beginning, that is to train pupils according to his fully detailed methods in a new spirit of renewed art. 'Lacking this', Craig added, 'I feel I can only improvise things as mediocre as those you can produce yourself at the present time.'

Those who related this anecdote pretended to be very amused by it. They saw it as an example of Craig's utopian ideas and a decisive proof of his intellectual estrangement.

In my eyes, Craig's answer was the only reasonable one. The fact that it was not taken seriously proves that the public mind has no notion of the fundamental conditions of dramatic renewal.

I see lunacy everywhere, among those numberless young men on both continents who give birth to big 'art theatres' out of amusement or excitement, without ever having learned or thought about anything, without knowing what they want or where they are going. They seize upon a formula; they undertake any enterprise from its most enticing aspect. After a while, they stop, abandoning the work when it gets to the test, rebuffed by the experiment which perhaps is about to teach them something. They toss around from right to left, because the fashion has changed and their mind with it, or simply because their lack of basic training and method prevents them from finding any order of development in their incoherent attempts.

You will ask how it is that I did not follow Craig's advice and open a School before opening a Theatre.

I did not do it because I was not able to do it, because I had neither the authority nor the means to do so. If, in October 1913, I had proposed the founding of a School, no-one would have listened to me. There was already enough scepticism surrounding our theatrical attempt. Craig was being logical. If I had been so, I should have remained in oblivion. I was deeply convinced that it was imperative to *exist* first of all. We had to familiarise the public with our utopian ideas. We had to give proof of what a company of actors, mostly novices, could give in a year's work in common, under direction. That is what we did from October 1913 to May 1914.

So, it is true that I started by making a concession to life's demands. But it was through caution, not ignorance. The idea of the School and the idea of the Theatre are one and the same; they were conceived together and described as such in my 'Attempt at Dramatic Renovation' (September 1913). In fact, since the founding of the Vieux Colombier, I have never ceased to consider the Theatre as a School, and, for better or for worse, to include the utmost of educational discipline in the often difficult necessities of the day-to-day production process. Our first attempts at education go back to the summer of 1913. The young actors of the Vieux Colombier had gathered at my side in the country, at Le Limon. Every day, for five hours, they studied the plays of the repertory. Two more hours were devoted to sight-reading out of doors, a kind of intellectual warming-up exercise, to vocal articulation, textual analysis and also to physical exercises.

To tell the truth, after two months of this, the advantages of such a system were only barely being felt. There was a lack of experience, clear ideas and methods on my part, of goodwill on the part of my unprepared pupils. They naturally felt a little out of their element. They still did not have much confidence in me, and certain among them appeared reluctant and even hostile.

Nevertheless, this preliminary training was to bear fruit. By the end of 1913–14, it could be considered to have produced a maximum return. I said *training*, not *education*.

At the time, my first experiments put me on the track of certain educational principles. But the only real result achieved on the eve of war, at least as I saw it, not without a certain emotion, was a kind of communication between my company and myself, the credence placed in me by these young people, the educational virtue in the largest sense, a product of their life and work together. And I was able to say that my original concept was not false, that it was now necessary at any cost to maintain this community, this continuity of influence by the same controlling intelligence upon the same individuals, and to make the one more solid and the other more profound. We were touching upon a real principle, one that was living and capable of creating something durable. From this time on, there was to be no circumstance, accident or progress in the life of the Theatre which did not have an effect on my idea of a future School.

[From 'L'Ecole du Vieux Colombier', Cahier No. 2, op. cit.]

1916: THE FIRST PLAN FOR THE VIEUX COLOMBIER SCHOOL

I. The founding of the Vieux Colombier Theatre in October 1913 and the success which crowned its efforts during the first season, showed that it is reasonable to hope for a renovation in France's great dramatic art based on the understanding and close collaboration between a group of selfless artists and an elite public.[7]

It is presumed that this renovation, after the war, will develop strongly and take on its full significance.

In order for such a renovation to be lasting, it must go back to the very sources of the ills it is combatting. It must destroy routine and *cabotinisme* in all branches of our art, and it is necessary to renew the personnel of theatre from top to bottom. This is what we call: 'raising a new theatre from absolutely secure foundations'. *If we do not do that, we shall have accomplished nothing.* [...]

II. The Vieux Colombier School calls upon two categories of pupils: 1. Children from 10–15 years; 2. young people from 15–20. [...]

III. We know that it is not possible, in the middle of the war, to realise all at once such an important and complex organisation. But we would like, in working for the future, to take advantage of this period of inaction that is imposed on us. We would like to see exist right now the embryo of the future Vieux Colombier School.

We have already formed that embryo with our own means, that is, without any financial resources: 1. bringing together, at the Club de Gymnastique Rythmique, a few children, boys and girls, whose first work gives us the certainty that, if it were carried out methodically, it would produce all the expected results;[8] 2. by meeting periodically in the Vieux Colombier Theatre to work with the women from the company and with a few young male professional actors who are exempt from military duty and who will join the Company when the Theatre re-opens.

But these efforts are being carried out under very unfavourable conditions. To be fruitful they must be continuous. The adults can only give us a small part of their time as they have to work for a living. The recruiting of the children presents difficulties which will not be resolved until the day we can offer the parents to take them away solely at our expense.

IV. For the moment, we are proposing to establish the Vieux Colombier School as a kind of *war-time relief organisation.*

It is agreed that, in the spring of 1916 (around April), we move to the country, into a big building furnished for this purpose:
1. a team of ten young pupils (recruited from needy families and, if necessary, from among the refugees from the occupied territories);
2. a team of ten adult pupils (five actors from the Vieux Colombier Company and five future candidates); 3. a team of five teachers; making a total of twenty-five people who would be supported (lodging, board, laundry) at the expense of the School.[9] [...]

V. The work of the Vieux Colombier School will be divided as follows:

1. For the children: reading aloud, poetic recitations, general instruction, games.
2. For the adults: reading aloud, poetic recitations, literature and theatre history, mime and improvisation, games, study of the repertoire, athletics, fencing.
3. For the adults and children: gymnastic technique, rhythmic gymnastics, dance, solfeggio and singing, various instruments, drawing, sewing and cutting, manual work.

Put down this outline of my School plan, as briefly as possible, on simple typed pages, in order to inform the few who might be interested in it. I read it to a few friends. It has not yet been distributed.

[Entry dated 21 January 1916 in Copeau's (unpublished) notebook 'L'Ecole du Vieux Colombier', op. cit., printed in part in *Registres I*, pp. 317–18]

WORK SESSIONS

I am remaining in Paris from 1 to 25 January [1916], which allows me to follow up my pupils more diligently.

1 The children

Their number is increasing. There are now twenty-two. Among them, four or five little Russian girls, one of whom has already worked with Isadora [Duncan]. No positive progress, but a livelier overall spirit, especially in the exercises they do with me. If I were to see them every day, if I were to work with them continuously, it would be something else entirely. That is what we must achieve. [...]

2 The adults

Periodic work sessions were inaugurated on 16 December 1915, at the Vieux Colombier, in the big workshop that will become my office. [...]

In attendance:[10] Blanche Albane, Jane Lory, Madeleine Geoffroy (taken on at the end of the 1913–14 season), Suzanne Bing, Jean Lambert (brought by Lory), Alice Desverges, Mme Bogaert-Lefebure (brought along by Vermoyal), Vermoyal (taken on at the end of the 1913–14 season), Nemo, André Chotin (noticed in an audition), Jean Sarment (from the Conservatoire), de Weck (a young Swiss from Friburg in love with the theatre who came to ask my advice and whom I have working with Suzanne), plus a few others, onlookers for the moment. [...]

The new arrivals are a little out of their element at first, and their relations are a little strained with the members of the Vieux Colombier Company, whom I see are so different and, I discover, a little protective of their moral prerogatives. This is felt in the work. It is a little untidy. It is not yet work. I incur a particular risk in seeking to make contacts and creating an atmosphere where individual suspicions would disappear. It all happens by itself, rather quickly.

Audition of scenes. Sight-readings. Readings of texts that I annotate and explain (Marivaux's *La Surprise de l'Amour*, *Macbeth* and *A Winter's Tale*). Group discussion. Exercises designed to force them to disregard their resources as actors, to approach a text humbly, to look at the text itself without making too much of themselves or the text. Simply the meaning and correct articulation. To prevent them from acting it straight off in order to impress me. Since we have the time, spelling it out unpretentiously. *Tabula rasa* of all the ready-made convenient methods that come out of one's bag of tricks.

Chotin seems to understand that. Already he achieves a kind of simplicity, a sincerity towards the text, on which he can build the interpretation of a character.

Albane is working on a scene from Henri Becque's *La Parisienne* in the same way, extending her resources and that stupid charming voice of hers that rings out in spite of herself and conveys nothing.

Mme Bogaert, who thinks she is natural, lives only by the methods of naturalness that she brings to all the texts, using a full voice and a lot of simple tricks.

Lory, still the same, attacks the text with an energy that is already that of a dress rehearsal.

Geoffroy, simple and intelligent, like her face. I have confidence in her.

Vermoyal, already fossilised in manner and aesthetics, but he has the sacred fire.

Desvergers, all enthusiasm and emotion, but with no resources and, I fear, no real talent.

Sarment gives me Musset's *Fantasio*, and reads the Harlequin of *La Surprise* at sight. Charming qualities of the lover and maybe of the young light comic. Voice and physique are good. Intelligent. He listens and understands. Can be straightforward. However, already spoiled by a year at the *Conservatoire*: a fake voice, behaviourisms, an imitation of the artistes of the *Comédie-Française*. I tell him that I'll engage him when we re-open, if he leaves the *Conservatoire*.

A trial improvisation on a short scene from a Spanish impromptu.

For a full quarter of an hour they do not make a sound. Then they begin, especially Geoffroy. But it has no form, no beginning, middle or end. And they always cue each other in the same rotation.

[From the notebook 'L'Ecole du Vieux Colombier', op. cit.]

THE SCHOOL IN EXILE

Cedar Court, Morristown, New Jersey
Thursday, 23 May 1918

After the 1917–18 season in New York, settled in at Morristown at the estate of Mr Otto Khan to spend the summer and to prepare the 1918–19 season. I am working with an ill-matched troupe and trying to break them in by various exercises outside of the regular rehearsals.

On 23 May, first series of exercises:

Mute action without props:

1. A man comes home, finds a letter and reads it; it's about some trouble he is in, a serious difficulty, a misfortune.
2. The same with a friend.
3. With an indifferent person.
4. A man is waiting for a woman who is late for their date (duration: two minutes).
5. A woman, same action, same time.
6. A man comes home (show his every-day face, what his present feelings are).
7. Movement class in the open air. Nausicaa episode (*Odyssey*).

In the fifth exercise, Lory shows some personality; Tessier[11] and Sarment some quality, inner purpose and some *continuity* of expression.

The important comment for the day is that there are two types of action in the actor's playing: discontinuous actions which seem to be intentional, artificial, theatrical, and the continuous actions which give an impression of portentousness and inner sincerity, real life and power.

Continuity and slowness as conditions for playing powerfully and sincerely.

Too many things in exercise 7, hence the confusion; to be repeated.

Wednesday, 24 May

1. Express a feeling or an emotion with the face only, very rapidly; to be guessed at by the others.
2. The beginning of an emotion, a feeling or a thought, developing through to the end.

Lucienne Bogaert successfully expresses the development of her emotion. Her face changes, and we see the progression as each successive facial trait appears. Little by little she lowers her head and her face darkens against the light.

3. With the back turned – astonishment, anxiety, depression, anger, sorrow, returning courage and hope. Not one of them succeeds in getting into the preliminary state of complete relaxation.

A few exercises in improvisation. From the first one (visits to the doctor), Millet shows himself to be an improviser in the role of a gabby Marseillais. I see the character of the 'bureaucrat' coming out of him.[12] [...]

16 June

Observation of animals.

Succession of attitudes. *Hold* each of these attitudes separately. Make sketches of them. Analyse by means of films.

Complete body gymnastics exercise. Analogy with the treatment of the mask. Example of the marionette. In the intense genres, tragedy and farce (particularly in farce – I know), the attitude and facial and bodily expression are always most intensively expressed. Not one should be indifferent. And the *time* between each attitude must be well observed. (The muscular time, as in purely acrobatic exercises.) Return to the preceding attitude after each movement has been completed. This is what clowns and comic dancers do so well. (Observation of a robin on the lawn of Cedar Court.)

In the New Comedy,[13] comparison of the characters of certain types with the appearance of certain animals.

Study of La Fontaine's *Fables*.

Les Brayes. Chambon de Tence. 13 August 1920

I have just re-read all this notebook.

How many things have happened since! What a struggle! How many trials! That terrible summer of 1918 in Morristown, when I thought everything was going under. The second New York season with its 25 plays in 25 weeks. The return, the re-grouping, finally that second Paris season which has just confirmed our existence so strongly. I have stayed here alone for the last twelve days, repeating to myself those eternal words: I have not yet accomplished anything – I go back to my *idée fixe* and say that nothing will exist so long as a School does not exist. We had an embryo of it this winter under the complete direction of Suzanne [Bing]. It must be established and organised for next year. I have neither the site nor the money. I have *one month* before me to think about its organisation, rules and methods; two months to ensure its material existence, consistent with my plans.

[From the notebook 'L'Ecole du Vieux Colombier', op. cit.]

4

THE VIEUX COLOMBIER SCHOOL

Thus Copeau returned from New York to France in June 1919 convinced that a reversal of the priority which the Vieux Colombier Theatre had so far taken over its School was the only way to progress towards his self-appointed goal of 'dramatic renovation'. Again, however, there was a compromise to be made. Although he had little stomach for creating yet more productions after the exhausting second season of 'weekly rep.' in New York, he was persuaded by pressure from his peer group (mainly associates from the NRF) that the restoration of French culture in the post-war period demanded the earliest possible return to public production at the Vieux Colombier. Gide, Martin du Gard and the other writers, although themselves now less interested in the potential of theatre than that of the novel, were unable to understand why their friend the theatre director might not want to get on with directing theatre. Copeau bowed to their logic. On 10 February 1920, the Vieux Colombier re-opened with a production of A Winter's Tale, *translated and adapted by Copeau and Suzanne Bing.[1]*

But if Copeau could not yet devote his working life io the School, as he longed to do, his collaborator could. Bing, although continuing to act in the company, now began to develop the teaching methods of the embryonic academy. Concurrent with the re-opening of the theatre she began a diction class for twenty students, including two actors from the company and six of its supernumaries. This course began again in December 1920, with seventeen students, including fourteen 'supers' from the company. The work took place at the Club Gymnastique in the Rue Vaugirard. There, something more than what is normally understood by 'diction' must have been attempted, since Bing, although not now working with children, used many of the exercises she had developed while working in a progressive infant school in New York,[2] an interest which had been carried forward from the earlier experiments under Copeau in Paris.

Between March and June 1921 Copeau himself gave a public lecture course entitled 'French Classical Theatre', the syllabus for which covered the study of text, characterisation, style and mise en scène *and acting technique. Finally, thanks to the success of the first season at the Theatre and to protracted negotiations with the Friends of the Vieux Colombier, the occasional experiment of the School became an institutional reality, opening in December 1921 under the directorship of Jules Romains,[3] eventually moving to newly acquired premises in the Rue du Cherche-Midi. The first documents which follow cover the period from then until the closure of the Vieux Colombier Theatre in 1924. During this period Copeau began more and more to regard the School as being synonymous with the development of the 'apprentice' group, working mainly under Bing. When Copeau closed the doors of the Vieux Colombier Theatre in Paris it was in order to concentrate his energies on the work of this 'school'. In what was to be his last attempt at de-urbanisation, he was accompanied by the pupils of the apprentice group and some of the younger actors from the Vieux Colombier company to search for old roots among the ancient vines and blackcurrants of Burgundy. This quest eventually resulted in the formation of a new company, nominally 'Les Copiaus', but in Copeau's mind still the Vieux Colombier School.*

IN SEARCH OF DRAMATIC UNITY

In founding the Vieux Colombier School, we are not deceiving ourselves concerning the extent of the educational development it will be possible for us to provide at first. We are well aware that we lack the rudiments with which to realise a full p⟩gramme, a model for professional dramatic teaching. But the very knowledge and experience we have of our limitations is a warrant of our sincerity. We shall proceed step by step, as we did for the theatre, advancing only on terrain that is certain and well organised, doing only what we are able to do, and trying to do it well. Our initial programme is not an outline of all our ambitions. It is adapted to acknowledged possibilities so that we may put into action only those tested means which are at our disposal.

Nothing is easier than writing up the particulars of a programme.

But drawing up a lesson plan is one thing, founding a School is another.

In order to found a School one needs a syllabus, teachers and pupils. Nothing is easier than opening an establishment that would attract flocks of individuals from all around, urged on by their vocation, fancy or curiosity.

Being a pupil is not given to everyone. It does not take much to want to be taught. He who claims the noble name of pupil or disciple comes in order to attach his person and life to a core of feelings and ideas: it will not be enough for him to lodge these in his brain but, as Montaigne says, he must 'espouse' them. The School will amount to nothing for the pupil if it is not the perfect place for him to choose, the pole of his existence and the source of his greatest joys. The strength of a school is known by its imprint on those who have left it and who never cease to be part of it.

We shall choose our pupils according to their degree of educability, their character, their origin, their individual qualities and aptitudes, with the idea of forming a harmonious ensemble. And we shall choose them as young as possible.

It is to the youngest that we shall devote all our effort. It is to them that we shall offer all our services, give the most complete teaching. They will live at the School, entirely separate from the Theatre, and be oriented from the start of their apprenticeship by special methods towards a series of new forms of dramatic expression. In three or four years we shall be able to judge the value of our School by the professional worth of these children, and to recognise a true *unity of spirit* in their training.

Nothing is easier than bringing together in the same enterprise a certain number of distinguished teachers, all competent in their specialities and able to ensure a varied teaching programme of music, dance, literature, fencing, the history of costume, etc. If one is content to add, to superimpose a more or less extended 'theoretical' teaching on the technical teaching, the results will not be very different from those of the *Conservatoire* where there also exists, I believe, a course in 'literature' and one in 'posture' alongside those in tragedy and comedy. It is not only a question of informing the actor-pupils, of enhancing their minds, or of developing such and such a possible virtuosity in them. It is not enough to have them do gymnastics or study literature so that they may be more agile or learned. All their teaching should be of a dramatic essence and intention, linked to a common dramatic idea and, consequently, taught by people who above all are either teachers of theatre or are preparing to be. There is the difficulty. And that is why also, instead of starting by drawing up a list of courses to be taught and then wondering which teacher is qualified for which course, we started by singling out from our midst competent collaborators and then set the number of courses accordingly. For only one thing can be productive in our opinion, and that is work which is well co-ordinated.

There will be a constant communication and exchange between the teachers of the School. No matter how learned they may be in their specialities, they will receive their real training from the common experience and from single overall leadership. In this way the *unity of doctrine* will emerge. [...]

The teaching subjects are detailed in the School prospectus. On the whole they aim at putting the complete instrument of dramatic expression in the hands of the creator, at raising today's actor out of his technical and intellectual impoverishment, at giving him the awareness of all his faculties, and of their utilisation within the unity of a stage production.

In a practical way, the teaching of dramatic feeling in the actor-pupil is conceived by analogy to the child's instinct for play. The example and model for this development were gathered from a close and lengthy observation of many children, one of whom, eighteen years old, is participating today in the work of the School. Upon entering the School, the young pupils will enter into a game which will last several years, where their surroundings will help them to awaken and stimulate all their faculties at once and in the same way, make all their inner imagining accessible to them, all inventiveness easy for them, and from which they will discover the secrets and rules by themselves.

One of the greatest difficulties I have encountered in this attempt to organise a drama school is finding a way to ensure unity of teaching: a technical and intellectual unity, one of principle, aim or intention.

I am not sure I have succeeded. It is on this point especially that experience will be our teacher. We shall record this in future accounts of our activity.

The unity of principle is presently being supplied by taking music as the basis and guide of dramatic instruction.

The unity of intention or aim can be linked only to the presentiment of a new dramatic form, already potentially contained in the methods being used and in the exercises being attempted. In order for the teaching and the resulting work to be fruitful and to attain perfect unity, it would be necessary to define and make known the intended aim and form being prepared. When they are, then the doctrine will be established, and from that, finally, will come the means to the newly discovered end.

As long as the doctrine is not established, we shall have to be content with a temporary unity, one of expectation, a kind of borrowed unity which will supply the teaching with its fulcrum, its centre and its axis.

I believe I have found this empirical unity in the linking of the preparatory teaching to a definite period in the history of theatre. For the first year, I have grouped the teaching subjects and the technical exercises around a study of the Greek theatre.

Let there be no misunderstanding, however, about my intention; this is not at all meant to fashion erudite minds in our pupils, nor to urge them towards being restorers of the past. I have too much enmity towards that uneasy aestheticism which goes round digging for inspiration in any source but its own native country or its own period. I have too much mistrust of affectation and pretence for that. Also I am too prejudiced against the momentary excitement of books which makes us accept as realities the mirages they inspire in us and which set us off down dead-end paths.

It is not a question of comparative history, where the past is compared to the present, like dead things to living ones. It is rather a close wedding of knowledge and practice, of renewing one's good faith in ancient traditions and rhythms, of reviving, not the actual forms of the past, but that spiritual bond which unfailingly puts us in contact with their principles.

[From 'L'Ecole du Vieux Colombier', Cahier No.2, November 1921, op. cit.]

PREPARING FOR THE OPENING

Notes before a meeting with Jules Romains, 2 and 3 September 1921

1. Speak to him about Maiène,[4] what I expect from her, what she is capable of doing. How she will be a link between him and me, and the living spirit of the education of the pupils.
2. Read to him what I have done from my notebook.

3. That we must always be perfectly sincere with one another.
4. That for a little while perhaps I will seem to be interfering with his functions. That he must not conclude as others have done too quickly that I do not want a collaborator and that I am an unreasoning authoritarian. Confess my tendency to be monarchic.
5. Question him closely about Chennevière[5] and his abilities.
6. Acquaint him with the general organisation, point out to him what my difficulties have been up to now, what a noble idea I have of my vocation and in what proportion I believe we shall be able to develop ourselves.
7. Insist on the character of the teaching and its unity, so that his class in poetic technique will be fully efficacious, at least as concerns the pupils.
8. Organisation. Buildings. Schedule. Office hours. Budget. Teachers' salaries. Scholarships for the pupils.
9. Programme of teaching: Music.

[The meeting took place at Saint-Clair, estate of the painter Théo van Rysselberghe, near Le Lavandou, on the Riviera; these notes published in *Cahiers Jules Romains*, 2, *Correspondance Jacques Copeau–Jules Romains*, Paris, Flammarion, 1978, p. 157]

THE FIRST YEAR PROSPECTUS
(December 1921 – July 1922)

Director: Jules Romains
Staff: Prosody, versification – J. Romains
    Poetic technique – Georges Chennevière
    Theory of the theatre, dramatic instinct – J. Copeau
    Reading, diction – Suzanne Bing and Romain Bouquet
    Acting, *mise en scène* – Romain Bouquet
    French language, memory – Marthe Esquerré/Line Noro
    Vieux Colombier Repertoire – André Bacqué, Georges Vitray
    Theatrical architecture – Louis Jouvet
    Music and song – Louis Brochard, D. Lazarus, Garcia Mansilla, Jane Bathori
    Acrobatics – The Fratellini Brothers
    Hébert method of physical education – M. Moyne
    Dance – Lucienne Lamballe
    Workshops in stagecraft – M.-H. Copeau and Emile Marque

41

(modelling), Ruppert (costumes), Suzanne de Coster (decor) Louis Jouvet (stage architecture)[6]

Aims of the School

The Vieux Colombier School is a technical school. It proposes to give its students a professional induction which is as methodical and complete as possible.

The centre of its programme is theatrical technique, envisaged in all its aspects. It gives greatest importance to the formation of accomplished actors. To this end, and without prejudice to future developments, the training it offers today includes all the knowledge and skills one can ask of an actor.

But it will also try to be a School of Dramatic Art in the largest sense of the term. Better still it does not despair of someday becoming, given careful expansion, a kind of general School of Theatre and of Literature, that is to say a place where a whole family of techniques are conserved, rediscovered and renewed, a place where public taste is purified and educated.

Although it is still far from achieving this vast goal, the School is already able to teach the young playwright, young poet and young critic, if not the whole of their profession, at least something essential to their profession.

It proffers welcome and interest to the lettered and to the amateur. Some of its courses round out the general cultural education of a university student, others will be capable of holding the attention of the scholar, the historian and the aesthete.

[The brochure (M-H D) continues with a description of the courses available which were developed the following year (with Copeau himself taking over the role of Director) as outlined in the prospectus given below]

THE SECOND YEAR PROSPECTUS

The Vieux Colombier School, 1922–3

General Director: Jacques Copeau
Director of Literary Studies: Jules Romains
Director of Dramatic Studies: Jacques Copeau
Director of Musical Studies: Daniel Lazarus
Director of Physical Culture: Lt Hébert
Administrator: Suzanne Bing

Secretary: Marie-Hélène Copeau

I
Apprenticeship Group

The apprenticeship group receives a professional training aimed at the formation of theatre artists (actors, stage-managers, designers, etc.) who are technically fully competent in their craft.

Courses for the Apprentice Group are absolutely closed. The only ones to be admitted – after examination and the receipt of proper references – are young people of both sexes at least fourteen and not more than twenty years of age.

The period of study is for a minimum of three years. Pupils are required to attend all classes and tutorials, from 9 a.m. to 12 p.m., and 2.00 to 5.30 p.m., and to respect all School regulations.

As the number of apprentices is limited, no places remain at present for new female students. Two places for male students are available subject to examination.

Courses and workshops for the Apprentice Group

1. *Theory of the Theatre.* Instructor: Jacques Copeau
   Religious origins and social significance.
   Birth and development of dramatic feeling, of the tragic form, of the instrument of theatre. The architecture and materials of the Theatre. Performance. The role of the actor and the arrangement of the stage. Written works.
2. *Dramatic Training.* Instructors: Jacques Copeau and Suzanne Bing
   Cultivation of spontaneity and invention in the adolescent. Story-telling, games to sharpen the mind, improvisation, impromptu dialogue, mimicry, mask-work, etc. Stage presentation of the various abilities acquired by the students in the course of their general instruction.
3. *Schools, Communities and Civilisation.* Instructor: Georges Chennevière
   The nation. Race. The spirit. Overall view of the history of civilisation. Great men and collectivities. Philosophical schools. Philosophical and religious communities. Literary and artistic schools. Corporations. Daily life of individuals, groups and cities. How it is expressed in poetry, music and theatre.
4. *Class in the French language.* Instructor: Line Noro
   Grammar exercises. Vocabulary. Textual analysis.

43

4a. *Memory exercises*. Rational cultivation of memory. Recitation of texts.

5. *Elocution, diction, declamation*. Instructor: Suzanne Bing
Mechanism of elocution. Syntax. Study of genres and styles. Ensembles.

6. *Music.* – under the direction of Daniel Lazarus
a. *Musical culture.* Study of ancient and medieval music. Annotated readings of the works of the great classical, romantic and modern composers.
b. *Singing.* – Instructor: Louis Brochard
Study of a *cappella* and accompanied chorus of the sixteenth, seventeenth and eighteenth centuries.
c. *Dance.* – Instructor: Mlle Lamballe
Technical study of the steps and figures of classical dance. Dramatic applications.

7. *Physical culture.* Monitor M. Moyne
Hygiene and training of the body. Open-air exercises. Suppleness. Breathing. Endurance. Stability.

8. *Acrobatics, games of strength and skill.* Instructors: Paul and François Fratellini
Work in the ring of the Medrano Circus.

9. *Craft workshops.*
a. Design, sketching, modelling and moulding. Drawing from life. Instructor: Emile Marque.
b. Costume. Instructor: M. Ruppert
c. Design. Study of materials. Technician: Marie-Hélène Copeau.
The work in the craftshops allows considerable freedom for individual initiative and for the student's own spontaneous aptitudes. Classes will be supplemented from time to time with readings, games, group outings (to museums, monuments, gardens, etc.).

II
Courses reserved for the Vieux Colombier Company

1. Study of poetic styles (in preparation for the Poetic Matinees.)[7]
Instructor: Jules Romains.
Exceptionally, upon application and prior examination, some amateurs will be admitted to attend these classes and choral recitations.

2. Principles of *mise en scène*. Instructor: Jacques Copeau.

3. Singing (individual and choral). Instructor: Louis Brochard.

4. Dance. Instructor: Mlle Lamballe.
5. Perfecting diction and stage practice (intended for the company's student-actors). Instructor: Suzanne Bing.

III
Classes reserved for outside professionals
Diction. Principles of *mise en scène*. Instructor: Georges Vitray. Under the direction of Jacques Copeau.
Tuition: 500 francs a year.

Public Courses of the Vieux Colombier
Under the direction of Jules Romains.

I
Permanent Courses
1. Poetic technique. Instructor: Georges Chennevière.
   Elements of prosody. Ancient prosody. Theory of classic French versification. Theory of modern versification. Analyses, demonstrations, practical exercises.
   First and third Fridays of each month at 5.30 p.m.
   Annual tuition: 100 francs.
2. History of the book. Instructor: Pierre Basset.
   First year: Generalities. History of manuscripts.
   Gutenberg and the beginnings of printing.
   Monday evenings at 9 p.m., from 20 November
   Annual tuition: 200 fr.

II
Dramatic Readings
Ten readings by Jacques Copeau.
1. *Antigone*, by Sophocles. 2. *Rudens*, by Plautus. 3. A Tibetan Mystery. 4. *El Médico de su honra*, by Calderon. 5. *The Maid's Tragedy*, by Beaumont and Fletcher, 6. *Bajazet*, by Racine. 7. Two Japanese Nohs. 8. *Faustus*, by Goethe. 9. *Atalanta*, by Swinburne.[8] 10. *Partage de Midi*, by Paul Claudel.
Saturdays at 5.30 p.m.

III
Forty-two Lessons on
Criticism, the Novel, Poetry and Theatre, by
MM. Albert Thibaudet, Benjamin Crémieux, Jacques Rivière,

Edmond Jaloux, Valéry Larbaud, André Gide, Paul Valéry, Henri Ghéon, Jules Romains.[9]

First Series: Criticism

Albert Thibaudet. 'The Art and Craft of the Critic'. Six lessons.

Jacques Rivière. 'Further progress in the study of the human heart' (Freud and Proust). Four lessons.

Second Series: The Novel

Edmond Jaloux. 'The novel's objective'. Four lessons.

Valéry Larbaud. 'Contemporary Spanish novelists'. Four lessons.

André Gide. 'The art of the novel'. Six lessons.

Third Series

Paul Valéry. 'Pure Poetry in the 20th Century'. Six lessons.

Fourth Series

Henri Ghéon. 'Spiritual and material conditions of a new dramatic art, and dramatic art in general'. Four lessons.

1. The author, the actor and the public. Closed theatre, open theatre.
2. France's dual tradition: Molière and Racine.
3. Poetry and plastic art. Modern theatre's rise and fall.
4. Theatre as a game; theatre as a cult. Popular and religious dramatic art.

Jules Romains. 'Substance and form in drama'. Four lessons.

THE APPRENTICE GROUP

The apprentice group consists of twelve pupils of both sexes, from fourteen to twenty years old. They receive a complete education appropriate to forming an artist of the theatre. The duration of apprenticeship is for a minimum of three years.

The first year is particularly concerned with the acquisition of fundamental concepts; the second year with a common general and vocational cultural development; the third concentrates on specific abilities and individual excellence; performance work is undertaken for the first time.

The teaching is based on *education of the body* (musical, gymnastic, acrobatic, dancing, games of strength and skill), with a progressive initiation into *craft skills* (drawing, modelling, decorative art, costume and props), *singing*, both choral and solo, *exercises in dramatic expression* (mask-work, physical games, physiognomy, mimicry), then to *improvisation* (*plastique* and with dialogue), to *elocution, diction and declamation*, to *general education* and to *dramatic theory* (laws of dramatic expression, study of the great epochs, scenic arts and crafts). Ultimately *free play* gives way to small-scale productions for which the pupils are left entirely to their own devices, as creators and workers.

Working and living communally, not excluding specialisation according to individual capabilities, has rapidly made a real little company from the twelve pupils of the apprentice group, with healthy ideals, a solid professional working basis, a remarkable *esprit de corps* and self-sufficiency.

In the course of the 1921–2 season, the group took part in the chorus of demons in *Saul*[10] for which they modelled and constructed the masks.

In July 1923, they present for an invited audience, on the Vieux Colombier stage, a complete presentation entirely produced in the own workshop, of a verse fantasy in one act by M. Georges Chennevière, *Chant du Jeudi*.

During the 1923–4 season, a small number of productions will be mounted by the School for the Vieux Colombier public.

No new pupils will be admitted to the apprentice group during the three years of its course of instruction.

A new, younger group, will eventually be set up.

Enrolment is now possible.

Pupils will be chosen after examination. They undertake to submit precisely to the rules of the School, to continue their education there for three years, and to receive no instruction other than that provided.

[From: 'L'Ecole du Vieux Colombier', in the Vieux Colombier programme for *La Locandiera*, January 1924]

THE JAPANESE NOH

In the course of its next season, the Vieux Colombier will present a production of a Japanese Noh play interpreted by the Vieux Colombier School which, on this occasion, will be having its first contact with the general public.

The word Noh (which means 'to be able', 'to have talent', hence 'an exhibition of talent', or 'performance')[11] designates a very ancient dramatic form whose origin goes back to the ninth century and which found its fullest expression during the fifteenth and sixteenth centuries. There is no equivalent to be found in our own theatre.[12] It is a sort of dramatic poem mingled with music and dance whose subject is usually taken from national history, from religion and from the most authentic popular traditions. It is composed of the following elements: declamation, song, dance, the performance of the principal actor who wears a mask, costume etc., structured according to traditions transmitted from one century to the next and combining, with moving simplicity, in a spectacle that is totally steeped in the noblest and purest of poetry.

The staging of such a production demands special preparation, for nothing in it is left to chance: the harmonisation of song, word and gesture, the intervention of music, the diversity of its rhythms; everything in it is regulated with minute precision.

The Noh, through the simplicity of its subject matter, the exquisite delicacy of the sentiments which it expresses, the measured way in which it makes use of the most diverse elements, reminds us of all the riches that our theatre has neglected and which make for the presentation of a visual feast, both for the soul and for the spirit.[13]

[From the Vieux Colombier programme, March 1924, op. cit.]

THE VIEUX COLOMBIER SCHOOL IN BURGUNDY

[*Copeau made little personal documentation of the work of the School in Burgundy from 1924–9, first at Morteuil, then (as 'Les Copiaus') in Pernand-Vergelesses. Le Journal de bord des Copiaus, 1924–9 – edited by Denis Gontard, Seghers, 1974 – is a carefully annotated, factual log of names, dates and events, recorded under Copeau's supervision by Léon Chancerel and Suzanne Bing, but containing little or no description of the pupils' daily work and training. The following description is extracted from an account of a visit to Pernand by Jacques Prénat, published in* Latinité *(December) 1930, pp. 377–400.]*[14]

A day in Pernand began at 9 a.m. For a good half-hour, in the wine-storage barn, the company would do gymnastics and acrobatics under the direction of Jean Dasté, former pupil of Lieutenant Hébert. From 10 a.m. till noon, the time was spent on mime exercises. Work resumed at 2.30 p.m. in the workshops: sewing, modelling, music or painting, and lasted until 4.30. Finally, from 5 till 7 p.m., time was devoted to the hard and difficult effort of improvisation, or in rehearsals for an entertainment.

'The predominant idea of my work', *Copeau told me*, 'is never to submit to any preconception. In what I was doing, there was always a close blending of experience and intellectualising. This is how, after years of working with actors, I arrived at the conviction that the problem of the actor is basically a corporeal one: the actor is standing on the stage. The defect of the official teaching system is to start by addressing itself to the actor's mind, to make him speak texts which he is incapable of understanding sincerely (*Phèdre*, for example): this leads to furnishing him with a certain collection of methods. Since the first problem is to make a given dramatic action legible, on a given stage, and since natural talents are not always sufficient, the first work will be to equip the actor with corporeal aptitudes relative to life on the stage. Hence, gymnastics. Certainly not aesthetic gymnastics, but with the aims of corporeal flexibility, control and balance of movements, and of breath control. Because the body, for the actor, starts out by being an obstacle. Afterwards, it becomes a terrible hurdle to link physical action with the text. In order to do it naturally, a prolonged effort is necessary.'

These words explain marvellously the reason that a day's work in Pernand began with a serious and difficult gymnastics lesson; why they pursued the effort to include acrobatics, even making perilous jumps above a straw-filled mattress. All that was done to give the young actors a sense of reliance in gesture, agility and the mastery of nerves and muscles. [...]

The rest of the morning, from 10 till 12, as we mentioned, was given to mime exercises. Copeau would propose themes to his young people or, most often, they invented some themselves: the storm, for example, or the vineyards, winter, spring, vegetation. And then they would freely compose short, mimed actions. In this way, intellect and poetic invention slipped into pure physical exercise and provided its form, in the same way that the sculptor informs his plastic substance. This prudent procedure will not be surprising when we observe that, in this manner, what the actors express is altogether true and pure. Obviously they can only bring to their compositions inner-felt feelings inspired by the given theme, and not plagiarised from a text. But, in return, this requirement forces them to look at the world around them and to create a substance which they can use later. So, they invent and become ingenious in organising this mass

*of knowledge. And, when the time comes to give life to a character,
these daily practice exercises will have greatly prepared them. This is
what Copeau meant when he told me: 'What* is important is not
working on a particular play, but that the dramatic imagination
should never stop working'.

*The manual labour which went on in the afternoon would not
have presented any difficulty if it had included only sewing, music,
carpentry or drawing. It is indispensable for a dramatic creator to
know the complete practice of his art. But what about modelling?
Since they wore masks in their exercises, why shouldn't they make
them themselves? This could only sharpen their knowledge of the
laws of facial expression. Their research, the tentative efforts of their
fingers in the ball of clay, must also ripen and deepen their knowledge
of man as revealed in his face; these are not unimportant supple-
mentary acquisitions. But it remains to be explained why, in returning
to Italian comedy and the classical theatre, Copeau is reviving the
mask.*

'When I had my beginners with me, altogether free from theatrical
influence and really spontaneous individuals, I was struck by their
excessive awkwardness. Even the most assiduous gymnastic training
could not overcome it. These supple and fresh organisms revealed,
in the mime exercises, a veritable corporeal impotence. So, I observed
them and looked for the reason: it was modesty. Indeed, the actor,
in tending to become unnatural while embodying a character, also
tends to distort himself: thus arises his inner resistance as a human
being. Looking back on the history of theatre, my deductions were
confirmed. In the early days of Greek drama, the people would
daub themselves with lees of wine. In Rome, behind the mask, the
audacity of the obscene mimes was multiplied and they ventured
gestures and postures they would never have dared with bare faces.
In our day, to indulge in debauchery, people disguise or distort
themselves. For the same reasons (but on a level of respect and
fear), the Egyptians would mask themselves when they wished to
represent the gods in their processions. All this explains how
Aeschylus seized upon the mask. So, in order to loosen up my
people at the School, I masked them. Immediately, I was able to
observe a transformation of the young actor. You understand that
the face, for us, is tormenting: the mask saves our dignity, our
freedom. The mask protects the soul from grimaces. Thence, by a
series of very explainable consequences, the wearer of the mask
acutely feels his possibilities of corporeal expression. It goes so far

that, in this manner, I cured a youngster paralysed by a morbid timidity.'

This account of the mask at the Vieux Colombier School shows us in striking fashion the accretive work which occurs, in Copeau's mind, around a correct idea. Thus, the first modelled masks are expressionless, impassive, completely according to the Greek rules, such as the one the Spirit of the Magician in L'Illusion *holds in his hands. The little expression it has comes from his making it bow or move. [...]*

THE ABSENT DEITY

A coherent organisation, a disciplined company, a creative process with a closely unified direction, a sincerity of *mise en scène*: I think these are the chief characteristics which made the Vieux Colombier what it is, and a few of the indispensable conditions for a dramatic renovation.

It is not up to me to recall the results we obtained which made us much envied. But you have the right to hear why, having obtained these results, already so far-reaching in comparison with the small size of our enterprise and which went far beyond the boundaries of our country, why, as I said, in spite of so many years of struggle, I suddenly broke the wand I had created with my own hands, dispersed my company and closed the doors of my theatre. I admit such an act had all the appearance of folly, and people did not hesitate to tell me so.

The first reason that comes to mind is that I had to give in to financial difficulties. It is one of the reasons, but not the one that decided me. I was always in need of money. My theatre was too small,[15] unworkably so. Even a full house did not bring in enough to give us a living. I had constantly to appeal to the support of generous friends. But, when all that is taken into account, my financial situation was no more desperate at the end of the 1923–4 season than in previous years. And, I maintain, that even if I had not had these money problems, which are anyway always surmountable, and had been materially prosperous, I should have done what I did; I should have stopped.

I shall tell you why.

First because I was being devoured by the craft which I had been practising for ten years. I should have died from overwork. I wanted to save my skin, not that I prize it, but I considered the sacrifice I could have made had ceased serving the idea to which I had devoted myself.

Indeed it is impossible, especially under such difficult material conditions, for the real work of dramatic creation to remain compatible with the overwhelming necessities of running a theatre. One's best efforts are quickly exhausted, and from then on there is no progress, and either one is oneself diminished, or one suffers abominably.

I do not mean to say that one is forced to make concessions, to follow the mood of the public, but whatever resistance is felt, the public makes its claims on one. It is demanding and unfair. It would like to see more and more productions, more and more definitive ones, which is futile. What hurts us more about the public is its inability to discern the authentically beautiful from the imitation or the counterfeit. Public favour tends to distort actors, and even frequent success chills their fervour. Everything which was once intoxicating becomes a torture for them: that constantly repeated effort; that unrelenting training day after day without respite for the artist to find himself again, to renew himself; that daily call on the best within him, that imperative of having to perform, almost always before being ready to do so, in order to be judged on a work he almost always feels he has not yet completely absorbed; and finally, that artificial light constantly glaring on a face which would prefer to find shadows into which to retreat.

These are a few of my reasons, and I could quote many more of the same. They have some importance, however they are not the most decisive ones.

The truth is that success, far from going to my head, continually sobered me. That is because, as I was learning my craft, I became acquainted with its difficulties and its resources; the more I worked, the more my demands and horizons grew, and the more I worked, the more I became dazzled by the possibilities of my art. New ideas filled my mind, discoveries enriched my imagination. And none of these things could have a place in our frenzied daily work which was slowly eroding my strength and was taking me away from myself. I was losing sight of myself, no longer knowing where I was. I had two existences, the one, at night, drawing me on to new paths and the other, during the day, holding my nose to the grindstone. Nothing within me or around me was satisfying any longer. I saw nothing but inadequacy everywhere.

I had been dreaming of an escape and a new beginning for the last three years, preparing for them all the while. Everything seemed to thwart me and to fight against my hopes; but, finally, I won.

I hesitate to go on, as it is already quite improper to have talked about what one has done. It becomes completely risky when one talks about what one is going to do. One runs the risk of overrating to oneself the importance of what is still in the project stage, and of making imprudent promises to one's listeners.

Allow me, however, if it is not possible for me to detail all the alternatives I have experienced, to outline for you the conclusions I have reached through experience and upon which I intend basing the new activity that I am on the verge of undertaking.

1. I believe that the conception of a new theatre such as those that have been realised under the name of *avant-garde*, art theatre or repertory theatre, does not represent much more than a compromise with classical theatre. I find proof of the malaise in the fact that such searchings for a new theatre waver among all the genres. After having extricated itself from the routine of the well-made play that was held in high esteem for a part of the nineteenth century, in order to adopt the more careless and so-called free composition of the novel, we see it today going to the other extremes and adopting the manner of the music hall or the circus. We have not yet produced a dramatic aesthetic to express our age.

2. I believe there no longer exists, strictly speaking, a creative force to express the concerns, the sudden changes and refinements of today's theatre. Its resources are dried up, and we shall not create new ones by stressing only the means of expression. The artists of the theatre are without aim or direction. It is the theatre's imperative objective to rediscover its function and its natural vocation.

3. I believe that in order to save the theatre, we must leave it. Those who want to stay in it will be condemned to being nothing but entertainers or aesthetes. As for us, we are not afraid to admit that we are tired of keeping alive a cult whose deity is absent, and we are going outdoors, on the road, to try to meet him there.

4. I believe that the theatre will not rediscover its grandeur until it ceases being an exploitation and becomes a ceremony. It is conceivable that the cinema, whose repeated performances are of a mechanical nature, can suffice to satisfy the needs for the provision of daily entertainment for the masses, and that the theatre could then be allowed its place only in special circumstances.

5. I know it was not enough to banish my little theatre out of the way on the left bank of the Seine in order to purify and renew the

notion of dramatic art in people's minds, nor in order to vanquish routine and destroy *cabotinage*. It has been necessary to leave the big city, where our austerity was only taken as an affectation, where all the bad influences were working to recapture us, and where the speculators had already seized upon our ideas in order to popularise them and make money from them.

6. I know that if we can, through work and restraint, discipline the actor, we cannot really educate him except by impressing on him from his childhood the notions of respect, grandeur and selflessness which are the basis of the total transformation we are seeking. There will be no new theatre which does not start from a school, where everything must be absorbed, from first principles.

7. Finally: I believe that within this school, and only there, will be realised that unity of all the dramatic elements of which we spoke, through the reconciliation of the creator with the director, and the identification of the author with the actor.[*]

---

[*]Nietzsche: 'This is what I have discovered: the only thing that all men really respect, and before which they bow, is a noble action. Never, never compromise. One cannot be truly successful unless one remains faithful to oneself. I already know what influence I have, and I see that if I were to become weaker or more sceptical, I should lessen both myself and all the others who are developing as I am.' (Letter to Baron Gersdorff, Basle, 15 April 1876)

[From: *Is a Dramatic Renovation Possible?*, lecture given in Brussels, 16 February 1926; transcribed in various versions, published under the title 'Une renaissance dramatique est-elle possible?', in *La Revue Générale*, Brussels (15 April), 1926. The version chosen here is that published in *Registres I*, pp. 253–73]

5

IDEAS IN COMMON: EMILE
JAQUES-DALCROZE

Copeau, coming as he did to the practice of theatre through literature, realised his lack of a conceptual base for the physical aspects of actor-training. The use of outdoor gymnastics, ultimately expressed in the adoption of the Hébert system of calisthenics at the Vieux Colombier School provided the students with general fitness and athletic exuber-ance. Yet he felt something more was needed, a discipline which would be integral to the performer's plasticity, rather than an adjunct to it. The key, Copeau believed, lay in rhythm, but where to find a training which would result in an expressive actor rather than dancer? For several years he thought to find a solution in the work of Dalcroze and his system of Eurhythmics, a method deriving from musical empathy with external forms, rather than movement to music.

Later, however (and partly as a result of his experiences with Eurhythmic training), Copeau turned against all separation of the vocabulary of theatre, not only as it went into the training, but also as forms (rather than Form) emergent from it. He was not in agreement, for example with the separatist development of mime by his former pupil Etienne Decroux. The whole had to be, as in his constant example of the Noh, greater than the sum of its parts. Any reduction of one of the contributory arts would be to lessen, not increase the potential expressiveness of the whole. And that is where, ultimately, the Dalcroze method was found lacking as a base training for the Vieux Colombier School. In an undated paper, probably written in the summer of 1920, Bing wrote:

The possibility of using music for exercises in bodily technique has been confirmed by Dalcroze's Rhythmic Gymnastics.

55

*However, a natural incompatibility very soon developed between
this conventional form and [...] my experiments.*

*Rhythmic gymnastics use <u>modern musical notation</u> to instil
into the body an equivalent notation through the practice of
movements which make up a form of gymnastics. Through this
bodily notation, the method instils into the individual the notions
of modern musical notation. [...]*

*Modern musical notation is a systematisation that im-
poverishes, imprisons and dries up the <u>inner feeling</u> of the
Rhythm found in declamation and Gregorian chant, and in the
way the Actor should come upon it in the great texts. [...]*

*The rhythmic sense must come from the inside. Exercises
are always unsatisfactory if they are not used exclusively to
exercise the outer manifestation of the <u>inner sense</u> that one
wants to develop.*

*We have seen some examples and made some experiments.
Maybe my objection is only valid for student-actors, but it
would be dangerous to ignore it. The very form of a certain
bodily technique for actors comes out gradually from this feeling
of danger. [...]*

*With Dalcroze, Music is reduced. Our art <u>is not reducible
to numbers and signs</u>. The Music we are trying to express by
cultivating ourselves as instruments is the same one we may
hear between an architectural form and <u>its environment,</u> and
the movement born from them. When Dalcroze speaks of
music, he means music reduced to its instrumental function.
When he deals with the human body, it is in order to incorporate
what he has learned from this music by means of a conventional
muscular translation of that music's conventional signs. In this
way, there is also a reduction of bodily expression: a kind of
<u>graphics</u>.*

The underlinings are Copeau's. Five years previously, however, he
had been full of enthusiasm for harnessing this new pedagogy...

FIRST IMPRESSIONS OF EURHYTHMICS

In the winter of 1913–14, the Vieux Colombier Theatre came into
contact with the Club de Gymnastique Rythmique, rue de Vaugirard,
founded and supported by my friend Emmanuel Couvreux,[1] for the
diffusion of Jaques-Dalcroze's method in Paris. Several

performances of Eurhythmics had been given at the Vieux Colombier and I had myself gone from time to time to the rue de Vaugirard where some of my pupils were taking courses, but my personal concerns did not allow me to pay sufficient attention to their work. I instinctively tended to be somewhat wary of the enthusiasm of some of them. However, I was struck by the exhilarating and healthy influence of the rhythmic exercises on the children, especially on my eldest daughter.

It was not until the spring of 1915, at Le Limon, that my eyes fell on an English language pamphlet, *The Eurhythmics of Jaques-Dalcroze*,[2] a gift from Emmanuel Couvreux.

Reading it was a veritable revelation for me, and I took an enthusiastic interest in it. In order to indicate a few of the ideas that inspired me, I content myself with copying here a few notes and quotations that I gathered while reading:

It is the pupil who should teach the master, not the reverse. The role of the master is rather to reveal to the pupil what it is that he has learned.

The master will constantly guide his teaching by the very responses to the educable material he has at hand and which will be an object of endless new discoveries.

One must not reshape the pupil but develop him.
...we do not think of initiating them into the art of elocution until they have got something to say... All modern educational-ists are agreed that the first step in a child's education should be to teach him to know himself, to accustom him to life, and to awaken in him sensations, feelings and emotions, before giving him the power of describing them.

Jaques-Dalcroze took the view that technique should be nothing but a means to art, that the aim of musical education should be, not the production of pianists, violinists, singers, but of musically developed <u>human beings</u>, and that therefore the student should not begin by specialising on any instrument, but by developing his musical faculties, thus producing a basis for specialised studies. [Copeau's underlining]

It is the same for the actor. Today, the actor is a specialist who, the more he develops, the further he gets from having a true devotion to his art. The 'great' actors being the most formidable enemies of great dramatic art, it is thus a question of de-specialising the actor, or as I have said elsewhere, de-histrionicising him. It is a question of making him more than he is through education, self-knowledge and the harmonious training of his faculties, and much less than he is by the position attributed to him in the service of his art.

The importance of musical education, which gives the sense of universality and develops plasticity. It allows one to adopt a view-point which bends the actors as a whole to the general rhythm of a dramatic work. The change of rhythm puts them on the track of a change of expression.

The analogy of staging with orchestral interpretation, of stage director with an orchestra conductor.[3]

The object here is to express by rhythmic movements and without hesitation rhythms perceived by the ear. The exactness of such expression will be in proportion to the number of movements of which the pupil has acquired automatic control. There is not time to analyse the music heard; the body must realise[4] before the mind has a clear impression of the movement image, just as in reading, words are understood and pronounced without a clear mental image of them having been formed.

When the realisation of a heard rhythm has become relatively easy, the pupil is taught to concentrate, by listening to, and forming a mental image of, a fresh rhythm while still performing the old one. In this manner, he obtains facility in rendering automatic groups of movements rhythmically arranged, and in keeping the mind free to take a fresh impression which in its turn can be rendered automatic.

Here again the process is analogous to that of reading, in which, while we are grasping the meaning of a sentence, the eye is already dealing with the next, preparing it in turn for comprehension.

In the preceding paragraph I have underlined the phrases which show an identity of means between certain methods of rhythmic training and those of dramatic reading, which I had established at the outset, almost instinctively, with the aim of breaking in my pupils to make them supple. That is only one detail, but it was probably the indication of a meeting of minds and a probable agreement.

In a general way, this first contact with Jaques-Dalcroze's ideas made me feel that the spirit of his method was not far from my own intuitions, and that rhythmic training as it is constituted and developed could perhaps provide that *first basis* which I was seeking for the training of the future actor. It remained for me to penetrate deeper into the understanding of the method and, in order to judge better his ideas, to know the man. The war had forced Jaques-Dalcroze to leave Hellerau and had brought him to his native Switzerland, to Geneva. I decided to visit him there.

[From the notebook 'L'Ecole du Vieux Colombier', op. cit.]

FIRST INTERVIEW WITH JAQUES-DALCROZE

Geneva, October 1915

The new Dalcroze Institute in Geneva had been opened since 1 October when I arrived on the 19th. Dalcroze said to me: 'I am very annoyed at having nothing interesting to show. We are beginning all over again.' I answered: 'Just let me attend your classes. I did not come here to see productions but to see you and your work. The more humble and elementary it is, the more interesting I shall find it.'

I recall one day when Craig repeated his famous words: 'You believe in the actor. I do not,' I had answered: 'I don't know whether I believe in the actor. In fact I have always detested him, especially the "great actor".[5] But I do believe in a new spirit which would transform the art of the actor. I believe in something I know about, that I have experienced, in something which, during an entire year of daily work, established itself between me and my company of young actors. It was on this "something" that I started to build.'

Well, here, from the first session, I found this something between Dalcroze and his pupils which exists between me and mine.

Dalcroze, personally, is perhaps not at all an artist. He is deserving only when he leaves himself behind and offers himself up as sustenance for others. He has a genius for teaching, essential to all born pedagogues; the gift of humanity, sympathy and complete self-sacrifice. The starting point of his teaching and of all his work is not in ideas but in himself. He needs to teach, to give of himself. He loves and understands people; he has the power of communicating with them, of understanding them, feeling with them, of coming forward to help them.

One must see him arriving at the Institute, trotting up the stairs, his big hands in the pockets of his overcoat, slightly flushed, with shining eyes, full of something he is going to share.

One must see him after class, unable to decide to leave the workplace, finding a thousand excuses to tarry with this one or that one, being considerate of the timid, encouraging with a friendly gesture or a word, searching in every glance for the need he hopes they have of him.

One must see him in his school, wearing little galoshes with the ends curled up by his big toe. He indicates a movement and his large body seems to throw off his weight; the *preciseness* of the indication lends him a certain grace. He rushes to the piano and improvises a rhythm without taking his eyes off the performers. He talks to them while playing and again becomes one with them. Obviously a distinct affection links him to the individuals he is teaching. This can be seen by his way of calling each one by his first name, saying 'tu' to them, of grasping a hand, squeezing a shoulder, leaning forward to hear a question.

Not the shadow of pedantry nor of dogmatism. Even in his vocabulary, Dalcroze tries to banish the slightest term that may smack of aestheticism. It may sometimes occur that in an article or a lecture the need to explain his system, to outline its general aspect and, also, to point out the series of consequences, he is led to use phraseology that seems pretentious. But that is not the real Dalcroze. He is the opposite of pretentiousness. He works from life, he is an experimenter. He knows nothing and induces nothing except from experience. Such is the force of his teaching and the fecundity of his work that they never stop, never reach conclusions. Results are added to results. And the method? It is inspired from life; it is life. And the goal? Each minute contains its own goal. One is constantly progressing towards the unknown, but on solid terrain which does not fade away behind you. With Dalcroze one is always in full improvisation, discovery, change; his teaching being limited only by the infinite combinations of his imagination and his fancy. It is a continual appeal to the forces of life and a renewal of them. It is also a complete exchange, for like a true master Dalcroze asks his pupils to teach him. He consults them, anticipates them and invites them to formulate their obscure feelings. He forces them to dare to feel and then gives back their feeling or observation in corrected, enriched and fuller form. The master and the pupil echo one another. A pupil executes a movement and Dalcroze invites the others to express their opinion and to form a critique of what has been done.

Certain classes are given by the pupils. The result is an endless interchange from which is created a union, an ease, a unanimity which lacks all personal affectation and stupid self-pride, ending in a joyful ensemble that is immediately striking.

Order, equability, eagerness, precision and discipline reign in this well-organised life.

Children's classes. Dalcroze lets them play. He has them execute the simplest movements collectively, rapidly and joyfully. Everything must begin with the child's play. The great difficulty is to ameliorate his play without his being aware of it. Everything must come from him; nothing must be imposed or taken away. Helping him without his noticing it.

Interpretation experiment: Dalcroze has them act out the essential episodes of *Snow White* while he tells them the story in words and rhythms.

Technique of the body. Collective exercises. Walking. Running. Climbing a staircase. Forward. Backward. Falling. The different ways of falling.

The general failure of the pupils: they put too much feeling in the movements they are executing. They need to summon up an idea that commands their attitude instead of achieving the union of body with music freely and spontaneously in time and space.

This is the great danger: the introduction of literature and aesthetic pedantry.

Unexpectedly, an adventitious exercise posed the question which interests me above all. A pupil recites a few verses, then she repeats them while accompanying them with movements meant to interpret them. The affectation was immediately obvious, even ridiculous. I say this to Dalcroze, that I do not believe anything interesting or instructive can come from such exercises. But the inversion of this exercise, for me, poses the great question. Moreover, in certain innervation exercises invented by Dalcroze, contraction and relaxation, some of the climaxes of the movements are accompanied, not yet by a sung syllable, but by an exclamation, and then, the exercise seems natural and necessary. It is beautiful; it produces emotions; it touches me. For I fancied seeking in this voice the sound of the human voice intervening at the extreme point of expression with movement that is completely in keeping with it. (It is again with the children that one must experiment, with the cries of the child at play.)

Is that the point where my method can be integrated with

Dalcroze's? I do not know yet, but I am convinced now that this juncture exists, is inevitable. I am sure from what I saw in Geneva, of the value of a general rhythmic training as a basis for the professional education of the actor. It was that certainty that I sought in Geneva.

It seems to me that agreement has been reached between Dalcroze and me on this ground: awakening in a collection of individuals a sense of an active, harmonious life, conscious of its strength and its resources.

We envisaged the future possibility of joint productions, and Dalcroze gave me all his writings, which I shall study.

[From the notebook 'L'Ecole du Vieux Colombier', op. cit., quoted in part in *Registres I*, pp. 300–2]

LATER REFLECTIONS ON THE DALCROZE METHOD

Letter from Copeau to Dalcroze, 26 July 1921

I am going to make the most of a period of relative leisure in order to write at length about many things which interest us and that we have in common. I hope you will answer me as freely and at length.

Since we met, I have worked and reflected tremendously. I cannot enumerate the details at present of all this work and reflection.

You are aware that, in a material sense, we have succeeded rather well in the past two years and have acquired a stability and influence that seems to bode well for the future.

However, I am far from satisfied. First, because of the necessity of constantly producing, of constantly confronting without concessions the requirements of an on-going production process made more difficult than ever since the war, and which stifles any possibility of renewal in the work. Then, the effort required personally in so many ways over the years tends to exhaust me. I need qualified fellow-workers who would be of more assistance to me. I am training them methodically, little by little, but more time is needed. It is obvious that my creation will only take the form I want when I shall have succeeded in creating a milieu where the training corresponds completely to my demands. This milieu is the Vieux Colombier School. It attempts to attract rather young elements. I have been working for six years to start up this school and I have not yet succeeded due to lack of time, money and qualified colleagues. Next winter, I hope to get a more satisfying result, but I am missing something fundamental. That is what I am going to explain to you.

You remember perhaps that in 1914–15 I became familiar with your work through a small pamphlet in which I found a resumé, probably imperfect, of your ideas and experiences, but which sufficed to show me the striking analogy and relationship between your researches and mine. I had a *presentiment* of what you already expressed with such technical competence. Suddenly the *need* that I was feeling was satisfied, the *deficiency* from which I was suffering was filled. I thought I had found the starting point of my dramatic teaching in eurhythmics.

I saw you in Geneva and we talked. I became more familiar with your work. Everything inclined me towards that union which I had foreseen at the outset.

In the winter of 1915–16 I conducted a few experiments in Paris with Paulet Thevenaz and Lili de Lanux.[6] I had seen you teach in Geneva, so I was able to judge how far they were from your spirit.

Later, I took Jessmin Howarth to America. It was fruitless and I had to dismiss her.

This year, in Paris, I tried out Jane Erb, who had approached me burning with desire to be one of us. The same profound disappointment. I dismissed her at the end of the season. More than once during these regrettable experiences I asked myself how I could have been mistaken in the confidence and hopes I had founded on eurhythmics.

In the peace and quiet of the last few days in this marvellous solitude, I read your book, *Rhythm, Music and Education*[7] with enthusiastic interest. All my enthusiasm and confidence was restored. There are times when your thoughts, identical to mine, are expressed in forms which I often used without knowing yours. Thus, there is an identity of hopes that must not be ignored, from which something living must emerge.

More than ever, I feel, see and proclaim that what I lack is *music*, that only music ought to provide the fundamental information for the young people we wish to initiate; music such as you teach it, Dalcroze, capable of musicalising the very being to the depths of its physical and moral constitution.

Therefore, how is it that, understanding this necessity, and having confidence in rhythmics, I was never able, satisfactorily, to find it in any of its pupils?

I speak to you frankly since this is a confession.

All the pupils of rhythmics I have known have seemed to me to be *inhuman*, or rather *dehumanised*. I mean that they no longer seemed to have the same faculties as ordinary mortals, nor the natural, instructive contact with ordinary, present-day life. They seemed to be terrifyingly personal, proud and even vain, undisciplined, solely concerned with their petty affairs and the effect to be produced; in short, spoiled by a specialisation which resembles histrionics, deprives them of all simple and living comprehension of the others they seem to despise and who, in turn, feel revolted by them. Far from seeing in them the equilibrium that a harmonious development should have given them, one finds them highly-strung, thin-skinned, anxious, almost unhinged, often frivolous and almost always tormented by the more or less self-conscious effects of sexual inhibition. They all, equally, lacked the power of being unaware of themselves, of forgetting themselves, of surrendering themselves, in short of *giving themselves*. They lacked the gift of living with others, of inspiring confidence and friendship, of making themselves both respected and loved. Lacking this natural authority, the one they lent to their functions became annoying, scoffing and offensive.

Was I just unlucky? Or are these traits that I mention generalised ones? I ask you as you are the only one who can enlighten me.

The fact is that today *I no longer dare* to apply to a pupil of rhythmics to put him in charge of instructing, for want of which, meanwhile, everything remains in abeyance and falls apart.

What I need is a master musician capable of and willing to work in agreement with me, in keeping with the general teaching of my school, keeping constantly in mind the *raison d'être* of the objective and conclusion of our efforts, which is *the drama*. The whole teaching of the school should be imbued and saturated with the dramatic spirit. The master in question should also give lessons in the rudiments of physiology and anatomy, solfeggio and singing, improvisation, the history of musical language, rhythmics, dance. He should even be able to teach certain instruments such as the drum, the dulcimer, the triangle, the rattle, the flute, etc. And all of this, I am sure you understand, with an eye to the dramatic realisation towards which our teaching constantly leads the pupil. The pupil will be, at once and in every fibre, *musicalised* and *dramatised*.

To my knowledge, this has never been done up to now. Rhythmics has been more or less, in experiments so far, brought in from the exterior, like an auxiliary or a complement to dramatic education. It has never been *incorporated* or *internalised*. Up to now, it has not animated the new teaching and has not had even modest effects or results. It is a *pretentiousness* added on to so many others, nothing real nor effective.

Who will come to my aid?

If I were younger or less weighed down by work, I should try to undertake my own education in order to give myself this fundamental teaching. It would be the solution. It is unthinkable.

Would you give me some advice, or your opinion of this grave question?

I now have an excellent staff, a solid organisation in some areas, the benefits of continuity, homogeneity, experience, in short, of a continuously controlled practice carried forward in the same direction over several years. The school, once it is well organised, will also make rapid progress, and when it begins to bear fruit, who knows what we shall realise?

I have spoken to you, my dear Dalcroze, with absolute frankness. It is understood that this conversation must remain between you and me. I await your answer impatiently.

DALCROZE'S RESPONSE

1 October 1921

You make a very harsh judgement of the teachers of my method that you have hired. You are right. However, I must assure you that, in general, my pupils do not have the faults you indicate, and unfortunately and tragically, you found yourself in contact with those pupils I should not myself have hired as teachers in my Institute. What characterises those pupils I consider really 'mine' is obviously a strong will, a great spirit of order, an absolute modesty and a lively imagination. Obviously, I cannot make complete individuals and artists of all of them, but I feel that those who have the faults you indicate are the exceptions. However, time will tell. [...]

How right you are to think and write that music is an indispensable complement to theatrical art! Not, certainly, the music of rules and theoretical combinations, but flooding music, orderly music, feeling music, balanced music. But you will admit that it is very difficult for me to develop both musical feeling and plastic imagination in my pupils. There are temperaments among them – determined, penned up, oriented by reason of natural laws – and it is very rare to find subjects inclined both towards music and towards plastic art, both dramatically and socially. In Geneva, I have three of that type of subject and, thanks to them, the milieu which I have created is beginning to develop and to take on definition.[...]

For the past two or three years, I have been engrossed in dramatic questions; I myself give the class in plastic movements and I think that all stagings need a music of lasting quality and accentuation, a common mental and musical rhythm *which gives unity to the displacements, organises the architectures of movements, balances the ensemble of gestures, establishes contrasts and harmonies. As concerns the solo actor, rhythmic training should not lead him to think out his own motricity, but simply allow him to attune it to that of the others. I consider the displacements, gestures, attitudes, group-ings as a kind of* orchestration, *i.e. to the art of making use of each instrument's individual tonal quality with an eye to the ensemble effect, so I am sure that the knowledge of certain laws of muscular economy, sacrifice of personal effects, influence on space, elimination of useless effort, co-ordination of attitudes and immediate adaptation to various atmospheres, should allow the actor to blend his tempera-ment with those of the ensemble and to regulate the relations between the soloist and the protagonists, as in a musical symphony.*

I shall be in Paris for a week at the end of November or the beginning of December. I am so shocked to see so many directors resort to the exterior *effects of my method (I do not mention any names!) that it would be very agreeable to me to explain to your 'company' what I call 'interior rhythm' and the prescience of ensemble movements.*

[From unpublished correspondence, Copeau–Dalcroze, M-H D]

FINAL THOUGHTS ON EURHYTHMICS

First, give the word Music its general meaning.

Let us say it is: the feeling for rapports. The Muses.

For the actor, it cannot be assumed that the word Music indicates something that comes to one first through the ear.

To start the actor with the study of Music is to immerse him in the universality of his art. To start him with rhythmics is to put him in touch with something particular. In the case of the pupil who is a natural musician, with or without a traditional musical education, rhythmic gymnastics give him an easy musical and bodily satisfaction. Rhythmics is another language, a speciality, and consequently a deformation.

Rhythmics leads to a personal idolatry of the body.

[Undated notes in Copeau's Journal]

Part II

THE THEATRE

6

THE PROBLEM OF THE ACTOR

In the Vieux Colombier School Copeau and his associates began a quest for a solution to the problem of the actor on the modern European stage through personal education and ensemble training. That search has been continued in other schools throughout the century. Lee Strasberg, for example, as well as his acknowledged debt to Stanislavsky in developing the teaching at the Actors Studio, also learned much from his contact with Copeau:

> One of the most brilliant descriptions of the actor's problem comes from Jacques Copeau. He describes the difficulties the actor has with his 'blood', as he calls it. The actor tells his arm, 'Come on now, arm, go out and make the gesture,' but the arm remains wooden. The 'blood' doesn't flow; the muscles don't move; the body fights within itself; it's a terrifying thing. To someone on the outside this sounds like verbalisation or poetry. But we know, because we have often felt what it means to stand on the stage, and know that what you are doing is not what you mean to do, that you meant to move your arm differently and you meant to come over to the audience with ease and warmth, and instead you're standing there like a stick. Copeau calls it 'the battle with the blood of the actor'.
>
> Copeau was also the first to bring to my attention the marvellous phrase Shakespeare used about acting. Remember what Hamlet says, 'Is it not monstrous that this player here, but in a fiction, in a dream of passion, could force his soul so to his own conceit...?' Isn't it monstrous that someone should have this capacity? The profession of acting, the basic art of acting, is a monstrous thing because it is done with the same flesh-and-blood muscles with which you perform ordinary deeds, real

71

deeds. The body with which you make real love is the same body with with which you make fictitious love with someone you don't like, whom you fight with, whom you hate, by whom you hate to be touched. And yet you throw yourself into his arms with the same kind of aliveness and zest and passion as with your real lover, with your realest lover. In no other art do you have this monstrous thing.[1]

Looking back on his career, both as director and actor, Copeau concluded simply: 'the problem of the actor is basically a corporeal one: the actor is standing on the stage.'[2] *It is a problem that actors should face in every generation. When they avoid its implications (which are spiritual as much as they are technical), Copeau argued that theatre loses its sincerity and falls at the mercy of fashion and commercialism.*

AN ACTOR'S THOUGHTS ON DIDEROT'S 'PARADOXE'

Diderot wrote with melancholy:[3] 'I have an exalted view of the great actor's talent – *this man is rare...*'

Indeed, all the rarer, and greater, when he appears on stage, as the craft he is practising is then even more of a threat to the integrity and uplifting of the humanity of his being.

Shakespeare wrote (*Hamlet*, II, ii) that an actor's nature is unnatural and horrible, while at the same time it is admirable. He described it in one word: *monstrous*.

What is horrible about the actor is not the lie, for he does not lie. It is not deceit, for he does not deceive. It is not hypocrisy, for he applies his monstrous sincerity to being what he is not, and not at all in expressing what he does not feel, but in feeling the make-believe.

What upsets Hamlet the philosopher, as much as his other hellish apparitions, is the diverting of natural faculties in the human being to a fantastic use.

The actor takes the risk of losing his face and his soul. He finds them falsified, or does not find them any longer, at the moment he needs them to recover consciousness. His features cannot pull themselves together, his behaviour and speech remain too sharp and detached, as if they were separated from his soul. The soul itself, having been too often upset by acting, too often carried away and offended by imaginary passions, contorted by artificial habits, feels irrelevant before reality. The whole being of the actor carries the stigmata of a strange relationship with the human world. When he returns among us, he looks as if he were coming from another world.

An actor's profession tends to pervert him. It is the consequence of an instinct which pushes a man to abandon himself and live a pretence. And yet it is a profession that men despise. They find it dangerous, immoral, and they condemn it for its mystery. This pharisaical attitude, which has not been eliminated in even the most tolerant societies, reflects a profound idea. That is, that the actor is doing something forbidden: he is playing with his humanness and making sport of it. His senses and his reasoning, his body and immortal soul, were not given to him so that he could use them thus as an instrument, forcing and turning them in every direction.

If the actor is an artist, he is among all artists the one who sacrifices the most of his being to the ministry he is exercising. He can give nothing but himself, not in effigy but in body and soul, with nothing in between. His creation is himself, both as subject and as object, beginning and end, matter and instrument. Therein lies the mystery: that a human being can think of himself and treat himself as artistic matter, play on himself like an instrument with which he must identify while never ceasing to be distinct from it, simultaneously active as a person and impersonating that activity, the natural man and the puppet. [...]

There is something about an actor which is dependent on what he is in himself, that certifies his authenticity, makes a tonal impression on us; knowing, from the moment he steps on stage, from his simple presence, even before he has spoken a word, that there is no possibility of deception. It is this something that distinguished an actress like Duse from her contemporaries. It is a natural quality that can be enhanced by art but cannot be imitated by it. [...]

It cannot be denied that actors do not always feel what they are playing; they may play the text without playing either the role or the situation, succeeding in giving seemingly faultless performances, that is to say ones which are more or less accurate and correct, even when experiencing no emotion. This is their downfall. This is the slope which the lazy and mediocre slither down. It is the martyrdom risked daily by the best, for none of them ever knows whether or not he will not suddenly feel devastated by dryness in one of those awful moments when he hears himself speaking, sees himself acting, or analyses what he is doing and the more he analyses the more distant he becomes from it. Diderot would say that he was 'moving all over the place without being at all moved'. If he were moving 'all over the place' it wouldn't actually- be because he was feeling nothing. It would be in order to *feel something.*[4]

One can easily smile at the idea of a feeling chasing after itself, of a spontaneity looking for itself, of a sincerity worrying about itself. Let us not be too quick to smile. Think rather on the nature of a craft where there is so much material to be handled. The sculptor's struggle with the clay he is handling is nothing if I compare it to the resistance felt by an actor from the oppositions of his body, his blood, his limbs, his mouth and all his organs.

I can imagine an actor confronted with a role he likes and understands, whose character is naturally suited to his own, whose style is right for his capabilities. He smiles with satisfaction. He can sight-read this role without even trying. The first reading that he gives of it is surprising in its correctness. Everything in it is masterfully indicated, not only the overall intention, but already even the nuances. And the author is delighted to have found the ideal interpreter who will carry his work to the heights. 'But wait,' the actor says to him, 'I haven't got it yet.' Because he himself has not been fooled by this first grasping of the role which has been effected by his mind alone.

Now he gets down to work. He rehearses, in a hushed tone, cautiously, as if he were afraid of upsetting something within himself. These private rehearsals still retain something of the quality of readings. The nuances of emotion are still perceptible in them for a few privileged listeners. The actor now has the role committed to memory. This is the moment when he begins to be a bit less in possession of the character. He can see what he is trying to do. He is composing and developing. He is setting in place the sequences, the transitions. He reasons out his movements, classifies his gestures, corrects his intonations. He watches himself and listens to himself. He detaches himself from himself. He judges himself. He seems no longer to be giving anything of himself. Sometimes he breaks off his work to say to himself, 'I'm not feeling that.' Often, correctly, he suggests a change in the wording, the inversion of a phrase, some alteration in the direction that would allow him, he believes, to feel it better. He is trying to find the means to put himself in the right attitude, a state of feeling: a starting point which might sometimes be a hand movement or a vocal intonation, a particular decontraction or a simple intake of breath... He tries to tune himself up. He sets out his nets. He is organising in order to capture something which he has known of and anticipated for a long time, but which has remained alien to him, has not yet entered into him, taken up residence inside him.... He listens without great attention to the basic instructions which are given to him from out front, about the emotions of his character, his motivations, his whole psychological make-up. And all this time his attention seems totally taken up with petty details.

That is when the author, with excessive politeness, takes his illustrious interpreter by the arm and whispers to him, 'But why don't you just stick to what you did the first day? That was perfect. Just be yourself.'

The actor is no longer himself. And he is not yet 'other'. The more he prepares for the role, the further he gets from what he was doing on the first day. He has had to give up the freshness, the naturalness, the nuances and all the pleasure that he got from his instant interpretation, to accomplish the difficult, thankless, pain-staking work of turning what is literally and psychologically true into what is theatrically true. He has had to set up, to master and assimilate all the processes of metamorphosis which simultaneously distance him from his role and lead him into it. It will be only when he has completed this study of himself in relation to a given character, articulated all of his capabilities, exerted all his being in the effort to serve the ideas he has conceived and the feelings for which he is paving the way within his body, his nerves, his mind, into the very depths of his heart, only then will he be able to get a new grip on himself, now transformed, and try to give his all.

At last the actor fills his role. He now finds nothing empty or factitious in it. He could live it without a text. He matches his sincerity against that beautiful 'interior silence' that Eleonora Duse spoke of.

Here is our man revealed on stage, put on show, exposed to critical judgement. He enters another state of being. He assumes responsibility for it. He renounces the cares, the discomforts, the sadness, the suffering of a real life for this one: or rather he is delivered from them by it. But now the way his partners handle themselves on stage, a movement in the audience, a noise backstage, a lamp blowing, a ruck in the carpet, a stage management slip-up, a forgotten prop, a snagged costume, a forgotten line, a slip of the tongue, a momentary loss of vital energy – everything threatens him, everything is against him, the one who, all on his own, must dominate the entire process. Any little thing can, at any moment, come between his sincerity (which nothing can force to return if it decides to slip away) and the acting that, willy-nilly, he has to do; any little thing can deprive him of the things he thought he had mastered through his long preparation, separate him from the character he has built from his own substance but which, like its original, can undergo sudden, profound changes.

The rise of the curtain has taken him by surprise... his first round has gone off rather involuntarily... now he is disconcerted. I can see him fiddling with the end of his tie. For a moment he loses the flow. He beats a retreat. He is looking for a point of support. He breathes deeply. I think he'll get it back because he knows his business. You will say that the way these unimportant incidents upset him proves that he was not feeling what he was doing. I believe, rather, that the more sensitive the actor, the more subject he is to such confusions. But he will get the feeling back – because he knows his business.

Let's suppose that he did not lose the flow. He is attaining fulfilment. But this fulfilment itself will have to be measured. There is a way of measuring sincerity, just as there is a measure of technique. Will it be said that the actor feels nothing because he knows how to make use of his emotions? That the flowing tears and the sobs are faked because they only interrupt his vocal interpretation for an instant and scarcely affect his speech? Should we not, on the contrary, while not even trying fully to understand it, rather admire this wonderful instinct, the gift of nature and reason which, a little while ago, put the disconcerted actor back into the emotional flow, yet is now preventing his feelings from disrupting the continuity of the play? Such acting requires a head 'made of iron', as Diderot says, but not 'made of ice', as he had originally written. It also requires flexible, resilient nerves, and very quick, very delicate, internal reflexes.

To deny that an actor has sensitivity, on account of his presence of mind, is to discount it in any artist who observes the laws of his art and refuses to allow the tumult of emotions to paralyse his soul. The artist, with a serene heart, rules over the disorder in his workshop and his materials. The more emotion rises within him and exalts him, the more lucid his brain becomes. This coldness and this trembling are compatible, just as they are in a fever or in a state of drunkenness.

'To embrace the full sweep of a great role, work out the light and dark passages in it, the smooth and the weak, to be equally good in the quiet moments or the animated ones, to give variety to details, to be harmonious and at one with the ensemble, and to develop one's own sustained delivery... this is the work of a cool head, profound judgement, exquisite taste, painful study, long experience, and an uncommon tenacity of memory.' Diderot is right: within the actor's mind, 'everything has been measured, worked out, learned, organised.' But if his playing is nothing but the expression of his mastery, the presentation, as it were, of technical excellence, he will either fall asleep in his routine performance or dissipate himself in the fireworks of virtuosity. The absurdity of the 'paradox' is that it sets the processes of the craft against the freedom of feeling and it denies, in the artist, the possibility of their coexistence and simultaneity.

For the actor, the whole art is the gift of himself. In order to give himself, he must first possess himself. Our craft, with the discipline it presupposes, the reflexes it has mastered and holds at its command, is the very warp and weft of our art, with the freedom it demands and the illuminations it encounters. Emotive expression grows out of correct expression. Not only does technique not exclude sensitivity: it authenticates and liberates it. It upholds and protects it. It is thanks to our craft that we are able to let ourselves go, because it is thanks to it that we will be able to find ourselves again. The study and observation of principles, an infallible mechanism, a dependable memory, obedient diction, regular breathing and relaxed nerves, clearness of the head and stomach, all of these give us the security that inspires us with durability. Constancy in our accents, our positions, our movements, maintains freshness, clarity, diversity, invention, evenness, renewal; it allows us to improvise.

In *Hamlet* (II, ii), Shakespeare the actor describes the bearing of a man who *is in action* while making a made-up character come alive.... Interpreting means, first of all, to insinuate oneself into the acquaintance of what is to be performed and to form a concept of it. Then, to possess the power of forcing one's soul to enter into this concept: 'force his soul... to his own conceit'. The intellect, educated by experience and reasoning, constructs coherent and varied ideas, animated and warmed by sensibility. The soul labours within the idea, respecting its limitations, and from this labour follows the precarious and mysterious operation, subject to all sorts of circumstances and peculiarities, which will clothe the idea more and more precisely – what Diderot calls the phantom – with the necessary forms and tangible signs by which the spectator will recognise the nature of what is going on within the actor, 'suiting with forms to his conceit'.... To the extent that these signs assert themselves with precision, accent, depth, as they take possession of the body and its habits, they stimulate in turn the inner feelings which settle more and more really in the actor's soul, filling it and supplanting it. It is at this degree of the work that is born, matures and develops a sincerity, an acquired and achieved spontaneity, which we can say acts like a second nature, inspiring in turn the physical reactions and giving them control, eloquence, naturalness and freedom.

> And all for nothing!
> For Hecuba?
> What's Hecuba to him, or he to Hecuba,
> That he should weep for her?

Where do we find the secret of an imagination that puts the actor on the level with Hamlet's torment or Oedipus' misfortunes, with incest and parricide?

There is one answer that can be found to this question. It is Goethe's: 'If I had not already felt the world within me *through presentiment*, I should have remained blind with my eyes opened.'[5]

[Extracted from *Réflexions d'un comédien sur le Paradoxe de Diderot*, Plon, 1929, reprinted in *Registres I*, pp. 205–13]

THE TRUE SPIRIT OF THE ART OF THE STAGE

Do not consider as a secret symbol the two doves facing each other on the coat of arms above our door. They adorn also a mosaic of San Miniato in Florence, where at the close of the day I often gazed at the hills of Italy, our mother. Do not search for a hidden meaning in this very simple title, 'Théâtre du Vieux Colombier'. All it means is that on 22 October 1913, a troupe of actors, fired by the love of their art, pitched their tent on the left bank of the Seine, in the street of the Vieux Colombier, halfway between the Place Bon-Marché and the Saint-Sulpice. Stories as old as time itself and theories long worn out are too often disguised under startling new names and presented to us over and over again. I kept an old name for something new – something quite small at present, but absolutely free and big with promise for the future. I shall tell you what is new in the house of the doves, and pure... and invincible: it is a new *spirit*. Now, how shall I define that new spirit? I dare not say a religious spirit, yet I know it is a spirit of love. Love for beauty, for simplicity and for the modest task we wish to perform; love for that life which breathes forever in the masterpieces of the past, which slumbers in our hearts and will inspire the unknown works of art of the morrow.

A great on-sweeping current of new ideas will soon regenerate the art of the stage. Precursors of great promise, such as Adolphe Appia and Gordon Craig, have centred our attention upon a few essential principles; we are invited to turn to the past and to blush at the abasement of our modern stage. We are many, in both hemispheres, who without having ever met and without even knowing of each other, are working for the same ideal. We agree to hate in all its forms the prostituting of the stage. We rebel at the vulgarity of current plays and at the lie imposed upon the public by a powerful commercial organisation which succeeds in labelling as worthy of admiration that which has no artistic value whatever. We have had enough of that absurd wealth of scenery and stage setting which draws the attention away from the play itself and stifles its spirit; enough of those conceited actors who are the parasites of our theatrical art, instead of being its servants. Artists, or simply cultured people, cannot meet and talk together for a few moments without coming to the conclusion that the modern stage is debased, and that it must, first of all, be purified and made worthy of our civilisation...

> *Et qu'il est pourtant temps, comme dit la chanson*
> *De sortir de ce siècle ou d'en avoir raison!*[6]

For the last twenty, ten, five years, and indeed almost every year, in every part of the world, small armies of courageous men have surged forth, and, as champions of the new stage, have been ready to fight for their ideals. Why none of these has succeeded is easily discerned. Some, when success begins to smile at them, yield to its lure and lose their ideal. Or a group of young artists, enamoured of beautiful ideas which they have been unable to develop, lack the sentiment of positive reality, that is to say, are insufficiently well prepared for the struggle. In another case, a well co-ordinated and vigorous leadership is wanting, or a well-defined programme, or patience and true self-abnegation. Elsewhere it may be that a leader has an excessive longing for singling himself out, and, under pretext of being original, is simply extravagant.

I came to the firm conviction that in our difficult undertaking of pulling the stage out of the mire in which it is sinking, a steadfast moral value must be put before anything else. And the so-called revolutionary principles, all the aesthetic ideals and the declarations of groups of artists who appear and disappear every week, all these will accomplish nothing, so long as our efforts do not succeed in banding together, under a leader worthy of that name, a 'brother-hood' of energetic and disinterested men, willing to work, willing to be led, willing to live and die for their art. Not a thing will be done until that new *spirit* has been infused into dramatic art.

Such is the first problem to be solved. Other questions are of secondary importance. In the Vieux Colombier I endeavoured to put into practice what I preach. Why did I succeed, in the eight months, from October 1913 to May 1914, in that Paris which is said to be so blasé, in forcing upon an ever-growing audience a repertoire made up entirely of French and foreign classical masterpieces and of the boldest plays of the present generation? It was because I was surrounded by fellow workers, men and women, whose pure souls and minds remained unsullied. I had inspired them with confidence at the start. Today, thanks to them, I am confident we have not undertaken this long voyage in vain.

These valorous young men are now risking on the battlefield lives consecrated to the service of art. They have faced the enemy for more than two years. But their thoughts ever return to the house of the doves. They keep watch over it, while they defend the national inheritance. Two have already fallen. One, who still risks his life every day, has just written to me: 'My dear and best friend, I am going to tell you what you must do; you must take everything upon your own shoulders... and calmly face the possibility of keeping up the work *without us*. I also may be killed. Do not be disheartened, as long as the Vieux Colombier survives...'[7] Such is the fervour of the *spirit* with which they are animated. No wonder I am proud to be delegated by them to tell our friends in America of our past efforts, and of the hope and faith we have in the future of the Vieux Colombier.

It seems to me, and I believe I am not alone in this opinion, that a company of earnest players, fired with the spirit of their art, will be able in the near future to give life to some new dramatic form. The theatre must achieve salvation from within, and not from insincere artists who approach their work with a grimace of commiseration, or perhaps with disguised contempt. I mean that it has been too often the case that an attempt has been made to salve the ills of dramatic art with the physic of literature. If our theatre is weak, we shall not be able to give back to it the grace and force of Apollo by offering it a pair of crutches. We must build up a new and healthy constitution for it. We must transform it from top to bottom. I am not suggesting a revolution, but a thorough and complete transformation.

Probably this has been said a great many times before, and it is obvious that the task will not be an easy one to accomplish. In order to fulfil our aim, the first step must be to obtain genuine dramatic artists, simple players, inspired with the true spirit and movement of the stage. They will have to be young and sturdy. Such a theatre then will be modern and active. Give me real actors, and, on a platform of plain rough-hewn boards, I will promise to produce real comedy.

[*Vanity Fair*, April 1917, p. 49]

THE ACTOR AS INSTRUMENT

The question of décor does not exist for me. Forming a troupe of actors, having them act anywhere, renewing the actor's mind and soul: *that is inimitable.*

No matter how we approach the problem of theatre, we come back to the problem of the actor as the instrument and perfect realiser of a dramatic idea.

[From the 5th Lecture (given in French) in the Little Theatre, New York, 26 March 1917, printed in *Registres III*, pp. 514–18]

7

SCENIC ARCHITECTURE

Often as Copeau reiterated the need to begin again at the beginning in the quest for a renovated theatrical medium, he remained uncertain (or perhaps unwilling to decide) whether to start with the actor or with the stage, for what he sought was their symbiosis as dramatic action. The previous section of this anthology deals with Copeau's search for the regeneration of the actor. The stage, as inherited by the twentieth century, he considered to be the domain of the scene painter and the technician, 'a cluttered up and mechanised theatre, [...] an enclosed space in which mind and matter constantly wage war on each other'.[1] *But the solution to this problem of the legacy of the proscenium arch and fourth-wall realism, could not, he argued, be found only through a new philosophy of design since, as he wrote in the 1913 manifesto:*

To hold to a particular theory of scenic design means that one approaches the theatre from a peripheral point of view.

Thus, as he explained on arriving in New York, where he was to strip the Garrick Theatre as bare of decorative encumbrances as he had the Athenée Saint-Germain in Paris:

If I stretch a grey cloth across the stage instead of décor, it is not because I think I have discovered a new decorative formula. It is a radical remedy, a purgation. It is because I want the stage to be naked and neutral in order that every fault may stand out; in order that the dramatic work may have a chance in a neutral atmosphere.[2]

On the other hand, as he had again stated in the 1913 manifesto, the truly dramatically significant should not be thrown out along with the deadweight of outworn decorative practices:

Let us be careful to give up nothing. One must not confuse scenic convention with dramatic convention. On the contrary! The obligations of the stage and its crude artifice will act on us as a discipline, by forcing us to concentrate all truth in the feelings and actions of our characters.

Which is, of course, to begin with the actor... During the company's exile in America, Copeau began to feel ready to add a first new 'crude artifice' to the enforced neutrality of the acting area which he and Louis Jouvet had created. This innovation was, in fact, a translocation of an image lodged in his mind since reading a description by Cervantes of Lope de Rueda's platform stage as consisting of 'four trestles and five planks'. A version of this tréteau nu *was placed upon the naked stage of the Garrick Theatre for the Vieux Colombier's opening production in 1917. On his return to post-war Paris, Copeau found this simple device for playing Molière's* commedia dell'arte *inspired farces needed a surprising amount of justification to supposedly sophisticated audiences. He wrote in the 1920 programme for* Les Fourberies de Scapin:

This is in no sense meant to be a reconstruction; even less is it the application of any theory.

At a certain moment in our interpretative work we felt a NEED for this *tréteau*. That is all.

We tried it out and as a result of it we have learned a great deal [...]

It seemed to us, or rather we have found proof, that this instrument brings a sense of exultation to the actors' performance, and that it gives form and vitality to the movement of the farce.

Two years later the tréteau *was tried outdoors in the Place Saint-Sulpice. A simpler version made its way to Burgundy, returning to its traditional place in local fairs and festivals, before touring Europe in Les Copiaus' production of Copeau's* l'Illusion. *Multiple versions of it were to appear in Copeau's large-scale outdoor religious productions in Florence and Beaune, designed by André Barsacq. These experiences finally led Copeau to the conclusion that, in order to establish truly contemporary dramatic conventions, it was not merely the nature of the stage itself that would need re-thinking as part of a total 'scenic architecture': to prepare for the popular theatre of the future, he wrote in 1941, the structure of the playhouse itself, not just the stage within it, would have to be called into question.*

THE MODERN IDEA OF SCENIC SIMPLICITY

It appears that the most modern exponents of scenic art have entirely turned their faces away from the realistic expression which was in such high favour twenty years ago.

Realism, in scenery, was a truth. It brought us to a fresh point of view. Its force today, however, has vanished. There no longer seems to be any life in it.

But let us beware lest the *new* idea, the idea of simplicity, which the modern chaps are making so much noise about, does not decay even more rapidly. It is already developing noticeable excesses.

The idea of scenic simplicity at the present time has been adopted by over-refined minds. Certain producers have made of it something which is really not simple at all, something which is, rather, very elaborate and pretentious. Where we might look for a work of art, complete, alive, inspired with movement, we are likely to find – because of this craze for simplicity – a sort of aesthetic demonstration, elaborate and cold. Any method of expressing the meaning of a dramatic work by over-emphasising its effects, by disclosing all its secrets, is, to my mind, a corrupt method. Too much scenic expression – whether 'simple' or realistic – is as inartistic as no scenic expression at all. When, at certain moments during a performance, the intensity and quality of the lighting are supposed to compel me to be more greatly affected by the play, I am merely reminded of the old-time melodramas in which all pathetic and sinister moments were accompanied by a dim lighting and by slow music from the orchestra. The two methods are really somewhat similar. Real drama can do without such disingenuous subterfuges as that.

The greatest drama possesses its own eloquence. The public need not be taken by the hand and guided through its emotional passages by a professor of dramatic sensibility.

[From *Vanity Fair*, June 1917, p.36]

THE VIEUX COLOMBIER STAGE

Our stage is such that it should be used without adding anything to it, no stairs, no moveable steps, no facile lighting effects; only the stage in all its truthfulness and implacability.

I noticed that it was more beautiful and moving when it was left alone.

I also noticed, as Jouvet and I had often remarked, that what suits it best, incontrovertibly, is *the action of the workmen on it*. A remark we had already made in New York in November 1917, when we installed the new stage. It was confirmed in 1919–20, at the time when we installed the present stage, and later, when we saw the carpenters or electricians at work, the fat Flemish cleaning woman dressed in grey and faded blue, standing or kneeling, sweeping the stage or polishing the stairs.

It is the opposite of other stages, where nothing is so sad as the absence of lighting, either before or after the performance, or after rehearsals when nothing is more out of place than the natural presence of anyone who is not an actor in action.

Real action is beautiful on our stage. The work being done by the artisans with their habitual movements, seems to be in its place on it. That is because they are really making something from what they are doing, and doing it well and consciously, absorbed in it. Their movements are sincere, in keeping with real time periods, and correspond to a useful purpose for which they are perfectly fitted.

The actor on stage never does anything real. He vaguely imitates certain activities, unconsciously, with a more or less skilful sense of the effect to be produced. During rehearsals, for many reasons (notably the absurd lack of props), we never see him do what he will be doing during the performance; we never see him do even the most elementary thing authentically. He thinks he will do it in the performance, that he will rediscover instinctively the theatrical equivalent which his never-changing habits have substituted for the authentic action. Even actors who are conscientious and like things to be well-ordered never follow a new piece of direction through to the end. They distort it by translating it. One supposes they lack the courage to do so, or that they simply do not let themselves go, as if their bodies on stage were suddenly exempt from the laws of gravity and duration.

The stage as we conceived it, and which we have only begun to put into action, i.e. disencumbered, as bare as possible, waiting for something and ready to receive the development of its own form of action, that stage is never so beautiful as in its natural, primitive and empty state, when nothing is happening on it, and when it stays there silently, weakly lit by the half-light of day. Once the season was over, that is the way I looked at it and understood it: real, with its flattened surface, already changed by the construction of a platform upon it, which is only a premature hypothesis of the needs of performance.

Last July, when I saw the stage again, in its natural state, I understood that everything that happened to it last season – props, costumes, actors, lights – had only disfigured it.

It is thus from the stage that we must proceed.

[From Copeau's *Journal*, 27 August 1920]

THE ROUGH-HEWN BOARDS

In the time of this celebrated Spaniard (Lope de Rueda) all the properties of a theatrical manager were contained in a sack, and consisted of four white pelices trimmed with gilded leather, and four beards and wigs, with four staffs, more or less. The plays were colloquies or eclogues between two or three shepherds and a shepherdess. They were set off by two or three *entremeses* (short farces or interludes), either that of the 'Negress', the 'Ruffian', the 'Fool' or the 'Biscayan', and these four characters and many others were acted by the said Lope with the greatest skill and propriety that one can imagine. At that time there were no *tramoyas* (theatrical machinery) nor duels between Moors and Christians either on foot or on horse. There were no figures arising or seeming to arise from the centre of the earth or through a trapdoor in the stage, which at that time consisted of four benches arranged in a square, with four or five boards upon them, rising about four spans from the ground; nor were there clouds of angels or souls descending from the skies. The furnishings of the stage were an old woollen blanket drawn by two cords from one side to the other, forming what was called a dressing room, behind which were the musicians, singing some old ballad without the accompaniment of a guitar.

Nothing moves me more, stirs my imagination so strongly, as the poverty of this stage. The musicians singing behind the blanket, 'singing some old ballad without the accompaniment of a guitar', tell me that I am on the right track...

But is it possible to go back, to ape such early naivety and penury? I say it is necessary. Let nothing remain. *We must.* Burn everything. Let nothing remain. Do not modify, improve, elaborate. *But abolish.*

[The preface by Cervantes to his *Eight Comedies and Eight New Interludes.* Copeau's notes, on reading a French translation, are from an unpublished notebook 'L'Art du Théâtre', November 1916, 78 typed pages, M-H D; printed in part in *Registres IV*, p. 156]

THE STAGE

The stage is the instrument of the dramatic creator.

It is the place for the drama, not the décor or the equipment. It belongs to the actors, not to the technicians or the scene-painters. It should always be ready for the actor and for action. The reforms which we have accomplished, and those which we have still to accomplish, have this in view and can thus be summarised: to put an instrument into the hands of the dramatic creator, create for him a free stage which he can use freely, with a minimum of intermediaries.

It is, today, invariably true that the dramatic creator is an *intruder* in the theatre, that everything opposes his conception, his efforts, even his existence. He is enslaved by that of which he should be the master. And, without him, the theatre today has no master. [...]

There are two distinct problems concerning the stage which are quite dissimilar. There is the problem of a new stage, which is bound up with the problem of the new dramatic form which it will engender. And there is the problem of a repertoire stage, an eclectic or cultural stage, which must lend itself in shape and in its resources to all scenic types from Antiquity down to the present day. In researching and establishing such an evolved, composite stage, the fundamental principle which should guide us is this: a dramatic work cannot be done justice in its presentation except in the intended or actual scenic conditions in which it was conceived by the poet.

That is why I could not continue to present a repertoire on stage.

Now, what I need is to create a stage in accord with the principles of a new drama.

[Notes in unpublished notebook, 'Scène 1940', M-H D, first printed in *Jacques Copeau et le Vieux Colombier* (exhibition catalogue), Bibliothèque Nationale, 1963, pp. xv-xvi; reprinted in part in *Registres I*, pp; 225–6]

AN EMPTY SPACE

Our work in the theatre permitted us to rediscover an aesthetic truth which has been bandied about ever since then by people who perhaps were not sufficiently aware of its meaning. It is this: that a given dramatic conception postulates a certain stage design; and just as much or even more: a given stage architecture calls forth, demands and gives rise to a certain dramatic conception and style of presentation. In this domain the reactions of the material on the spiritual, and vice versa, are close and constant so that it is difficult at first to say which is responsible for the formation of a particular style, the form of the drama or the form of the theatre. But it is certain that a clearly defined, deeply rooted, dramatic genre corresponds to a clearly defined and stable theatre architecture and cannot dispense with it. We cannot conceive of Greek tragedy independent of the Greek stage, nor Shakespearian drama detached from the Elizabethan stage. The moment that stage structure becomes fluid, dramatic poetry begins to lose its foothold.

People might answer that it would be paradoxical to build theatres today for a dramatic form which does not yet exist and which no one can yet say much about.

As a matter of fact, we have undertaken enough imperfect experiments, we have put forward enough blemished efforts, we have struggled, invented, worked enough for thirty years in an attempt to get away from the theatrical conventions that keep us prisoners, to have at least a feeling and a foretaste of this new dramatic form, of this *Mystery of Modern Times* around which, little by little, poets and pioneers of today's theatre in all countries are turning, and towards which they are approaching.

Moreover we are no longer in a primitivistic state. We possess a desire for a renaissance. A proposal must be made. It will be made consciously, by an effort of the spirit and of the will.

We can make this proposal, trying at the same time to spare

existing theatres. But an experiment undertaken under such conditions will always be imperfect and inconclusive. It will be sumptuary, artificial and, I believe, doomed to failure, if we propose to build permanent buildings according to new plans.

We must not build according to hard-and-fast plans. We must leave a margin for evolution, an empty space for the poet to fill in sooner or later.

We must not simply refine what is already built [...], without any real inner necessity. All such undertakings are outdated.

We don't need the 'last word'. We need the *first word*.

It is not simply a question of building the most perfect theatre in the world, but the simplest and healthiest, a house conforming to our present-day poverty and, if you wish, to the humbleness of our present state.

What we need is not a masterpiece of stage machinery. We need a masterpiece of architectonic articulation.

[From *Le Théâtre Populaire*, PUF, 1941, pp. 61–4, reprinted in *Registres I*, pp. 277–313]

THE CLOISTER OF SANTA CROCE

In 1932, Sylvio d'Amico, the dramatic critic, asked me if I would be willing to participate in the Maggio Fiorentino that year. I made a visit to get acquainted with the locale, because for me, a dramatic representation, what is called a '*mise en scène*', is primarily and above all a certain locale, as well defined as possible. The production that was offered me to stage was a late sixteenth-century mystery, the *Mystery of Saint Uliva*, and the locale was the cloister of Santa Croce.

When I got off the train, a sort of miracle occurred. I cannot think of another word to describe the sudden revelation I had of how the production would turn out... and through no intellectual research or deduction on my part. All at once, I repeat, I was permeated, inhabited by a certainty. Where did it come from? From the architecture. Primarily from the purity of Brunelleschi's architecture, of its ineluctable beauty, of the impossibility of resisting it and, what's more, of cheating with it. It forbade me to introduce the slightest element of décor or to erect any elevated structure in front of its pure arches. It advised me to place two-thirds of my audience under the cloister arcades and to make use of the edifice's open court, which was very austerely designed. In the centre, a big stone well raised on three steps, around which were four lawns bordered by box-wood hedges, separated by two stone paths in the form of a cross. By opening out the levels around the well, we made the central stage, the largest one. In the middle of the four lawns, we constructed four stages of identical size. This gave us five principal stages, connected by slender walkways, not to mention the approaches beneath them, as well as what remained of the green lawns around these four secondary stages.

Excuse me for furnishing so many details which may seem superfluous, but for me they were exciting. I should say, for us! For André Barsacq was with me. From my first visit to Florence I had shown him a plan and a photograph of the site. With these documents, he began to work and had brought with him the complete construction plans which he supervised himself, explaining everything to the workers in an Italian he had just learned.

The actors at my disposition were not without talent or submissiveness. But this old play, written in obsolete Italian, as far from modern realistic methods as could be, made them smile. To tell the truth, they thought it was a little ridiculous, and they were afraid that the audience would fail to understand the story of this princess, both of whose hands are burned off and then grow back. Added to this, I was sharing the company with another director, Max Reinhardt (Hitler's Germany was already becoming dear to the hearts of Fascist Italy). Reinhardt had been invited to stage a Shakespeare comedy, *A Midsummer Night's Dream*, in the Boboli Gardens. (Also, I had, for the choreography, the collaboration of Maja Lex and her school from Munich. I must say that she was a charming girl, an untiring worker with an admirable professional conscientiousness, and that we both had as much trouble in accepting and putting up with the unpunctuality, fussiness and slovenliness of my Latin brothers.)

Now, we were working in the full noon-day sun of Santa Croce. As for Reinhardt, he was able to take his actors in the late afternoon under the big trees in the Boboli Gardens.

In a little less than two months, the result was two productions as opposed in character as could be. In the magic hands of Reinhardt, the *Midsummer Night's Dream* had become expanded and taken on an amplitude and a weight much greater than in Shakespeare. It was already an outline of the film that Reinhardt was later to make in Hollywood. In comparison, in my poor little *Mystery of Saint Uliva*, there was no amplification, not the least eloquence, nothing which did not come out of an inner feeling and was not piously designed, like a primitive painting. And yet, against all expectations, that rather spare and awkward thing, pious and old-fashioned, did more than bear comparison with my German colleague's grand display. The evening of the première was a victory for France.

I learned from this, although I already knew it, that the only valid law for a work of art is that of sincerity, provided it has an adequate technique at its disposition. In the Boboli Gardens, the scenic methods and technical expertise, if I may say so, went far beyond what the artist had to express. The result was a deal of amplification, even systematisation.

On the other hand, in the Santa Croce cloister, it was the dramatic, emotional and religious matter which was, in a way, tightened in expression, extending beyond it on all sides.

The Shakespearean density was impoverished by a spectacular intention. That of the old unknown Italian author found itself heightened by the fact that scenic problems constantly came up which had no foreseeable solution in the present system of the theatre. So it was necessary to admit one's powerlessness and look elsewhere. It was necessary to *invent* something that had not become trite on the stage, something which was perhaps not of a theatrical nature, but which as a result of a particular circumstance, seemed to emerge from it in all its freshness and with the radiance of the unexpected. [...]

Duse was not with us, that evening [...] as she had often been in our Paris theatre [...]; but I remember two kind accolades which impressed me: Luigi Pirandello's and Arturo Toscanini's.

[From typed MS of 'Souvenirs pour la radio', a series of fifteen broadcasts, May–June 1945, M-H D]

8

IDEAS IN COMMON:
ADOLPHE APPIA

The third visit that Copeau made to a leading innovator in European theatre during the enforced wartime closure of the Vieux Colombier was not planned in the same way as those to Craig and Dalcroze. It was at Dalcroze's suggestion that he went to Rivaz, on the shore of Lake Geneva to meet Adolphe Appia, and Copeau's notes admit how ill-prepared he was for the encounter with the 53 year-old author of Die Musik und die Inscenierung. *At first Copeau convinced himself that he had nothing to learn from Appia, especially in terms of the use of music as a well-spring of actor training and performance. On returning to Geneva, however, he read a letter from Appia to Dalcroze concerning his current preoccupation with architectural unity between stage and auditorium, which prompted a second visit to Rivaz. The tone of Copeau's notes, however, remains dismissive. Yet Appia was to remain an ardent supporter of Copeau's work until his death in 1928. By this time Copeau, with the frustrations and impatience of the war years behind him, had come to realise just how seminal Appia's ideas had been, influencing in particular the* dispositif fixe *of the second conversion of the Vieux Colombier with its permanent levels, stairs and steps joining stage to auditorium. His obituary for the Swiss artist, printed below, also reveals an admiration for a personality some aspects of which he had at first found aversive.*

FIRST VISIT: Rivaz, Thursday, 28 October 1915

Splendid weather. Joined Dalcroze and his wife at noon. We leave for Rivaz.

I see Adolphe Appia coming down the hill to meet me. To the right of this tall, weather-beaten greybeard stretched the golden vineyards of autumn; to his left, the transparent waters of the lake. A smart, vigorous gait. Youthful legs in black stockings. A light-coloured suit and a tight-fitting rose-coloured jersey.

When we approached one another I saw a smile full of intelligence and kindness flowing from his face, from his eyes to his mouth. A handsome and vigorous man, erect, slim, hardy and reticent, elegant and natural, his whole body radiating an extraordinary liveliness, fluid as it were, not like water but like fire, an upright flame. Always moving and always erect. Such is the image which sticks in my mind and sums up the man. All the words that I could add would only add to that image: purity, youth and even childishness. A character perfectly *whole* and completely *devoted*. Devoted to his research for its own sake and to his inspiration; unblemished by any menial task.

Quickly, Appia leads us towards his old castle tower on the edge of the lake. He guides us through the tangle of plants and faded flowers which have grown in profusion the past summer. He stops us, gesturing and laughing, under the bower, to look across the smooth surface of the lake up towards the grey mountain. Then, on a path covered by an enormous tree-trunk uprooted by the wind, through the fragrant woodpile, we reach the stairs at the top of which is Appia's apartment. Two rooms, one of which serves as a store-room and a kitchen (a spirit-stove and a few utensils). The other overlooks the lake, bathed in a glorious light. A vase containing the last nasturtiums of the season sits on the windowsill. On the wall, some prints and photographs. A bed, a large table decorated with foliage. On a shelf, a few books. I come nearer. A row of a set of books attracts my eye. It is Dickens. I cannot help turning a look of recognition towards Appia with a smile of deliverance. Dickens welcoming me under this Wagnerian roof! Dalcroze sees my delight. He takes down one of the volumes, reads aloud a short passage and winks knowingly. Already a kind of intimacy arises among us.

Appia sets down the tea which he had brewed, a few cakes, a bottle of wine given to him by his landlord, and we talk. My first words are to convey greetings from Craig. He speaks of him with affection, a little irony and with a soundness that makes me admire his intellect. There is nothing constrained, no conceit. Moderation and energy, delicate feelings, faith in his intelligence. In conclusion, *a humane tone*... It starts with a smile. I tell Appia how Craig had disconcerted me at first. 'Yes, yes', he answered, 'you see, I was never able to communicate very well with him. He does not speak a word of my language, nor I his. We conversed by signs, or by drawing symbols. I remember one day when Craig summed up our differences in the following way:

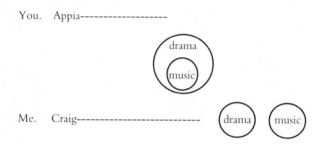

'I was amused by his paradoxes to the point of saying: "Yes, yes, I understand you: the theatre of the future: music? no; words? no; dance? no; the actors? no; the audience? no, not the audience either".' [...]

I cannot copy out this sketchy conversation exactly. I am only putting down the parts which struck me most. For example, this note, on Craig's character, which coincides exactly with my own impressions: 'It is impossible', says Appia, 'not to give in to the sincere passion which emanates from him in his better moments, and which, in a way, fills in the gaps left by so many inconsistencies... But, sometimes he pulls himself up severely. I know of the *two faces* you mention, and of his way of forcing, of inflating the importance of things. Yes, he is a bit of an actor, in spite of everything, and also a bit of a bl- bluffer.' With this last word, Appia hides his stuttering by lowering his voice a little.

On this date of 28 October 1915, I truly knew *absolutely nothing* definite of Appia's ideas and work, except for a few reproductions of his sketches in Jacques Rouché's brochure, *L'Art théatrale moderne*, and the originals of his most recent work exhibited in the foyer of the Dalcroze Institute in Geneva. Unable to question him competently, I asked him to show us his drawings. He spread out before me about thirty of his sketches from the Wagnerian period. I cannot say that I appreciated them very much. He flipped through them discontentedly with a modest haste. Two of his most recent compositions struck me the most. I do not know whether I really understood them.

All of Appia's present activity seems tied up with Dalcroze. I left them to chat together as we returned to the boat landing.

While waiting for the boat, we resumed our talk. Here are a few scraps which I recall. I note them in order to re-read some day when I will be more familiar with Appia's thinking:

> The whole problem today is the creation of equipment which is simple, basic and capable of lending itself to the infinite combinations of technicians and experimenters.... You see, we are in a period of transition. Impossible to say exactly where we are going. But what is certain is that only music can give us a direction. I do not say that because I am a musician. It is not a question of preference or of talent. It is a question of *necessity*. I do not know what part nor what place music will have in the drama of the future, once it is achieved, whether it will be incorporated into it or rejected. But I am sure that music is our only guide for the present and it is the sole steady base of our research.

As a commentary on Appia's words which struck me as being a resumé of all his ideas, but which I understood only on reflection, I must copy here a few lines of a letter which I have just written to Craig on 6 December 1915. It is about a performance of *Carmen*:

> You say: 'I was excited – the orchestra work is so very wonderful' ... Don't you find the stage-work to be quite as wonderful? To be rather the *same* work, in its way, provided the director takes hold of the whole drama in his mind, in the same way as the conductor does of the whole score. I expect my company to answer my suggestion, in the right key and tone, when I lift up my arm, as the violins or trumpets obey the baton in the hand of the musician ... But you will say that human beings could never serve an artistic purpose as instruments do. They will, if they become instruments. I mean if they are in full possession of their bodies, voice and mind, of movement and expression, even to the finest shade, if they have *developed* their personality and *mastered* it enough to release it into more powerful hands. Don't you see that the conductor lives and acts the music, I should say almost *speaks the music*, strives to get out of himself, looks to be, by his action and

desire for manifold actions, a figure of music, in a form of expression which is not music. Words do not allow me to tell you how I feel about that orchestra – music is to me the nearest, the keenest representation of an ideal dramatic action. Appia, when I met him, told me in these words: 'I don't know what place music will hold in the theatre of the future, when it becomes reality at last, whether we shall incorporate music into our drama, or cast it off. But what I know is that, *now*, music and music alone may be our guide, and the basis for our research.' You understand now, my dear Craig, in which way I think that Appia is right. That is something: music, the basis – drama, the aim. I am far from being a musician. But I dare say that, from the beginning, I always thought of drama musically.

[From the notebook, 'L'Ecole du Vieux Colombier', op. cit., printed in part in *Registres III*, pp. 303–6]

SECOND VISIT: Sunday, 25 June 1916

Everything about his reception of me is in exquisite taste. I recognise certain impressions from my first visit, but I modify them by newer and more well-founded observations. I sum up the man.

Appia disclaims all dogmatism. He was instinctively inclined towards it. He claims that Dalcroze cured him. Imperfectly, however, for I often balk at the excesses of his imagination. There is one thing which separates us on the very points where we should be most inclined to agree, that is in the nature of his thinking, which is deeply and forever imbued with Germanicism (his manner also, that display of sentimentality and weeping easily, his conventionalism which passes for cordiality, not a true simplicity).

He speaks to me of Hellerau and the rehearsals of *Orpheus*.[1]

Although he had no official role there, it was his impassioned opposition which succeeded in having the girls from Dalcroze's Institute, who were playing the role of the Furies, dressed in their simple, black work-jerseys rather than in fancy costumes. He defended 'the dignity' of the pupils against everyone – even Dalcroze. 'It was too beautiful,' he said, 'we could not allow it to be spoiled.' He added: 'I never wept so much in my life. I was ill for a week.'

He told me that his extremely strict family would not allow the word 'theatre' to be spoken. One had to say 'the hot-house'.

He said of himself: 'I am unfulfilled.'

Unable to do anything else, he began to write. But writing is a very painful task for him. I can well imagine that; he never seems to *pursue* an idea.

He agrees to write a summary of his work for the Vieux Colombier review.

In short, during these two days of continuous conversation and exchanges, he has taught me absolutely nothing. He told me nothing I did not already know after eight months of experience and almost two months of meditation on that experience. The reason is that for one who works in the real world, the problems are self-evident.

The most striking thing he told me was his famous 'Music is our only guide today. Let us not abandon it.' He does, however, see it as an integral part of a production. When he speaks of hoping that I could collaborate with Dalcroze (whose most serious faults he is not aware of) it is with a production in mind. I see this link with music as an auxiliary in the education of the actor. Interiorisation of music into the organs, into all of the actor's faculties, in order to obtain precision and freedom.

The idea of stage settings emerging from the text, from the inner spirit of the dramatic work. It is a truism which he discovered before we did. To tell the truth I do not think I learned it either from him or from Craig; I discovered it by myself. How much more important it is in relation to the movement and actions of an actual production.

As for decoration, he constantly repeats, like Craig, his hatred of painters, of their intrusion into a field they know nothing of. We are in agreement on that. I tell him: 'The solution is an architectural one.' He agrees.

I talk to him a little about my actors and my new improvisational comedy[2] which, in one fell swoop, could resolve in a simple, humane and life-like way all sorts of questions pertaining to the stage, the actors and the public from both an aesthetic and a speculative point of view. Something is born, grows, and by its very existence resolves all the problems and casts out all difficulties. Appia grimaces with joy and astonishment, grasps the window frame against which he is leaning, jumps for joy and cries: 'Ah! ah! you excite me very much. I have been *thinking* of that all along... and here you bring it to me!'

Communication with the audience. It is his present pre-occupation, his latest idea, his dream for the future.

Appia would like to raze the entire structure of modern theatre. No more separation between the stage and the auditorium. And even no stage at all. Only a great auditorium, in the midst of which would rise in an appropriate place a podium upon which the performers would play, and when they were not playing, would mix with the audience. It was this, I think, which was conceived at Hellerau.

He speaks again of the monstrousness of the disparity between the auditorium and the stage. The former is luxurious, comfortable or at least decently appointed. The latter, behind the sets pasted with newspapers, is poor, miserable and ugly. For the dignity of the art and of the actor, he wants both to be of the same simplicity. He describes his ideal arrangement of the wings. But here there is also the whiff of German organisation, of *Kultur*. I do not think that the shabbiness of the back-stage has ever degraded the artist; for me this odour of poverty is exhilarating. But soon I interrupt Appia in his plans, saying: 'What surprises and worries me is that you and Craig are constructing the theatre of the future without knowing who will be in it. What sort of artists are you going to have on the stage, inhabiting this theatre which you wish to be more worthy of receiving them? It seems to me, Appia, that I am the only one who began by turning my attention to forming a company of actors.'

[From the notebook 'L'Ecole du Vieux Colombier', op. cit., printed in *Registres III*, pp. 350–3]

A TESTIMONY

Appia's greatest merit, one which he shares with Craig, is that he left the theatre and made us leave it with him. Because of his love for this living art, he denied and repudiated it. He uprooted it and replanted it elsewhere than on the dusty boards of the desecrated stage. He pierced the ceiling of that box of mediocre glamour; the air came in and we saw the sky. Thoughts of life, grandeur and style lighted up for us and, in order to serve them, we returned to the eternal truths.

Both musician and architect, Appia teaches us that the tempo of music, which envelops, commands and regulates the dramatic action, creates at the same time the space in which it unfolds. For him, the art of staging in its pure sense is nothing else but the configuration of a gesture or a piece of music rendered tangible by the living action of the human body and by its reaction to the opposing architectural volumes. Hence, the banishment from the stage of all inanimate decoration, of all painted backcloths, the dominance of the moveable prop and the active role of light.

When that is said, we have said almost everything. We have a *radical* reform – Appia readily used that term – we are provided with a theatrical fact which links us up to the most ancient traditions whose consequences and variations can be developed indefinitely. We are at ease, or at least we shall be. We can work on the play and the actor instead of eternally chasing after more or less original decorative formulas, more or less novel methods of presentation, all of which make us lose sight of the essential objective.

Appia's basic principle: an action in keeping with a form of architecture should be sufficient to create masterpieces, if the directors know what a play is, if the dramatists know what the stage is, if the actors have bodies and souls authentically imbued with music and poetry, with the words pronounced and with living rhythms.

It would be a mistake to think that Appia's principle of subordinating all dramatic *substance* to the measured elocution of the actor, that is to the spirit of the play he incarnates with his voice and gestures, applies only to musical action. Spoken action obeys the same laws. Tragedy, comedy, drama, if they are well conceived for the stage by a real dramatist (which is extremely rare), articulated in accordance with the movements, developed in accordance with the rhythms, organised in accordance with the architecture, are not only analogous to music but are the essence of music. Declamation in the classic theatre was written, as for example that of Japanese Noh today. Notation is always postulated in the verse-form of great drama. Molière attempts to rediscover it for his pupil Baron and Racine for La Champmeslé.[3] Even the divisions in free prose have a tendency to such formal shaping. A dramatic dialogue is not altogether expressive unless it is completely harmonious. It attains this harmony only by its spatial relationships, which control the elocution that is intimately linked to the action at hand and is a fact or function of space. After considering poetic expression, we end up considering the stage and the utilisation of space, the two notions indissolubly linked in Appia's opinion. In 1922, after a performance of Corneille's *Le Menteur*, he wrote to me: 'Finally, finally, the actor and only the actor! How good you made me feel. It is so obvious that that is truth! You possess it in your field... I have it in mine... and the principle remains exactly the same!'

Pursuing to the extreme this idea of a three-dimensional stage, an architectural stage instead of the *trompe-l'oeil* given to us by the Italians, we should reach the moment of examining the *permanent* stage, of a permanent architectural device conceived as a complete dramatic organism, self-sufficient like a 'great instrument' as Diderot had already termed it in conjunction with the Greek stage: 'I should only ask for a similar monument', he wrote, 'in order to kindle a multitude of poems, and perhaps, *to produce a few new genres*.'[4] Undoubtedly this subordination of the renewal of dramatic genres to that of theatrical architecture will be surprising. It is, nevertheless, an essential and well-founded question which the modern theatre movement is in the process of solving. Appia did not go that far. We talked about it a few times in Nyon, but he did not pursue it. He had already accomplished what he could. He had liberated us and, now, he was enjoying watching the young follow the path he had opened up. Until his last days he remained perfectly incapable of jealousy. One of his last thoughts was whether he had ever hurt or upset anyone, for which he asked their forgiveness. He was not only a great artist, but a great man, whose spirit was sustained by enthusiasm and love. If those who follow us succeed in restoring the dignity and *éclat* of the supreme art of the theatre, they can gauge what is due to the genius, simplicity and modesty of Appia.

['Adolphe Appia et l'art de la Scène (16 Avril)', written in 1928, on the death of Appia, pub. in *CRB*, x, 1955, and in *Registres I*, pp. 66–8]

AN OBITUARY

Dear Appia, we were going to meet again soon, as we have every year. Now I shall no longer see you. No longer shall we have those interminable conversations which used to leave us exhausted with enthusiasm and friendship. You will no longer come to welcome my little company at the railway platform in Geneva, nor visit my dressing-room before the performance in order to check on the details of my costume. No longer will you stand, clothed in your Ibsenian frock-coat, near the stage box in the Lausanne Theatre, closely examining the audience as if you were mounting guard at the door of the performance that your friends were about to give. You will no longer replay the play afterwards for us, reproducing our slightest gestures and all of our intonations, enjoying with child-like glee the most subtle meanings and often enlightening us on some artistic point which remained so obscure to us.

Appia, I shall no longer see your great white head in the door of the railway carriage which was returning us to France, still nodding to us with that exquisite courtesy which was the flower of your natural nobility... But you will not cease to exist for us, missed, adored, consulted and heeded.

[From 'L'Art et l'Oeuvre d'Adolphe Appia, Pernand, 6 Mars', *Comoedia*, 12 March 1928]

9

THE POET IN THE
THEATRE

Copeau's stripping down of the Garrick and Vieux Colombier stages, with the later additions of the dispositif fixe *and the* tréteau nu, *made way for the primacy of the actor rather than the designer as the medium of expression in the quest for a 'renovated' dramatic art. But what was that art to express? Copeau's conviction was that the true content of theatre was not the concern of the director (except in so far as the selection of a repertoire was concerned), but of the writer, or, as he preferred to put it, the Poet. He said of his own career:*

If I have brought anything to the theatre, if I have at least indicated what could be brought to it, it pleases me to think that it is [...] a releasing of the human spirit on to the stage by means of a profound and well-assimilated technique which has, as its consequence, the direct domination by the poet of the dramatic instrument.[1]

The purification, both physical and ideological, of the stage and the education of the actor as human being as well as technical exponent, were thus to be simply necessary preparations for the coming of the Poet, the new Aeschylus, the new Shakespeare, the new Molière.

PLATITUDES

In the face of today's morality, one wonders what can be the function of dramatic criticism – whether it is not complaisant or venal?

Under the heading of *Theatre News*, you will find anecdotes about actors, directors and a few fashionable authors; backstage gossip; the balance-sheet of gate receipts; rumours about monopolies and actions for infringement; insulting correspondence from writers; descriptions of décors; publicity for costumiers; notes and sensational announcements at so much per line, etc.; everything, in short, that concerns the theatrical life of our time. The rest is of no interest.

Now and then, if the critic must interrupt to call attention to a work of art that has appeared unexpectedly or through some misunderstanding, he is usually only able, truth to say, to demonstrate his monotonous vexation.

Sometimes one hears talk about a *dramatic movement*. This is a journalistic term; handy for certain merchants, in order to puff up the excellence of the product they are selling to a few young men whose future they want to confiscate at the expense of their vague aspirations. It does not correspond to any present-day reality.

A confusing abundance of productions; a growing mêlée of impresarios, authors, actors, many of whom are getting rich, the eagerness of the crowds in the theatres; the blooming of a thousand parasitical industries on both sides of the stage... But must we consent to call this restless and sterile *theatrical agitation* a *dramatic movement*?

The latter would have as its motive to encourage talent, with the aim of a perfect dramatic realisation of life's synthetic forms. The only motive of the former is the ruthless competition of greed, the sole stake being *money*.

For a long time we have been deprived of manifestos which speak of decadence, inertia, obscurantism, prophesying emancipations, renaissances. The new cry of the Poets breaks a silence which was beginning to weigh on us. They are proclaiming the supremacy of verse drama or, as they call it, *idealistic theatre*. They differentiate – at last! – between the body and the soul. They want to address themselves to the soul. They will awaken the national spirit, ennoble and guide it. They will be the seers and the apostles, following Victor Hugo's dictum. They will move the Isle of Patmos to the Théâtre des Bouffes-Parisiens.

Oh, our times!... may the goodwill of these adolescents, with their romantic nobility and incoherent resolutions be sufficient publicity for them! But it would be tempting to beseech them above all to be, since they write for the theatre, dramatic authors. 'Let a man *accomplish his work*; the fruit of this work and its care belong to another.'

As for me, nothing shocks me more than the glorification of a genre, the affectation of a style which *a priori* and systematically excludes from dramatic art such and such an aspect of human truth or aspiration to beauty. Poetic theatre, realistic theatre, psychological plays, plays with ideas, comedy of manners, character comedy... So many classifications invented by the dominant laziness of schools and temperaments. Specialisation is only the failure and not the aim of our spirit. Rule out nothing from drama. Its capacity is infinite. I should like to feel a *total* ambition in the rising generation. Nature in all its confusion; life in all its expansiveness; reality in its depth and movement – tangible and secret, plastic, lyrical, musical; the truth of the world which is ours: such is the substance offered up to the creator. To be sure, a poet will know how to unite his genius to it. Only a poet can absorb it and make a masterpiece from it. A *dramatic poet*: a perfect title we must dream about. But *poetic theatre*: this phrase is meaningless. There is only: *drama*, the synthetic image of humanity. Let all the means of expression join with it...

Modern man has not yet had his tragic expression.

The profound movements of contemporary thought; the nascent, the still uncertain and all the more troubling modifications of sensitivity that they give rise to, have not influenced dramaturgy at all. Except for some occasional experiments, considered chimerical, the efforts of today's artists have not influenced theatre.

Could it be any different?

Theatre, even the kind called *serious*, has fallen to the lowest ranks of frivolous occupation. The most deadly inspiration that can befall an artist today is dramatic inspiration. He knows it and turns away from it. If he persists, he will be assuredly reduced to capitulation or starvation.

The fickleness of the public and the laziness of the critic are accomplices in this state of affairs.

The directors and their numerous lackeys have no other concern before a new manuscript than: will this play make money or no? For they have heavy expenses to bear, the most crushing being the greed of the actors.

Vain and arrogant, they are the true masters at the present time. Their whims and despotic ignorance rule the stage. In their hands, a work becomes unrecognisable. They modify the text, adding or crossing out lines at will, remake entire scenes and change the endings of plays. They are considered to be the writers' collaborators while they are in fact their hangmen.

But the authors whose plays are being produced want only to be produced. Their ideas are not essential, only provisional and vague. They invent characters in sympathy with the actors who will play them and who will be the only real *creators*. Whether the characters change is of no importance, as long as the actors remain.

A choice must be made between art and a theatre which corrupts those it receives. It is necessary to give in and lower oneself to the conventional or the scandalous. We could name an author, once representative of our hopes. He is successful. Each one of his new productions gives proof of the progress of his as yet unconscious downfall. Each of his successes is a defeat.

Consequently originality, sincerity, truth, style and the standards of the conscience, everything that makes of the artist a philosopher, a novelist or a poet, is forbidden to him as a dramatist. Theatre is a special craft, a kind of closed shop. Alone, he is the prisoner of conventions, prejudices, an abstract formula, for whom life does not exist, who does not evolve nor progress, but who remains unchanged in death. The 'man of the theatre' is a being apart, custodian of a certain mysterious secret: the craft; slave of the masses, whose entertainment he provides, exiled from beauty, con-demned eternally to fake the same plots, to putting make-up on the same puppets, to re-writing the same play according to popular taste.

The forced abstention of the artists seems to be a sufficient explanation for there being no dramatic art.

Realism gave our vision precision and colour; symbolism opened it up and made it flexible. Both of them revealed new possibilities of dramatic art, widened its field, enriched its means of investigation and expression.

There was Becque (especially the Becque of *Les Corbeaux*); there was Ibsen (whose prodigious example was not understood, be-trayed in France by his translators, interpreters and admirers); there was Hauptmann (notably, *Lonely Souls*); there was Maeterlinck (the one before *Monna Vanna*); there was Paul Claudel, enormous by his power of suggestion.

And why not add that Richard Wagner has given us the giddiness and fascination of Drama?

There has been a shifting of mediocrity in the theatre. Public taste is no longer exclusively concerned with frivolous plays. It has pretensions to literature. Thought has been lowered to meet it.

In spite of the violence it sometimes affects, the problem play does not trouble the middle class because it does not produce real images of life. Opinions and speeches are substituted for them. That is why it is more like a newpaper article or a public meeting. It puts the audience on the same level of familiarity as the author, and a dialogue is established between them. It flatters those with a modicum of education by initiating them into philosophic jargon. It is easy to follow: everything is explained, simplified and resolved through discussion. It is conceived along the lines of the old plays, and the choices of its pathos are not of any higher quality. The vicissitudes of reasoning replace those of action. It's an ideological melodrama. It excites the passions of the mind. And the good citizen believes he is accomplishing a duty by listening to it.

Emile Zola wrote in 1881: 'Nothing entices our middle class like the alleged daring which generally ends in a sermon.' He added 'Mr Dumas inevitably became the idol of the Parisian public who found him to be *the writer of genius whom it could understand and discuss.*'

Flaubert said, 'It is easy, with a conventional jargon and two or three popular ideas, to pass as a socially-minded humanitarian or a renovating writer... It's the latest craze to be ashamed of one's craft. Openly to write verses, write a novel, carve marble, oh for shame! It was acceptable in the past when one did not have the social *mission* of the poet; now, each work has to have some moral significance, a progressive teaching: a sonnet must have a philosophical meaning, a play should take to task the heads of state, and a water-colour should tone down the *mores*. Pettifoggery creeps in everywhere, the rage for speechifying, arguing...'

I do not know whether 'one is ashamed of one's craft'. The truth is that *one does not know his craft*. Everyone has ideas these days, and it is less difficult to sew them together than to construct a work of art. [...]

Great art portrays native resemblances, 'a simple portrait', like *The Misanthrope*. One must 'create dreams' by evoking and suggesting their multiplicity and mystery of life, by extracting their inner expression from things and beings, by not blocking man's perspective with tedious moralising [...] by being simple, familiar, 'loving, fair, brotherly to all' (as Carlyle judges Shakespeare), by knowing how, if I may say, to lack ideas, to lack wit – and to *see*.

One cannot, after all, bring oneself to despair of theatre. [...]

So many false revolutions have taught us by their failures. But they have awakened our suspicions. We do not dare to speak of a renaissance.

Let us strive modestly to prepare and motivate it with all of our zeal and our faith. A criticism which is pitiless towards daily depravities, which is competent, sincere, daring, itself artistic, would be able to help artists. It would keep them in touch with tradition; it would know how, by being positive even in its negations, to extract for their use the assimilated truth found in each incomplete system; it would point out the great examples, and finally, by analysis, it would widen the possibilities of creation.

[From 'Lieux communs', *L'Ermitage*, 15 February 1905, reprinted in *Registres I*, pp. 93–9]

CRAFT IN THE THEATRE

As long as a craft is sound, it does not permit evaluation. But when, through attrition, it reveals that it is tired and worn, one sees appearing, with belated admiration of them, those secret cultural adjustments, which are going to degenerate, either in the hands of the decaying artist – and it becomes formula – or in those of an idle posterity – and it becomes cliché. For if craft is the most positive acquisition of culture, it is also the most dangerous.

The older a culture is, the more difficult it is to handle. It does not reach the point of its maturity and refinement without discomfort. From that point, a twofold danger menaces it: to be corrupted by the masses or to fidget in the lap of an elite. It is either too alarming or too inviting. To some, it gives an abundance and ease of resources which spare them from original research and personal merit. To others, it prompts only exaggerated scruples and the distrust of excessively tractable forms which lend themselves complacently to the puniest of enterprises. Because the latter adopted straight off, brazenly, a banal form of expression, we saw the former assuming it their duty to stumble about with deliberate restrictions and to concentrate their laborious nobility on a sort of 'impossibility' of language. And while the severest artisans of technique pretend to disdain *savoir-faire*, thousands of undisciplined producers will eternally accuse a few chary creators of an impotence from which they themselves are a little too bereft. So much so that, in the common opinion, the abstract divorce between two inseparable ideas becomes more serious: the idea of art and the idea of craft.

Nowhere better than in the theatre is this disastrous misunderstanding more felt. Forty years ago, Alexandre Dumas *fils* wrote, in the preface to his *Père Prodigue*: 'A man with no value as a thinker, a moralist, a philosopher, or a writer, can be a first-class man as a dramatist.'

This absurd maxim has spread into the mores of the theatre. It has degraded it by pronouncing that a fool could take precedence over a man of genius, that an empty work could be considered a well-written work. This prompted the cynical covetousness and muddle-headed activities which are meddling with the stage in sterile fervour. The artist who strays into it collides on all sides with lack of culture, ignorance, flightiness, baseness and formidable interests. So it is in disgust that he gives up his place to 'tradesmen'.

Tradesmen: authors, actors, directors, critics and the theatre-going public itself. Everything that comes into contact with the theatre is immediately diminished, distorted and corrupted in such an atmosphere.

A 'man of the theatre' must not turn his attention towards the world, nor familiarise his mind with feelings or ideas. He must be educated only by the theatre. He must keep his eyes only on the public, to whose greediness he must ceaselessly offer himself, and which is in itself all of theatre, declaring its taste once and for all, commanding the receipts and insisting on being obeyed.

What some call 'craft' is not an exigency the author feels within himself, it is an outside constraint. The cult of craft is nothing else but public idolatry. The alleged secrets and rules of craft are, in the final analysis, the totality of the public's attitudes imposed on entertainers.

For that matter, some day, the dramatist will be chased from the theatre by the actors to whom he is enslaved and who have, when all is said and done, even more than he 'the habit of the stage and the audience'. More and more they are replacing him, and their craft impinges on him. Some of them become authors. Others even offer opinions, when they are not imposing their collaboration. Back-stage slang has taken on the force of aesthetic laws. And, are not all the plays being performed more or less the sole work of the actors they glorify? They have the same shape and the same wry face.

Craft without that art which is its *raison d'être* is nothing but an idling motor. Art deprived of the craft which ensures its strength and durability is an elusive phantom.

We reject the old and futile distinction in an intellectual work between what is material and what is spiritual, between form and substance. In the same way, we refuse to conceive of an artificial dissociation between art and craft.

To tell the truth, and to put a name to the mysterious talisman that dramatists think they have adopted, we ought to say, not *craft*, but *formula*.

Bernard Palissy once said: 'There is no nature that produces its fruit without intense work, and even pain.'

Craft is that work of the personality struggling against its own attainments, art in the act of creating. It is also that 'long patience' of genius.

It is said of a painter (and why not of all artists as well?) that he possesses 'a beautiful technique'. No more than we praise a writer for his correct spelling, nor a poet for his perfect metre, do we think here of rating highly the *savoir-faire* of schooling, but only of an original method, something new that the painter has drawn from his fundamental qualities, whose value is his alone, and is unique because it is personal.

If we give the term its proper dignity, craft is what distinguishes an artist from all the others – *the proof of invention*.

Formula, on the other hand, is that which makes all mediocre productions look alike: the parody of a decrepit craft, the appropriation of a faculty by anonymous figures which, in their hands, becomes a method, falling from the domain of art into that of industry.

On the other hand, formula writing is common to all mediocre productions: the parody of a craft in its decrepitude. It is the dead hand of the anonymous on a creative faculty which, from the moment they take hold of it, proceeds to moult and fall from the realm of art into that of industry.

'Invention does not exist for us. We have nothing to invent; we have only to see.' This amusing shaft comes from Dumas *fils* again.

'To see', for an artist; is it anything else but 'to invent'? Thus we would readily concede that, indeed, all you had to do was see. But you see 'theatre'. You have, as you call it, 'an eye trained in a certain way'. That is, it is perverted, as your taste is poisoned, by habitual artifice and experienced trickery. You think you see, while it is the formula that jumps out at you, disguising all appearances from you and shrivelling all sincerity. You want above all to write a play. This preoccupation commands you in the choice of materials, the grouping of proportions and the disposition of effects. It strains your gestures and alters your voice. A good subject or human character in your hands is soon reduced to that kind of theatre, because you anticipate on their behalf, the murmurs, the applause, all the public reactions which you thought you had mastered but which in fact control, almost automatically, your spontaneity. You can already hear the purring in the theatre even before your characters have spoken a word. If it should happen that you succeed in deceiving the masses, it is not because you have deviated from the common rules but because you have flagrantly applied them, through a lack of virtuosity that makes impudent jugglers of the best among you.

By thus condemning a literature that is only theatrical, we do not mean to disregard the requirements of a 'special form', nor the rules which formed Racine and Molière. There is no greater enemy than we of what would want unduly to substitute itself for dramatic merit in theatre; I mean certain literary refinements or philosophical and moral arguments, or even those psychological discourses linking melodramatic episodes to them.

We are rebelling against false craft which exhibits only itself and expresses nothing, and we favour real craft, so closely associated with art that it cannot be distinguished from it, and without which nothing can be expressed. Dramatic craft draws its necessity, form and cohesion only from dramatic invention. All original creations demand an authentic and new expression. Whenever the truth and sincerity of the characters is missing, the form loses all its value by being made empty of any meaning.

As long as they will never have *created*, as long as they will patch together the same plots and make travesties of their characters, dramatists will exhaust themselves in vain by manipulating a precarious instrument which lends itself to everything. It is so dispersed that it gives the impression of having an extreme adaptability. One can do anything with it and it will be nothing but frivolous, illogical and superfluous.

['Le Métier au théâtre', *NRF*, 1 May 1909, reprinted in *Registres I*, pp. 100–4]

THEATRE'S CALL FOR POETRY

Theatre's call for poetry is essentially a call for freedom, I do not say for imagination, because imagination is an intensely personal gift, strange and spontaneous, a divine gift that all poets do not necessarily possess, and that it would be as dangerous as it is absurd to make into a rule. But the theatre lives by freedom, all sorts of freedoms: the freedom to choose a subject, that is to escape from routine. It is not true that some subjects are theatrical and others are not. Any subject will become theatrical provided it is subjected to a proper technique. This opening up to all themes is one of the refreshments that our art thirsts for above all. The greatness of the most notable dramatists is to have assimilated everything into the quality of drama: love, politics, history, fables and gratuitous play. The freedom to choose characters, from those which are historically or psychologically accurate like Mark Antony, Alcestis or Berenice, to the products of the most delightful imagination, like Ariel. The freedom to choose a tone, that is the form of the dialogue, the colour of the language, the treatment of the action and the development of the characters, but above all, the freedom of invention, the use of all of theatre's possible resources, divorced from the shackles of realism. This is where poetic truth is opposed to the lies of Realism, whence emerge spiritual reality, true creativity, and the real gift of life. But in order for it to develop all its inspirations, it must not collide with material obstacles, complications and heaviness. We must give the poet what Mallarmé called 'the uncluttered stage open to fictions'.[2]

Our generation received drama from the hands of Naturalism. I do not deny that the Naturalistic reaction was necessary and that it produced some successful results. [...] The Théâtre Libre movement served a few authors who have not left very much behind them. It infiltrated the Boulevard theatre. When it attempted poetic works under the pretext of returning them to the truth, the failure was complete. At the time we took over, Naturalism was a dead weight on dramatic inspiration. It had made the stage uninhabitable for poetry by overloading it with properties and décors and exploiting to the point of absurdity what it thought was progress in *mise en scène*. We showed much lack of respect for these marvels and we destroyed them. We decongested the dramatic arena and denuded the stage. At about the same time, Meyerhold in Russia and myself in France were expressing the same unlimited dramatic ambition by

111

asking for *a bare stage*. This famous stage aroused much controversy: we were accused of being Jansenists. When I recall those heroic times, it seems to me that the most favourable critics, authors and members of the public never saw this instrument as anything but makeshift. However that may be, the only important thing is that such a rigorous purge of all stage superfluity freed the poetry of Molière and Shakespeare. It allowed us to revive works we thought were dead, to restore delights to works we thought were unplayable. It was then that a few poets who had turned away from the stage, and others who had never come close to it, began thinking of honouring it again. Everyone was talking about poetry.

Whence came this renewal, this refreshening? Simply from the fact that we had returned to the ancient laws of the theatre and to its original traditions. We were on the way to establishing a *convention*. Those who stay away from theatre and despise it under the pretext that it is a conventional art do not understand anything about it. They are thinking of base artifices and vulgar fakes, which have nothing to do with living theatre. What we call convention is a lofty creation of the mind, a cultural fruit, one of the eternal sources of style. This is what gives force and nobility to Molière's comedies, purity to Racine's tragedies; it is the classic chorus and structure of the Japanese Noh; it is Shakespeare's stage, free from the slavery of time and space, where dramatic intensity vies with epic grandeur. What I call theatrical convention is the use of infinite combinations of very limited material signs and means, which give the mind a limitless freedom, thus leaving poetic imagination its full fluidity.

Do you think Shakespeare would have conceived, or even dreamed, of the storm scene in *King Lear* if he had had to ask for the material means, lighting effects and off-stage noises, to create it on the stage? No, but Lear pitting himself against the tempest, echoing it while defying it, becomes for us, without ceasing to be himself, an image and an incarnation of the furious elements. He *dramatically creates* the storm. He is one with it, and so are we, and he becomes for us both Lear and the storm. That is what a Naturalist, as clever a professional as he may be, will never understand. All his art will aim at replacing Shakespearian poetry with the virtuosity of scene-shifters, and the result will be that instead of opening our minds to the sublime expressions of a human being in distress, we shall be thinking only of closing our eyes and blocking our ears.

Such is the difference between a convention that respects poetry and a poetry stifled by the grossness of Naturalistic theatre.

[From 'El teatro llama a la poesía', *La Nación*, Buenos Aires, 19 June 1938; reprinted in French, 'L'Appel du théâtre à la poésie', in Copeau Exhibition Catalogue, op. cit., pp. ix-xiii, and in *Registres I*, pp. 162-7]

HOW THE POET IS OBLIGED TO WORK

Let us enter the theatre together; we are going to see how the poet works. I invite you to a rehearsal, a privilege the public envies the professionals. I presume that you are sensitive, that you are delighted to uncover the secrets of our art, and that you did all you could to be on time... We have an appointment for 1.30 and it is now 1.35; let's go in... Naturally you come in on tip-toe, holding your breath for fear of disturbing the work that is undoubtedly going on... The auditorium is dark; the stage is dimly lit, bare of sets, furnished with a little table and two or three chairs; it is completely uninhabited. As our eyes become used to the dark, we see a form sitting all huddled up in the fourth or fifth row of the orchestra stalls. It is wrapped in a coat, wearing a battered hat. I think this lonely exiled figure is the poet. He turned to look at us when we came in, but now he turns back, shifts his seat and looks at his watch. Time passes. A cat crosses the stage. It's the porter's cat. Look how much he seems at home on it, how naturally he walks!... But look, to the left of the stage, just near the harlequin jacket, a head is leaning round, surrounded by a scarf and hat. It goes back into the wings, not even having shown its body. It is probably one of the actors, certainly a young actor, an insignificant one of no importance, since he takes his work seriously enough to be on time. He shares this kind of naivety and guilelessness with the author, who also attaches a certain importance, even an altogether exceptional one, to the rehearsal of his play. He had much trouble in writing his play, and even more trouble attracting the attention of the Director in order to have it accepted. He has never yet had the good fortune, and may never have it in his lifetime, of being performed. This little actor and this author are not yet quite professionals. This is what excuses their impatient concern and fervour. But for the theatre professionals, from the porter and his cat who have seen so many sets and scene-shifters come and go, so many manuscripts and so many authors, to the actors who have acted in so many plays, who were performing again last night, who rehearse and will continue performing every day and every night of their lives to the very end – from these people you cannot ask that this thing be taken tragically or even seriously. They are paying little heed to it. They have a good memory and a pretty good bag of tricks; they will always get along. There is the same difference between them and the author as there is between the department-store salesman who sells a hundred pairs of socks every day of the year with great detachment, and the customer like you or me who once every year anxiously selects a pair of shoes from among hundreds.

So, we have been waiting for almost an hour and nothing has happened yet. But, there, the actors are arriving little by little. They are forming small animated groups on stage, the men smoking cigarettes, the women smelling one another's flowers and holding out their new handbags to be admired. The author is making visible efforts to interest himself in all this. He is very nice, that's the least we can say. He tries to get along with everyone and offers compliments to one and all. Moreover his play is found to be rather lovely, though perhaps not 'theatrical' enough. In any case, there are some tedious passages that will certainly have to be cut. *Cut*, here is the actor's principal pre-occupation, the key to his aesthetics. He is like Polonius, all of whose feelings in regard to poetry are reduced to this formula: '*This is too long.*' Hamlet says of him: 'He's for a jig or a tale of bawdry, or he sleeps' (II, ii). Each actor tends to find the entire play too long and his own role too short... 'We'll see, we'll see,' says the author, 'maybe you're right... we'll fix it.' It is 2.45. The stage manager says, 'How about starting?' The coats fly off, the scripts come out of the pockets, the pages rustle; they are going to start... But the great actress is not there; she is never there. Now, naturally, hers is the principal role; they start without her. The stage manager will take his cigar out of his mouth long enough to read the great actress's lines. They start... The author has retreated into the shadows. He is pacing the aisles, hunching his shoulders and, from time to time, making the face of someone whose best tooth is being pulled... The great actress arrives; they start again. She excuses herself, but everyone excuses himself because she has to excuse herself. The author kisses her hand. The leading man tries to remove her coat. 'No, not yet...' She shivers. She is out of breath. It's a whole story... But let's get to work, let's get to work! And she begins courageously, barely taking the time to open and close her compact, to shake her powder puff, to apply a little lipstick, to run a moistened finger over her eyebrow. She swims through her role, with large strokes, in spite of the horrible headache which wrinkles her brow, in spite of the dressmaker who has earned her anger, in spite of the exasperation at being late; she who is so conscientious, in spite of – ah! this play in which she has no confidence, this role which is not at all written for her, whose lines she cannot succeed in getting into her head...

It is 4.15.

I am a little ashamed at betraying my colleagues by unfolding before you this ludicrous spectacle they offer us. I ask your pardon for having brought you here. But I can guess what you are saying to yourselves. 'He is exaggerating in order to amuse us. It is not like this in reality...' Don't you believe it! My little tableau shows you only a very small part of the disorder that usually presides over stage work. I could go on and show you many other extravagances. You would see disputes, laughing fits, breakdowns in the staging caused by non-existent difficulties; you would hear the silly suggestions made by the director; you would not be able to keep a straight face at seeing the threadbare methods and absurd working materials. For it is customary at rehearsals for nothing to correspond to the conditions of the actual performance. I am not talking only about the lack of scenery, the uncertain entrances and exits, the costumes not yet fitted, the lights not yet adjusted for the opening night. But even the smallest stage prop, during these so-called working days, seems meant to give the actor a false idea of its use and invites him not to take what he is doing seriously. That is why a chair will almost always be replaced by a stool. A rectangular table which should measure 42 inches long will be replaced by one 24 inches across, in such a way that the actors gathered around today, jostling one another, will suddenly find themselves during the performance separated by a space that their acting no longer fills. Is a heavy object needed? It's a light one that you will get in the meantime. If you need a fan, they bring you a feather duster in its place, while the fan is elsewhere passing as a feather duster.

These are hardly parodies, but they make one laugh. From outside they are a part of that kind of dusty poetry that is considered theatre. Is it not, however, a sorry thing to see a badly performed work? For someone who has respect for craft, is it not revolting to see this particular one, one of the most beautiful in that it is one that exalts reality, wrongly practised and desecrated? For one who really loves theatre, is it not humiliating to see the poet's work caricatured in this way as soon as it approaches the stage?

And the poet in all this, what is he? The poet is the one who interests us... If he is a smoker, he smokes; if he is a ladies' man, he becomes intimately acquainted with one of the young ladies while she is off the stage. When he is young he does it with ardour and awkwardness; when young no longer, with nonchalance and cynicism.

Alas! I am sorry to have to say it, but most often the poet accepts anything in order to be performed. He accepts delays and risky improvisations; he bemoans the betrayals, but hardly resists them, and even ends up adopting them, inventing good reasons to find them legitimate. Sometimes he intervenes, in a shaky voice, but he is quickly persuaded that he knows nothing about stagecraft. Having no influence on those who have seized upon his work, he recites it silently to himself as a consolation. If he is too touchy, he bursts out briefly, then goes and cries in a corner. If this poor unhappy poet still has a little dignity he will end up slamming the door behind him. He will go away to breathe a little fresh air and try to adjust his dreams, no longer to theatre plots but to the novel. You see how the poet is shown the door to the theatre.

But you will say that I'm painting the portrait of a poet without authority or courage, of a coward who does not know how to defend his work and to impose it on those who should serve it. A real poet, a great one, rises above this tribe of quacks.

[*Copeau goes on to quote Hamlet's advice to the players and Molière's to his actors in* L'Impromptu de Versailles].

With Molière and Shakespeare we have the purpose of our speech: the poet in the theatre, the theatre become man – the living poet and, through him, the living stage work. They were born on it, they possess it and they rule it. Because of them, there is no longer an intermediary between creation and its proper technical and theatrical realisation. Dramatic invention and its *mise en scène* are but two aspects of a single act. Thus there is no longer any conflict, nor even any difference in the ideas of the poet, the actor and the director. What's more, there is an identity of means and expression. The poet does not nurture an inert and distant masterpiece that addresses itself only to the mind, but to the breath of the lines and their slightest motions, outbursts and silences; not only to the characters but to the actors in the play. And the poet finds naturally in his voice, his face and his body, all the means to speak to the eyes and to the senses. [...]

I am not saying that an actor should expect everything from the poet, that he should stand there inert, waiting to be shaken. No, in fact there should always remain between the poet's direction and the actor's playing a certain distance, a free space for original inflection and natural inspiration. But I want the poet, having to express himself through the actor, to be as close to him as possible, as associated and incorporated with him as possible, so that the art of one joins with the art of the other. Sometimes you express your satisfaction as listeners and spectators by saying that a company plays *in tune*. You mean that all the actors in the company, whatever their individual differences and original characteristics are in accord with a certain tone that seems commanded by the nature of the work they are interpreting. And what is this certain tone of the work if it is not the voice of the poet himself which, though divided among numerous interpreters, does not deviate from its unity. What you admire in a perfect performance is the fidelity of the actors to the poet. It is even more than that, it is the presence of the poet among them... So I say that in order to recognise the sovereign delicacy of the poet in this way, he must have known the actor in him. In order for the actor to play for the poet, the poet must know how to write for the actor. If we require of the actor that he understand the peculiarities of a character, the meaning of a situation, the mechanism of the stage, the phrasing of a line, in short that he enter to a certain point into the process of a poet's art, it is only fair, and even more necessary, that we ask the poet to absorb as much as possible of the process of the actor, not in order to thwart it, but on the contrary to release it, to encourage its perfection by playing on the most sensitive and correct key.

One must not confuse this good understanding of the means of expression, instinctive in the great dramatic author, with a willingness on the part of the poet to follow the actor's routine. On the contrary, the more the poet knows about stagecraft, the more he is well placed to detect in the actor the resistances resulting from his laziness or his lack of comprehension, the more he will know to indicate to him the latest and most daring acting through the use of the technique which he possesses. Each time the baffled actor stops and, with a great air of exasperation and disgust, says to the poet: 'Sir, I cannot play that', the poet must be able to answer the actor. He must do so, but not in the writer's usual way: 'Well, my friend, what do you want... do something else... I don't know'; nor by giving him psychological or metaphysical explanations, nor reasons from pre-history that justify his 'Bonjour, Madame'... No, the poet must get up on the stage and assure the actor: 'Sir, what you are asking is very simple, and here is how to go about expressing this nuance or that movement which I want and which cannot be replaced: this, and nothing else.'

If actors give us tepid performances so often, if audience responses become routine, it is largely due to the technical incompetence of the poet, who goes around complaining that his play has been betrayed, his lines torn to shreds, but who would be unable to correct the errors he is condemning.

Not only must the poet control the individual who becomes his instrument, but in order to place his acting on the stage which is his podium, and to render it intelligible and poignant for a whole audience, he must deal expertly with that inanimate individual: the stage.

The theatre is a world, a perfect world, as a geometric shape is perfect, as are all creations of an accomplished art. It communicates with the real world, borrowing its forms, colours and its accents, but gives it back an image composed only from its own resources.

To be more exact, I should say that the theatre is architecture, with its dimensions, its plans, its volumes, its strengths, its features, its perspective, its acoustics, its lighting, and its own atmosphere and system. It reconstructs the world and time, mankind and life, as the cathedral translates nature, the soul and God. One must belong to this world to know its symbols and practise its rites.

Theatre is an art with roots as deep as the architect's, and its equilibrium is just as mathematically planned. It allows for no falseness. It cannot exist without a subtle and strong craft, like all arts which rest on a mutual confidence between the spiritual and the material. The poet who approaches the theatre, whether it be the building or the stage without having sized it up carefully or foreseen its lasting qualities, in the little time he is given, foreseen its move-ments on an unrelenting surface where everything is done in order to be seen, the poet who does not possess the mechanics of the stage like an actor or a stage-hand, runs the risk of seeing his work deformed as soon as it is performed. The configuration of a master-piece on the stage is at the mercy of the most trivial accident. The purity of the performance rests on an exquisite discipline of all the material elements. The more elevated the poet's art, the more his craft must be infallible. It is the invisible and profound perfection of the craft which allows art to rise without yielding.

[From 'Le Poète au Théâtre', *La Revue des Vivants*, nos 5 and 6 (May, June) 1930, reprinted in *Registres I*, pp. 169–83]

FREEDOM AND SERVITUDE

Some authors are truly incredible cowards in the face of their own plays. They give in to the least objection and surrender before the first difficulty. This is because nothing irresistible nor deeply necessary inspired them to write such rather than something else; it is also because they have not explored or inhabited the perfect universe of the theatre. They passed through it like performers chasing after an adventure. They are not at home in it. They are so intoxicated at seeing themselves performed that they find the best excuses to praise the refusals they receive, and they gratefully adopt their adulterated work. They must be protected from themselves.

Others, on the contrary, profess an unlimited idolatry for their text. They can no more detach it from themselves than they can become detached from it. They refuse to allow it to go on to the stage, to the actors, or to that new life it will get from them. They cannot manage to force themselves to be quiet in order to listen to their characters, and they reproach the actor for any intonation that does not slavishly reproduce their own. They should be operated on for this selfishness.

Does the author complain at not being free? The proper accent of his art lies in the servitudes imposed by acting. Everything can be spoken in the theatre, providing it is expressed according to the theatrical form. Very little is needed to enlighten the mind of the spectator or to stir his senses and to capture his imagination. But a choice trait, a necessary word or movement will be as nothing unless it comes in such a place or such a moment in the life of the play.

These days, when there is so much talent around, many authors are coming to the stage in their first flush of youth with a plan to invent everything... They often find that the theatrical instrument, its personnel and its machinery, resist them more brutally than the blank page before their wordy ideas. One of them said to me one day: 'I am no longer going into the theatre. Every time I have dared to, I felt diminished by it.' I answered: 'As much of a musician as you claim to be, try to play the violin without learning how. I should be surprised if you did not feel diminished by it...' Everything is acceptable in a book, at least provisionally, but what is not made to work on the stage stumbles immediately.

[From 'Le metteur en scène', *Nouvelles Littéraires*, 15 October 1932, reprinted in *Registres I*, pp. 183–4]

AN INVITATION TO THE COMIC POET

In today's world, where people are increasingly engrossed by material worry and social anxiety, in this topsy-turvy world we are in, let us admit at least that these varied conflicts make up the liveliest and most exciting spectacle. Society, which is badly in need of re-adaptation and re-orientation, has never been more interesting to the observer for the eccentricity and extraordinary confusion of its manners and styles. It has never produced more varied, brand-new and pronounced types. If then, in these times, tragedy, like the epic of old, has failed us, why do we not at least take part in the birth of a *comedy*? Why do we not have a great comic poet?

Perhaps, very simply, because a society that is troubled, worried and disoriented does not favour the comic spirit. It can produce documentary pictures, works of imagination and fantasy, amuse-ments, dramas and perhaps farces, but no Comedy. Because comedy is the flower of a culture, evidence of an order, proof of an equilibrium, it needs to be founded on reason. Comic force takes root in a philosophy. It rests on a well-established conception of mankind and on the general acceptance of this conception by the majority. 'Ridiculous' is what we call anything that is different from this conception, either through lack or excess. In order for all the spectators to enjoy Comedy, to laugh in the right places, in the same places, they must all be in agreement, without consulting one another, on what is ridiculous, and consequently comical. Now, in our day, the so-called 'cultured' spectator has a tendency to set himself apart, to make himself conspicuous by not approving a dramatic work unless he thinks it is rare, exquisite, or I daresay, divorced from the common sensibility, not on the level of the public at large, but especially meant for his own remarkable intelli-gence... Ridiculousness exists as long as there are conventions, and Comedy exists as long as these conventions sanction a judgement of the world. When there is a general tendency towards free morals, individual fancy, social equality, disdain for culture and tradition; when everything becomes confused, the sense of ridicule is lost and the comic spirit fades and crumbles away.

France has not had a comic poet for three centuries; since 17 February 1673, to be exact, when Molière died. [...]

Since then (as Boileau wrote in his eulogy), Comedy could no longer wear its traditional buskin; it had lost its stature. The great comic plan was abandoned, and neither Regnard, Marivaux, Beaumarchais, Le Sage nor Diderot, as distinguished writers as they were, could restore the prestige and rank of the genre that Molière seemed to have exhausted by raising it to perfection. [...]

If we go back to the nineteenth century, we find that neither Emile Augier nor Alexandre Dumas *fils*, continuators of the 'bourgeois comedy' now out of favour with the public, were able to recover that great comic tone of the Greeks and Romans, almost reached by the *Commedia dell'Arte*, and which Molière used in ten of his unequalled and definitive masterpieces.

Look at a more recent period, the theatre of our fathers. Naturalism, and what was called the Théâtre Libre School, followed in the steps of Balzac and, under the influence of Zola and the Goncourts, stood opposed to comic tone and to anything that that form of expression might include in the way of freedom, detachment, impulse and even spontaneity. Naturalism aims low and it lowers itself to its subject; it is bad-tempered and substitutes *detestation* for irony. Henry Becque is strong and talkative; he has the shoulders and weight for it. He attacks public morals by claiming to follow his master, Molière, but he lacks the ease, variety and flair. He is tainted by pessimism and 'blackness'; his verve is not aroused, but gets bogged down. Starting with light comedy and genre tableaux, by way of melodrama, he ends up with a picture in two tones, made from disagreeable and 'narrow' subject matter. [...]

We shall not find the comic poet in the symbolist generation either, not in Maeterlinck nor in Claudel. [...]

Feydeau had all the sparkle of a farceur, but his *drumfire*, well-constructed plots are inhabited only by puppets.[...][3]

You must not think I look down on the authors that I have just named. Almost all of them are talented, some of them very much so. I only meant to say that I do not see among them the great comic poet that I am looking for, and that Comedy in France, since Molière, has not found its greatness. But I could say as well that there is, in France, an uninterrupted comic tradition, a latent comic vein. According to the times, it can become changed or diminished, but it will never disappear, for we have it in our blood. When we speak of a possible renewal of our theatre and try to encourage it, it seems there is where we should turn. This is our point of orientation, wherein lies our secret strength. We must turn to our tradition for the remedy to our ills and not ask for exotic drugs that some claim will galvanise the invalid, who is perhaps not as ill as all that.

[From 'Invitaçion al poeta comico', *La Nación*, Buenos Aires, 30 December 1928, reprinted in *Registres I*, pp. 188–91]

1 The flagstone in the church of San Miniato in Tuscany from which
the Vieux Colombier's logo was derived.

2 Gymnastics class in the garden at Le Limon, 1913.

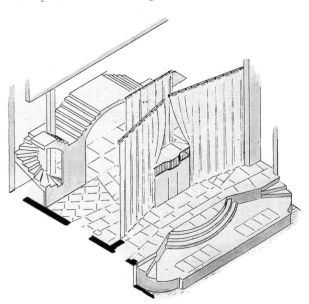

3 Louis Jouvet's projection of the Vieux Colombier, showing curtains
in position for *La Jalousie du Barbouillé* by Molière.

4 *La Jalousie du Barbouillé*, photograph, 1914.

5 *La Jalousie du Barbouillé*, drawing by Dulac.

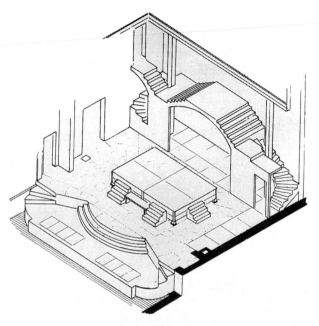

6 Louis Jouvet's projection of the Vieux Colombier, showing the *tréteau*
in position for *Les Fourberies de Scapin* by Molière.

7 *Les Fourberies de Scapin* in performance, with the *tréteau* placed
outside in the Place Saint Sulpice, near the Vieux Colombier, 1922
(Robert Allard deputising for Copeau in the role of Scapin).

8 Copeau at the time of *L'Illusion* (1926) holding the mask of the Magician,
by Paul-Albert Laurens.

9 Copeau as Plébère in *L'Illusion*.

10 Schematic plan, by André Barsacq, for *Le Miracle du Pain Doré* in the courtyard of the Hospices de Beaune (1943).

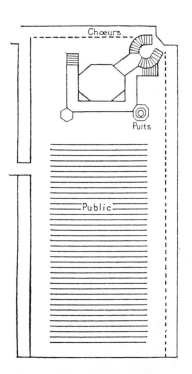

11 *Le Miracle du Pain Doré*, Copeau seated in background, chorus above.

12 *Le Miracle du Pain Doré*, Copeau as Le Meneur du Jeu.

10

THE DIRECTOR

The ubiquity of the director in theatre and film is today as un-questioned as that of the sea-captain: every ship must have one. But when Copeau, at the age of thirty-five, gave up the role of dramatic critic for that of metteur en scène in 1913 the job had only been thought of as desirable, let alone necessary, for three decades or so. His immediate Parisian predecessors were Antoine (the 'master' of Realism) and Lugné-Poë, nominally a Symbolist, but more eclectic in taste, who had, for example, somehow allowed the iconoclastic Père Ubu through the doors of his Théâtre de l'Oeuvre. Although Copeau's tastes were catholic also, he was at heart a traditionalist and his vocation was, he believed, to restore the classics through a dedication of his abilities as a director. In the process both he, his actors and, if not his own theatre, then that of some future director, would become ready for the works of the future. In the interim he would work also with contemporary authors and attempt to raise their consciousness of the task in hand.

Initially, then, he saw his responsibility as being twofold: to the author/Poet and to the actor. The analogy to which he often returned was with the role of the conductor immersing himself in a classic score and then being the medium of its release to an ensemble of skilled players. That he himself also often played the lead (first violin, as it were) is an indication of how difficult he found it to restrict the dominion of this new role: with the models of Aeschylus, Shakespeare and Molière always in mind and particularly conscious of the living example of Stanislavsky, he found the boundaries between directing and writing on the one hand and acting on the other were relative to the work in hand, rather than to semantic absolutes. At the Vieux Colombier, complete self-dedication transcended the traditional role distinctions of theatre.

THE ROLE OF THE DIRECTOR

When a director finds himself in front of a dramatic work, his role is not to say: 'What am I going to do with it?' – his role is to say: 'What is it going to do with me?...'

[From 'Le Théâtre du Vieux Colombier', speech in Lyons, 21 December 1920, published in part in *Forces Vives*, IV, 1953; MS in FC, reprinted in *Registres I*, p. 194]

ESPOUSAL

Undoubtedly we do have our principles, the ones we learned from our work and our experience, to which, fortunately, we do not always adhere, and from which we are sometimes lucky enough to escape.

Someone once asked a charming young woman what she did always to have such pretty dresses. She answered innocently: 'I put myself into them.'

When, around my thirty-fifth year, I entered the practice of theatre, I had no single principle. I just put myself into it in all good faith and with love.

And, for the past twenty-seven years, I have tried to preserve that freshness. Whatever work is to be performed, whether a thousand years old, three centuries or brand new, I try to enter into it without any preconceived notions or ready-made ideas. I do all I can to espouse it as it is and to live with it.

[From a lecture in the Royal Theatre of Athens, August 1937; MS in FC, pub. in part in *Registres I*, pp. 201–2]

CURRENT TRENDS

Direction has played so prominent a part in the work of the contemporary theatre; it has aroused so much curiosity; it has given rise to so much research, effort and striving; and it has helped shed light on so many basic problems that it has often – and wrongly – been considered an art in itself. Some have asserted that the director possesses universal talents, ranging from those of the actor to those of the creative writer, and including those of the painter and composer. As a matter of fact, that is a portrait of the ideal director. But this ideal has turned the head of more than one director.

In the cinema as in the theatre, there is a conflict between technicians and writers for the realisation of unity under the guidance of a master-creator. As cinema techniques develop and improve, and as the cinema establishes its own traditions, the director tends increasingly to take the place of the writer. But that place was left vacant; for one cannot really say that up to now we have had masters of the cinema. We usually say that the dramatist is the master in the theatre, and fundamentally, of course, everything does depend on the creative writer. Thus far there has been no split between creator and realiser: there is a perfect unity in simplicity. But an increasing simplicity in the means of realisation will bring about a division of labour. The unity thus lost will be found again only in exceptional cases.

In principle there is no reason why a first-rate dramatist, with rich experience in the theatre, should not also be a first-rate director, quite capable of directing his plays admirably. Up to a certain point, his experience as a director may usefully influence his concepts of drama. But it must be acknowledged that in our day the playwright is usually a master who has let slip the instrument of his mastery. This has come about for many reasons not all of which are his fault. He writes for the stage; yet the stage may repel him or baffle him. He finds it indispensable to get help from a method of inter-pretation. So he turns to the specialist in this method: the director.

Hence the director is the playwright's right-hand man, or sub-stitute in the matter of producing the play. His work is based on an agreement, a kind of contract which he is able to sign because of his insight and to which he is bound because of his sincerity. But trouble arises the moment he makes use of some of his professional skills to distort the playwright's work, to introduce into the fabric of that work his own ideas, intentions, fantasies and doctrines.

Technical competence, profound understanding and genuine en-thusiasm can and should develop in the director a second inspiration, which is released when he makes contact with another's work. To this extent he participates in creation. He is also a critic and often better able than the playwright himself to discern errors in play-wrighting.

It is easy to understand why a gifted director is tempted to conceal the playwright's lack of skill by means of his own technical resources. Admittedly too he becomes impatient when certain masterpieces are said to be unplayable; so he toys with the idea of revising them or removing the difficulties in them. It need not surprise us, therefore, if he proceeds boldly to the very source of creation and convinces himself that he can shape the entire process.

It is true that creating a dramatic work in words and actually mounting it on stage with live actors are but two phases of one and the same operation. And it is also true that all great dramatists, from Aeschylus to Shakespeare, from Aristophanes to Molière, and from Racine to Ibsen, have been directors. We could cite many others of lesser genius – Voltaire, Diderot, etc. – who had original ideas about directing. The fusion of dramatist and director, however, is in a *descending* line; it is difficult to see how this order could be reversed.

Let us hope for a dramatist who replaces or eliminates the director, and personally takes over the directing; rather than for professional directors who pretend to be dramatists. (No matter how experienced a craftsman he may be, he is immediately too much the professional.) But since we lack great dramatists who stage their own plays personally and with authority, the great director shows his mettle only when he confronts a written masterpiece, particularly when that masterpiece is considered unplayable. Because he believes in it, he understands it; and because he has insight and respects it, he wrests its secret from it.

Does not perfection in directing arise from the friendly conflict between a great creator and his great interpreter? Whenever this salutary conflict is avoided; whenever the technician of the theatre, freed from restraints, visualises things like an actor, and only in terms of the acting, his production thins out and dries up. It resembles that of the musical virtuoso who composes solely for his own instrument. He obtains perfection without depth, without nuances, without mystery. An added dimension is lacking. And artistic creation suffers a mortal blow.

[From: 'La Mise en scène', *Encyclopédie Française*, op. cit., reprinted in part in *Registres I*, p. 195]

MUSICAL ESSENCE

The great orchestra conductor does not stress his own conception nor display the prestige of his virtuosity on a musical text. He goes deeply into the music and emerges with all its secrets. He subordinates all his artistic means, all the resources of his craft, to the correct expression of its values; he makes us hear everything and adds nothing. He is the master whose originality consists of communing with the original; the interpretive genius who, in order to translate the written text into the world of sound, follows the identical process to the composer's in organising in silence the world of musical signs.

But the essence, the reality and the truth of a piece of music are inscribed in the music itself, and the main guides to executing it are in the score.

If it is a matter of a literary text, particularly of a dramatic one, how will we be guided, by what sign will we know the hidden way, the true one?

For, in all realisations, there exists a true way, the one the author took, and the one it is our mission to find and to follow.

What's more, we shall recognise the value of a dramatic text by its call for fidelity, by the little freedom it allows us, by the commandments it gives us, and by the servitude it imposes. It is by working within these limitations, by struggling within these bonds, that we shall find the master's confidence and life's secret.

By what operation, it is difficult to say. I shall not go into technical considerations. What interests me here is the attitude of a supreme interpreter before a supreme work. I define this attitude by its use of such intellectual gifts as intelligence and attentiveness, but above all in its moral qualities, the rarest and the most precious of which are simplicity and humility. As these gifts or qualities become enlightened through study and strengthened through work, they produce in us what we call by a word that must be well understood, as it says it all: sincerity.

It is sincerity that introduces us to profound knowledge, though this very knowledge remains almost undefinable. It is not quite like intellectual knowledge and cannot be obtained either through scholarly principles or through logical reasoning, or even through applying special methods. It is a faculty of contact, a natural intuition, a revelation, I daresay, of a musical essence.

For the contemporary mind to realise an identification with a centuries-old work of poetic creation, the director will have two dangers to avoid: a lifeless reconstruction due to his excessive respect and an extravagant modernisation under the guise of giving it a personal interpretation.

It is simply a matter of being sensitive enough to discover its life and revive its style.

Putting new life into the style is only possible by creating the performance conditions analogous but not identical to those of the original work being revived, either because it requires a narrow constraint or it needs a great freedom of the stage to expand.

In a word, I think we need to take our inspiration from the conventions of the period, within which we shall try to make life flow and circulate in the natural fashion that will be recognised by a contemporary public, and never be flattered by those facile and vulgar anachronisms so much in style today.

[From: 'L'Interprétation des ouvrages dramatiques du passé', speech before the Musical Congress of the Maggio Fiorentino, Florence, May 1938; MS in FC, published in *CRB*, 25 bis (1963), reprinted in *Registres I*, pp. 197–201]

MUSICALITY AND THE ACTOR/DIRECTOR

I don't understand anything about music. As a child, I was not forced to learn the piano, and that was a big handicap in my profession. Unable to read even a simple score; almost unbelievable. Yet, I often took part in musical performances, the most noteworthy of which was Honnegger's *King David*. In most cases I would wait in anguish for the conductor's gesture to indicate when I should start, and I was never sure of stopping at the right moment. As kind as they were, the composers were astonished at my ignorance. It did not prevent Mme Ida Rubenstein, in spite of my protests, from entrusting me with the direction of several of her ballets. I failed completely, moreover. What is rather surprising is that I believe I feel strongly the musicality of a text. In my long dramatic readings, especially of the Greek tragedies, I succeed in inventing and even improvising cadences and rhythms which are musical, and in rendering the choruses I even go almost as far as song. When working on a *mise en scène*, even for a realistic play, it is always a musical feeling which inspires me. Or, rather, I anticipate the music. But the simple idea of having to follow a melodic line upsets all my faculties. When I played Figaro in the *Marriage*, as you know a role which requires several songs, I would make my fellow actors laugh by boldly plunging into a different melody with each performance. [...]

It was quite another thing when I decided to take the role of Sganarelle in *Le Médecin Malgré lui*. You recall that the character enters singing a drinking song. [...] It's a very simple air, very popular, all the more hazardous since everyone knows it, and one risks making a fool of oneself. Also, if one hums it off-stage, just before going on, there is a chance, at least for me, that I would sing it in two different keys. I stood there anxiously behind the curtain awaiting my cue, repeating my air endlessly to myself. And, what is awful is that, within me, I was singing on key. Then the cue came, and I was singing off key!

But, you will say, why did you have to play parts that included singing when you knew you could not do them properly?

Obviously, it was a mistake. An actor-director makes many of them. The more intelligent he is, the more there is a chance of error, and there is always an abyss in the theatre between understanding a character and acting it. The younger and more ardent he is, the more dangerous are his inspirations. The more sincere he is, the more imprudent he becomes. Noble illusions lead one astray. One says to oneself: how could the audience criticise me for a mistake when I am giving myself to it with such ardour; be so severe towards a blunder which it knows is not inspired by *cabotinage*? More than once, not finding in my company any actor I deemed adequate to play such and such a role, I would take it on myself in the belief that I could do it better. And I was mistaken; and my detractors would gloat at this unhappy result. My best-intentioned friends, seeing my fatigue, would insist that I give up acting comedy. It is true, though, that when I limited myself to acting it for others, that is when I would establish the outline of a role for the rest of the actors, indicating the essential means of expression, or of passing on to the company the spirit of a work, the result was generally better. In order to make a first-class *metteur en scène*, one needs a potential actor who is at the same time on the stage and in the hall, who is alive to the best possible use and the fullest output of each person. But do not expect the *metteur en scène* to penetrate deeply into a character, or to use that power of deep concentration which seems to be reserved for great actors, if he is not an actor.

[From 'Souvenirs pour la radio', May–June 1945, op. cit.]

THE DIRECTOR AS PARTLY ACTOR

I am not quite an actor. He who is 100 per cent actor cannot live away from the stage. I am doing very well without having set foot on it for several years. There is a type of actor whose ignorance of other arts and techniques does not bother him at all, but my curiosity for these things is almost infinite. The true actor enters into his role and becomes its prisoner, unable to leave it. I have known some actors whose faculty for persistent metamorphosis was something hallucinating; Zacconi,[1] for example. I believe that my own dominant faculty is that of dual personality, for however important my role, my ears and eyes could not avoid being aware of my partners. One day, when I was playing Alcestis in *The Misanthrope*, the actor who was playing Oronte came on stage with one of his shoelaces untied. Immediately, my eyes became so fixed on those laces that my unfortunate comrade forgot his lines. In this presence of mind, this sang-froid, this refusal to forget oneself, there is the sign of a personality that objects to following the basic law of dramatic interpretation. It is like a leak in the actor's painfully worked-out system of creating an illusion for himself, his confederates and for the spectators. This is a problem that has always been and probably always will be subject to much controversy.

The first difficulty for an actor is to get the idea of the role he intends to take on. The second is to find the means to enter into it. I may add that there is a third difficulty, perhaps the greatest of all, and that is to come out of it once we have entered. Some actors are very skilful in sketching out their role, but not only do they make no progress during rehearsals, on the contrary, to the extent that they exert themselves, one could say that they forget it, that their role escapes them, and the wild efforts they make to recapture it are useless. It is rather common to see an actor lost in his role.

The art of helping the actor, of showing him his way and clearing it for him, is perhaps the most pleasant and successful one I have ever practised. It is a delicate art that requires an actor, but not too much of a one. The instructions must be slight, for the slighter they are, the more effective they become. One must know the man or woman being instructed well, and one must treat them tactfully. It is also important that they know you well, that they like you and have confidence in you. This is relatively easy when working with the same ones. With my Vieux Colombier company, rehearsals were a kind of game. According to my mood, or theirs, I knew how to shake them up, lecture to them or encourage them. I also knew how to protect them from authors, for authors are always in a hurry. Either they try to stir the actors up with flattery, or they discourage them by asking them at the outset to do things they cannot do, things that they must be allowed the pleasure of discovering for themselves. Perhaps they won't find them until the twentieth rehearsal or even until they face the public. The director's primary quality is patience. One cannot imagine how much is needed for certain inner states, the simplest movements or the most elementary gestures to mature in an actor. The second quality of a director is discretion. One must never take the place of the author under the pretext of helping the actor. It is enough to call forth or engender in him certain feelings, to point out certain actions which express them, but without doing them, for there are things which are not fully or really expressed except through his own means and temperament, his own personality. That is why I said that a good director should be part actor, but not completely. He is there to smooth the way that leads to the role and to brush away the undergrowth. But once reaching a certain point, it is advisable to leave the actor alone to penetrate his role. In any case, a time always comes when the director can do no more for the actor. That has often been my experience. [...]

The role of the director then, both his duty and his privilege, is to be present everywhere and yet be invisible, without oppressing the actor's personality nor offending the author's intention, and to use his genius only to serve both. All his effort is directed to composing and building a perfectly coherent and proportional object, solid and harmonious, like those tiny cathedrals in the hands of the kneeling donor in the old altar-pieces.

[From: 'Souvenirs pour la radio', May/June 1945 op. cit., published in *Notes sur le Métier de Comédien*, M. Brient, 1955, pp. 41–4; and in *Registres I*, pp. 195–6]

11

THE PUBLIC

At the height of its success, the Vieux Colombier seated only 365 spectators. Were it not for the argument that it was a necessary refuge, a laboratory in which to prepare for the theatre of the future (and the fact that seat prices were the cheapest in Paris) Copeau might have found it hard to defend his theatre against charges of cultural elitism. From the outset, however, he stated that the new theatre would need a new kind of audience:

We considered it would be foolish to try to set up in the midst of the fashionable theatres and to try to compete with their levels of expenditure, which would soon exhaust our resources. How could we make ourselves heard among the milling crowds of the Boulevards, in the midst of a plethora of cries, appeals and conflicting advertisements? On the contrary, we had to remove ourselves from the kind of places where cinema vies with theatre for the attention of an impressionable public. [...]

The audience we are seeking to attract at first 'is a "minority" audience, composed partly of intelligent theatre-lovers, partly of people who no longer wish to encourage the banality and insincerity of commercial theatre, and partly by a new cross-section of the public.'[1]

And, as we have seen, the Vieux Colombier School was as persistent in its attempts to educate its audience through public lectures and readings as it was to develop the individual talents and esprit de corps *of its actor/pupils. Copeau himself never ceased to give public lectures and play readings all over Europe and the United States throughout his career. And in his later work he became even more convinced that the theatre should be open to the sky, a public celebration rather than a private séance. But the natural growth of a large new public for the Vieux Colombier round the nucleus of its official 'Friends' did not take place at a rate which could create development programmes for work which eschewed subsidy as much as it disdained commercialism. Copeau eventually came to the conclusion that a new popular theatre would have to be created by other means (see Part Three: Popular Theatre).*

THE TRUE PUBLIC

We know very well what a public is because, as I have said before, when what we lovingly call our true public is there in the auditorium, having rushed to attend the first performances, we no longer need to see them face to face to know they are there, with their special quality and particular vibrations. We feel them and we know they are there, even before the curtain goes up. We act the play ten or twenty times before this public, and everything becomes transformed because the solution comes naturally; because on the one hand, there are those who have something to say and say it with all sincerity and with all their powers, and on the other hand, there are those who came for that reason and whose face and hands stretch out to us to receive it. That is a public! Even if, later, the house is sold out and the box office receipts are good, we know that in spite of the 400 faces before us, there is no one there, there is no public.

[From 'Le Renouvellement Dramatique', lecture in Paris, 26 March 1922, M-H D]

BELONGING TO A COMMUNITY

Then we turned to our rapports with the public, which were based on a very high respect which we never refuted. As these rapports were facilitated by the openness, regularity and politeness of our organisation, and as the public became used to us through their feeling of belonging to our community, we slowly won them over, collectively and individually, by creating for them certain advertising methods and means of subscription – in no way comparable with the usual blatant publicity – in which they could find the same kind of quality and perfection that we were trying to give to our plays.

[From 'Une renaissance dramatique est-elle possible?', 1926, op. cit.]

LOOKING BACK ON THE LITTLE THEATRES

The nature of the public, its number, its social composition – that is the essential, the first postulate in the problem of the theatre.

We did not understand this thirty years ago as well as we do today, but we already could feel it when we tried to give a new stimulus to dramatic art. That is why we made such an effort to bring together and to satisfy a new public. But since it was our ambition to do everything anew and to remain pure, it seemed important for us to escape as much as possible from commercial pressures and to take refuge in little theatres. The avant-garde movement of 1919 was a movement of little theatres. We did what we could. It was not our fault if the time was not yet ripe. And God knows how much effort was expended in this difficult work. But since I have never deluded myself regarding the profound results of purely artistic efforts, I realise today that these little theatres were only technical laboratories, conservatories where the noblest traditions of the stage came to life again. To be true theatres they would have needed a true public.

On the fringe of the boulevards we found our public. It discovered with us pleasures of a rare quality. But they were de luxe pleasures, selfish pleasures; they had no more meaning than the pleasures of the mob.

[From *Le Théâtre Populaire*, op. cit., pp. 17–18]

AN APPEAL TO THE FRIENDS OF THE VIEUX COLOMBIER

A theatre with a mission, complying with its duties, holding itself accountable to public culture, will always need to be subsidised. This is the way our national theatres are run. They receive a subsidy because they have a mission. If they fulfilled it we should not dream of attempting to do so in their stead. In order to do so, subsidy will always be necessary and we shall continue to ask for ours directly from the community and the audience, first from the elite and then one day from the general public.

That is why, for those of you who are seeking to recruit new members, you must know that the Vieux Colombier does not want complacent friends. It is not a matter of *drumming up* support from people and then running off with a grudging contribution from people for work they will soon forget about. That is too easy and serves no purpose. The idea that the *nouveau riche* should pay for the rest does not interest us. The person who gives 10,000 or 50,000 francs in order to be enlisted as a Founder of the Vieux Colombier, yet spends all his evenings in the Music Hall, does not interest us. The person who purchases a 300-franc subscription in the hope of selling us on some script or girl friend is out of the question. Such supporters would not add two centimes to the Vieux Colombier's *raison d'être*. Now what we are seeking, and what you must seek with us, is the growth of our material resources. We want the monetary aid that is offered to us to be real evidence of friendship, in proportion to the means of the donor. We are requesting financial support from the very people who are attracted to our artistic commitment. There should be no cheating on that. Let us be realistic. It is important that each one of those who drops his coin in our hat *knows what he is doing*.

There will be no new theatre as long as new working conditions have not been established. And they will be so only through the formulation and application of new methods.

The Vieux Colombier has a doctrine that has stood the test of time, a programme for the future which will become clear to the public as we shape our means of production before its eyes.

By helping us to create these means, you are effectively collaborating... not only in the uplifting or renewal of today's theatre, but in the birth of the theatre of tomorrow. Each time one of our friends brings along an extra friend, he is contributing to the formation of a *new public*, without which our concern for the future would be only a dream.

Everything depends on proper publicity.

To encourage those who are creating it, to preserve them if I can from scepticism, I might say to them that they will never be mocked as much as I was at a time when *no one* believed it possible to find 300 people in Paris to provide benevolent support for an enterprise like ours. This number was attained, then exceeded; today it has advanced to more than 500. It has grown in a natural and regular manner, and we are far from having reached all those that we should. The movement is only beginning. It will extend even further as the Association appeals, not to a restricted category of the public, the privileged class, but to the entire public. That is why we set such a store by the little annual contributions of 20 francs. In our eyes they mark the beginning of a popular membership. Their number can increase almost indefinitely. That is where the future development of the association can be found. It is from there that our enterprise will gain its strength and stability. The day when the 20,000 or 30,000 people who make up the faithful public of the Vieux Colombier will have understood that we need them as supporters and allies in order to retain our creative independence and to remain worthy of our mission; the day when these 20,000 or 30,000 francs of subsidy will not only mean our good fortune, they will signify the solidity of our existence: they will proclaim our *raison d'être*.

[From *Les Amis du Vieux Colombier*. 1ère année. Les Cahiers du Vieux Colombier, no. 1 (November 1920), Editions de la *NRF*, 1920, pp. 37–41]

SOLEMNITY

The primordial dignity of theatre stems from its solemnity. You know how attractive forbidden pleasures are. The difficulty which one encounters in procuring them gives them a savour which can be perverse. Indeed, who does not know the dreary debauchery of such pleasures for sale as are within the means of anyone who carries a coin clenched in his fist, at the bottom of his pocket. The daily diversions that money can buy, not only at all times of the year, but also at every hour of the day are nothing more, in fact, than diversions, having no other *raison d'être* than that of distracting us from ourselves. The signification of a theatrical spectacle goes beyond the immediate: its connection with certain seasons, certain dates in the year, certain social circumstances, certain celebrations of national life, those are what provide nourishment that we respect for the mind and for the imagination. The individual imagination, in order to collaborate in a dramatic celebration, needs proper preparation, initiation.

In order better to understand this need, let us go back to our childhood memories. The promise of [being taken to] a show, the anticipation of it as a reward, released in us the most poignant sources of the imagination. Remember what waiting was like, and how any delays added a delicious impatience and fervour. Remember the state of mind in which you went to bed the night before, woke up on the day of the performance, in which you travelled the distance which separated you from the theatre, entered the auditorium, breathed in its atmosphere, took your seat, waited for curtain up and finally watched it rise and bring you another world, and the resonances that were stirred in you as the first words were spoken. And once the marvel was over, silence fell, the curtain down, normal life resumed, that infinite prolongation of memory through which you could relive emotions that were more real than those of everyday experience, which has neither the harmony, nor the continuity, nor the fullness of a dramatic creation. We can gauge the solemn power of theatre through its effect on a young mind, a fresh spirit. We can gauge it again, to some degree, in its effect on that small public which is the true public, I mean on that section of it which is least privileged, least fortunate. The almost daily abuse of dramatic enjoyment creates a routine in the public analogous to that which deadens and destroys the professional actor, the actor jaded by his profession. There is a professional public (in the pejorative sense) in the same way that there are professional actors and professional authors. They have lost their sincerity. Theatre needs sincerity, authenticity on its stage. It needs it no less in the auditorium. A factitious public engenders factitious acting. We play with the public and the public plays with us. A blasé public which goes to the theatre with indifference, without knowing why it does so, without the need to do so, without love or respect, which arrives late, makes a noise coming in, doesn't even wait for the end of the last act before turning away from the stage and reaching for its overcoat, such a public is not a public. It holds us in contempt. And we return it. That is why, so often, we find true recompense in the understanding of the gallery, of those people who have really wanted to come to the theatre, who don't come every day, who have made a sacrifice in order to be able to come, who have come by public transport, or on foot. That is the kind of build-up of expectation, the kind of singularity of feeling, the kind of freshness and the kind of sincerity of understanding, that I find to an even more vital extent among my French countryfolk when my little troupe goes among them to celebrate, in their villages on the occasion of some seasonal solemnity, their countryside, their labour, their customs. Thus our art rediscovers a little of its lost signification, it re-establishes its place in the city, its station in culture, its power and its nobility, each time it comes near to the primitive conditions which, in ancient Greece, at the time of the Great Dionysia, constituted a religious festival of theatre.

[From the third lecture at the American Laboratory Theatre, 26 January 1927, published in *Registres I*, pp. 135–44, 157–8]

Part III

PAST
AND
FUTURE FORMS

12

MOLIERE

The vehemence with which Copeau rejected much of contemporary French theatre did not lead him into innovative isolationism; today he would perhaps be tagged as 'post-modernist' in his views, since he had a sense of collaboration, not only with contemporary masters such as Antoine and Stanislavsky (see appendices A and B), but also with those of the European tradition. He admired Aeschylus (but did not stage him), found a new style of presentation of Shakespearean comedy for French audiences on which his reputation as a director was initially founded, and, most constantly, kept Molière at his side as the example of the dramaturgical and human values that he was seeking. For him, Molière was not a dead, but a living example. Commenting on Mascarille's line 'Listen, here, unadorned, is the end of a true and pure comedy', (L'Etourdi, V, ix) in his edition of Molière's complete works, Copeau wrote:

Indeed, *pure comedy* [...]. Abundant, quick, joyous, full of incidents and accidents, inexhaustible movements, dazzling, it is from beginning to end wrought by the force of the dance which, even in his major works, completely regulates Molière's rhythm. Disguises, meetings, fictitious letters: it is a gratuitous form of playing, absolutely free, playing with everything: honour, love, respect, death. Already a master comedy, full of seeds and possibilities which could become too disciplined. *Young* comedy. [...]

The language and the style have the same gaiety and happiness, a sparkling contrast. The imagery is familiar, direct, full to bursting, always moving, like the dialogue which is sown with incidents, surprises, discoveries, as in the action. Everything is carried off with the same inspiration, as in life.[1]

The repertoire of the Vieux Colombier, and that of the Copiaus reflects the centrality of Molière's position in Copeau's thinking, in particular the rediscoveries to be made from playing the short farces. In 1921 he wrote in his Journal:

It was under the invocation of Molière that the Vieux Colombier was founded, and it was he who provided its first production, in October 1913, *L'Amour Médecin.*

Returning in 1931 to give two talks under the title of 'Souvenirs', he said:

Molière guided our first steps in the practice of an art which, while not at all ignoring those tendencies we call modern, is concerned to remain French, I would even say: classical, if I was not afraid of being misunderstood. Molière teaches us the rules of the game. (p. 26)

L'Amour Médecin *was followed shortly by* L'Avare, *with Dullin triumphing in the title role, and* La Jalousie du Barbouillé. *The New York season opened in 1917 with an* Impromptu du Vieux Colombier, *based on* L'Impromptu de Versailles *followed by the key mise en scène of* Les Fourberies de Scapin, *with Jouvet as Géronte. In March 1917,* L'Amour Médecin *and* L'Avare *were brought back and the 1918/19 season saw the addition of* Le Médecin malgré lui *and* Le Misanthrope. Scapin *reappeared in Paris in 1920 and it and all the preceding productions were reprised at various times up to the 1924 closure. In August 1926, Copeau introduced* Le Médecin malgré lui *again, this time to strengthen the repertoire of his emergent young troupe of 'Copiaus' as they performed in the towns and villages of Burgundy. A new piece,* L'Ecole des Maris *was added that winter, a measure of the company's growth to maturity. George Dandin *was in rehearsal when the Copiaus disbanded in 1929. And, in 1936, now at the Comédie-Française, Copeau returned once again to* Le Misanthrope.

However, Copeau's work on the short farces of Molière cannot in general be said to have led on to a renewal of the master works, rather back towards their comedic roots in the commedia dell'arte, *thus setting off another quest which informs the next chapter of this anthology.*

A PERFECT MODEL

Molière is our perfect model because he is essentially an infallible *metteur en scène*, that is, a man whose imagination takes fire from the possibilities of theatre, who concentrates his genius on turning these possibilities to the best account, who sees straight off the whole perspective afforded him by the stage, is never at a loss over a movement or a phrase, and knows how to do all that it is possible to do within a given *genre*.

With Racine, Shakespeare or Molière, we know where we stand, what the questions and answers must be. Masterpieces speak in the clearest and most intelligible language. It is enough to listen to it well in order to understand it. Knowing how to listen is the beginning of sincerity, but in order to be sincere, one must have integrity, a knowledge of one's craft and be practising it honestly.

It is always easy to run away, to dodge the question, to be carried away with an idea. The most beautiful parts of a *mise en scène* are the hidden inventions. Almost no one notices them. [...]

Let us recognise in good faith that the inventions of the directors, their technical questings, their concern for the past, their anticipations of the future, and even, one might say, their trespasses, have to a certain extent given an impetus to dramatic inspiration.

But these rediscovered truths must not be used to express lies, puerility, facile pretentions, empty methods or, in a word, fall into the trap of vanity. It would be absurd to think that we have saved the theatre from the *cabotinage* of the actor only to have abandoned it to the more despicable one of the director. [...]

A good dramatic work does not have to adapt itself to the stage. It was born there, so to speak. It occupies and owns it naturally. The action remains in suspense in the text, like a waiting dancer already inspired by the rhythm which will release him.

[From 'Metteur en scène', *Nouvelles Littéraires*, 15 October 1932; reprinted in *Registres II*, pp. 59–60]

MOLIERE'S *MISE EN SCENE*

A play must be read for its feel; this feeling is what produces, after a certain time, the lively and joyous blossoming of an interpretation.

Working on interpretation is like working with wood.

There is a *mise en scène* which is *felt* or *imposed*; it works, it gives, in the way that wood gives. [...]

[Copeau] defends himself against the objection made against him that he is too 'analytical':

That is to object to the intellect, to the critical mind, which Baudelaire calls the creative spirit. It is a discriminating, dissociating faculty, a sense of vision, of introspection.

This defect is (*for the dramatic renovation which he is attempting*), obligatory, it is a discipline for the mind.

Dramatic sense is a blend of the critical mind and delight. [...]

Only the text counts; nothing but the text!

It is only through the text that a man from 1660 will be able to signal to those of the year 2000...

If it is a dramatic work, all they will need to do is to read it.

Expect nothing except from the text!

Stay with Molière for an understanding of the stage, he is an actor. He does not write one word without hearing it and without making it act.

Molière never created a mundane character, a stock character, as we say, or a fill-in, because he was a man of the theatre and he wrote for actors.[...]

There is a 'scenic' principle in certain Molière plays. It is a constant movement which tends towards dance.

There is a physical necessity made on the actor to be a dancer, feelingly to manifest this physical quality.

There are constant intermezzos within the action (as between the acts themselves). This dance is in the the text. It is not imagined. The way that Sylvestre and Octave walk in the first scene [of *Les Fourberies de Scapin*], I can read in the text,[2] it is not an invention, it is a sort of obedience to the text.

When a text is created for dramatic life, there is a necessary *mise en scène* within the work itself. That is probably not true but it is an agreeable and fertile thought.

[From 'La Mise en scène de Molière'. Notes taken by Louis Jouvet during Copeau's lecture course at the Ecole du Vieux Colombier, 30 March 1921, published in his preface to *La Mise en Scène des Fourberies de Scapin*, Seuil, 1951, pp. 22–3. Jouvet's interpolations in italics, reprinted in part in *Registres II*, pp. 71–2]

HOW TO STAGE MOLIERE

It is often repeated that I intend to break with tradition. The exact opposite is true. I am seeking to bring works closer to the 'true tradition' by freeing them from the contributions loaded on them for three centuries by the official actors [of the Comédie-Française]. The important tradition is the original one.

A difficult task, obviously, to rediscover the movement which existed at the creation of a comedy! Difficult to teach these old plays to actors who have fretted and brooded over them since childhood, to make them understand the true meaning of words taken from life! Thus, with my young students, I never work from the text. I give them scenarios and I teach them to improvise. I ask them to play the characters before speaking the text, while the traditionally trained actors speak the text rather than play the character.Up to now, I have played mostly Molière's farces, plays with much movement, because they are the ones which are least adaptable to the cold, fixed, half-dead interpretation inflicted by the official theatres. Two years ago, I put on *Les Fourberies de Scapin*. In order to revive the movement with which the play was presented, I thought it advisable to conceive a stage lay-out which forcibly produced movement. So I imagined the *tréteau*, surrounded on four sides by steps, built in the centre of the stage, in order to compel the actors constantly to change position. The result, as you know, was a happy one, and we succeeded in communicating to the public such high spirits that this old play was enthusiastically applauded as if it had been written today by a young Molière.

Joy, acting joyfully, there is no other secret.

For the costumes, I admit to not having an absolute rule. I rid Scapin of his traditional red and white-striped costume, and I dressed him like Brighella, his ancestor in the Italian comedy, whose tight-fitting costume, white or yellow, with green Brandenburgs, was embellished with a small cape. That is the way Molière played Sganarelle. Here again, I am trying to reach back to the oldest tradition and cleanse it of the modifications from which it suffered through the ages. Once that is done, I am not afraid to add a *je ne sais quoi* of modernity. For example, in *Les Fourberies*, Jouvet, in the role of Géronte, carried a parasol. Are we not in Naples, the region of perfect weather, sun and heat? With this parasol Jouvet obtained the most amusing effects.

Finally, for me, there are no unimportant characters in Molière.

The most minor ones are interesting to compose: Lucas, for example, the husband of the buxom nurse in *Le Médecin malgré lui*; Monsieur Robert in the same play. What has usually been done with this exellent Monsieur Robert? A bit part. He has, however, such an amusing personality!

['Comment mettre Molière en scène', interview published in *Lectures pour tous*, January 1922; reprinted in *Registres II*, pp. 73–4]

THE RENEWAL OF MOLIERE

The strange undertaking of speaking about Molière's *mise en scène*, of claiming to bring new light to the subject. Is it not a matter that has been settled for more than two centuries? [...]

Astounding that a new theatre company should dedicate itself to the classic repetoire?

It shows evidence of youth and innovation to give life, not only to the modern repertoire, but also to the old, tired repertoire, defaced by a so-called tradition.

Nothing more difficult: to give life and to maintain life throughout. That is: the springing forth, the spontaneity, freedom, imagination, fantasy – finally, that divine thing: movement.

Not a learned method, with more or less well-executed principles. But the very feeling of the style of the work, the communion with the mind that gave it birth. Invention in the interpretation. And let it have that savour, that taste of discovery which fills us – that sort of jubilation which accompanies our deepest feelings, takes hold of us when we see and really understand something in nature *which pleases us*. [...]

Renewal of Molière. Antoine at the Odéon.[3]

A more realistic décor. Furniture on the stage. Antoine and his milieu theory: 'For a long while, the milieu was considered as a collection of properties of no importance. It was generally sacrificed to the concern for not interfering with a classic and, equally, the false acting of it by the actors. But I thought it was better to start by truthfully creating the milieu, the atmosphere in which the characters were to move about, and only then could these characters enter – not to act, moreover, but to live in it.'[4]

The theory as tried in Molière. Acting with furniture and props.
Le Médecin malgré lui at the Thèâtre Antoine.

Les Femmes Savantes at the Comédie-Française. Renewal in the realistic sense. Stairway. Vestibule. Little footmen. Fireplace. Bookcase with books. Realistic movements stuck on the interpretation, not at all required by the action. Renewal from the outside. Timid and revolutionary treatment.

Le Misanthrope. Eclairs are passed round in the portrait scene. [II, iv]

Les Fourberies de Scapin at the Moscow Art Theatre.[5]

Renewal with preconceived ideas. Romantic inflation. Mixture of realism and stylisation. German methods.[6]

How to play Molière well?

Play him in his style, fully, as it is written. With its incongruities, its blend of stark reality and mad fantasy, its music, its diversions. Do not disguise him in any way. Be faithful to him. No restorations.

Put oneself into a state of sensitivity.

Enter deeply into the understanding of the work. The director does not understand it in the same way as the historian or the critic. He has a special faculty. He studies the characters, the peripeteia, the details of the dialogue. But it is a more direct grasp which puts him in possession of the character of the work. He perceives straight off the general style, the tone, the movement, which, little by little, is conceived, lends a meaning to every scene and dialogue.

No need for erudition, not even for profound analysis, for the creator of stage movement to discover instinctively the original *spirit* and meaning of true tradition.

Very often I thought I had invented things in the interpretation of Molière and Shakespeare. And later, something revealed that I had put my finger on a detail from the original interpretation.

True classical interpretation rejects outward affectations of a so-called realistic or aesthetic novelty as much as it does the droning of a lifeless tradition. It does not stick to the letter of certain rites, box-office receipts or stage tricks handed down by the actors. It is all spirit. It lives only by sensitivity and invention. [...]

Thus, understanding of the text.

Comprehension of the character of the work.

And a good company of actors, young, solidly in the hands of the director. The Vieux Colombier company. Our friendship. Necessary to play comedy well.

Molière's company, by its composition, gave the impression of a large family rather than of a circumstantial company. Molière and the Béjarts formed its solid core. He always lived with them.

Attended to them. Advised them, egged them on, helped them, exerted himself unstintingly, communicated his movement, his spirit to them: *L'Impromptu de Versailles.*

Molière a bad actor? I don't think so. Spirituality. He was *theatre.*

Draw up a list of Molière's instructions on acting, delivery, *mise en scène.*

Molière invents technical means: he drew up a system of written notation for the use of the young actors he was training. According to reports, the young Baron, who became such an eminent actor, owed the naturalness of his diction to Molière's teaching method and to the system he had invented. Thus he fashions the material he needs.

The same is done at the Vieux Colombier. [...]

Movement.

Molière owes the movement in his theatre primarily to the Italians. I have a high opinion of this movement, these *cascate.* It is altogether lost on our stages.

Through our productions, bring Molière closer to the Italians. The only way to rejuvenate and invigorate him.

Indispensable youth. Mimes.

Physical training of our actors. Awkwardness of modern actors. Will not kneel because of their trousers. Banality of all the movements. Stage tricks.

The scenarios of the *commedia dell'arte* are not very funny. The *spirit* is in the movement. The same as in certain comic scenes of Shakespeare. Don Juan's valet (in the banquet scene) does a somersault without spilling his wine.

Acrobatics, jumping, juggling. Example and training of the clowns. [...]

[From 'L'Interprétation et la mise en scène de Molière', notes for a lecture before the Institute of Arts and Sciences, Columbia University, 23 March 1917; printed in *Registres II*, pp. 61–70]

13

IMPROVISED COMEDY

In the second half of the twentieth century the Italian improvised comedy of the sixteenth-eighteenth centuries based on stock characters, the commedia dell'arte, *has been fully restored to its place in the spectrum of theatrical possibility. Following the reconstructions of such directors as, amongst others, Meyerhold, Reinhardt and Strehler,[1] small troupes have sprung up again all over Europe and America specialising in* commedia *performance. Some are even applying its techniques to the quest for new stock characters as an alternative way of bridging the nineteenth- and early twentieth-century gap in the living tradition of the original form. All this interest and activity was pre-figured in the work of the Vieux Colombier School and the performances of Les Copiaus and its successor company, La Compagnie des Quinze.* 'It was', *Copeau noted,* 'the study of Molière that led me to the Italian comedy. I had an inkling of the style of farce and, in order to magnify its movements, brought it back in my mind to the* tréteau *of its origins.' (Souvenirs du Vieux Colombier, op. cit. p. 76)*

The work on commedia, *the reconstruction and re-animation of an improvised form, was an alternative (but, he hoped, ultimately complementary) proposition to Copeau's purgation of the formal stage in preparation for the advent of the Poet. Properly understood, the retreat to Burgundy with his pupils and the rump of his troupe can then be seen as a positive quest rather than, as it is often represented, a negation of urban values in despair at theatre's inability to enhance them. Certainly, despite the high proportion of new works in its repertoire, the Vieux Colombier had not discovered a playwright/poet of the calibre that Copeau sought. Rather than a Shakespeare or a Molière, what he had really lacked was someone to play Chekhov to his Stanislavsky. As he wrote:*

Stanislavsky's exceptional luck as an actor and director was to meet Anton Chekhov... From 1898 to Chekhov's death, no season at the Art Theatre was without a play by the famous writer. In order to present them to the public, Stanislavsky exhausted his whole art. He was thus disconcerted the day he no longer had a Chekhov work to present.[2]

Even worse, in André Gide's opinion, it was not only a Chekhov that Copeau lacked, but an increasing dearth of worthwhile new writing:

The real desertion, the one from which he had most to suffer (but it was hard for him to speak of this), was that of the authors. He could hope, and I hoped with him that the only thing lacking was the instrument (which he was providing) for a renascence of the theatre to take place; new works, strong and young, called forth by the need he had of them, were of necessity going to pour in... and I thought so too. Nothing of the sort happened. And his immense effort remained without any direct relation to the epoch. He was struggling against the epoch, as any good artist must do.[3]

As early as January 1916, possibly taking inspiration from his visit to Craig in Florence, Copeau had started a notebook devoted to the possibilities of a new alternative theatre, one in which the writer would come last rather than first. Separate correspondences with Louis Jouvet and Charles Dullin (who were at the front), as well as long conversations with André Gide and Roger Martin du Gard[4] helped to define the possibility: if the new Molière was not imminent, why not go back to a form which had been vital to his apprenticeship, a form which, in its original state had had a place for the sceno-grapher, but not yet the poet: the commedia dell'arte. *Again, however, he was later to suffer the theatrical inadequacy of the authors available to him as they came up with a succession of pale literary distortions of his original idea; for example Roger Martin du Gard* (Le Testament du Père Leleu), *René Benjamin (*Il faut que Chacun soit à sa Place) *and Georges Duhamel* (L'Oeuvre des Athlètes). *Copeau intended, and tried actively to seek, something much more Aristophanic or rustically Atellan.*

His appreciation of all types of contemporary popular entertainment can be traced as far back as his early years as a drama critic in the period known as 'la Belle Epoque', the Paris of the 1900s celebrated in the posters by Toulouse-Lautrec and others. In an article on the 'Cafés-Concerts' (July 1906, MS M-H D), Copeau noted:

Of course, the entertainment one comes to see there is not meant to edify those who are enjoying it. It appeals to the fatigued and worried minds, to the pleasure-sated nerves depressed by the first heat of summer. [...] But to intellectualise the café-concert, as some have tried, as well as to moralise about it, I think rather unconvincingly, would it not at the same time be taking away that secret savour, that indefinable space which excites and fascinates us?

During the Vieux Colombier's first season in Paris, again in New York, and twice in the post-war Paris seasons, Copeau presented Molière's farce, La Jalousie du Barbouillé *to enthusiastic audiences. He wrote in a programme note (27 October 1920):*

Each time we revived the *Barbouillé*, we found new delights in it. In this sense it can be said that this little farce taught us a great deal by inciting us to renew, vary and shade our interpretation on a given subject. And, perhaps because of it, we found ourselves starting to explore a very summary and free comical genre which, by giving back to the actor the feel for his own resources and giving full reign to his inventive fantasies, would some day make him rediscover a little of that professional joy that we no longer see except with the circus clowns or the music-hall 'fantaisistes'.

In 1917, in New York, he invited the famous 'diseuse', Yvette Guilbert, to give a series of seven matinée recitals at the start of the first season at the Garrick Theatre. While in New York, he also took delight in visiting vaudeville theatre and musical comedy:

Somebody asked Jacques Copeau, the distinguished French producer, what he had seen in our theatres and the visitor replied that he had seen Canary Cottage *at the Morosco and that he liked it very much. The man who put the question was shocked, for Copeau is one of the leaders of the little theatre movement in France and* Canary Cottage *is a somewhat loud and rowdy musical-comedy. At least, the objector said it was when he took Copeau to task. But Copeau stood his ground. He said he could not fail to like* Canary Cottage *in spite of obvious crudities, because it was fun not only for the audience, but for the actors too. There was joy in it. There may be joy without art, but there can be no art without joy.*[5]

AN INAUGURAL FARCE

Introduction of the characters in the new comedy by their ancestors from the Italian comedy and the French farce. They evict from the theatre: the poet who comes offering his written play, the pretentious actor, the prompter from his box, etc. Finally the *director* appears, looking sad, constantly searching for a good literary play. He is alarmed and upset by his troupe's revolution, indoctrinated and converted enthusiastically as he was by the new comedy. They tear off his wig and his beard, revealing his natural face. They rid him of his director's clothes and he appears in the costume of a jester. And the improvisation begins...

IMPROVISATION

This is an art which I do not know, but whose history I am going to study. But I see, I feel, I understand that we must restore this art, revive it, help it to live again; that only it can give us back a living theatre, a comedy and actors.

Leave literature aside. I am in the theatre, amid my actors, those future theatre artists whom I am educating by dedicating myself to them.

To create a brotherhood of actors. I had really felt from the outset that this was the problem. People living together, working together, playing together; but I had forgotten that other phrase, the one which inevitably remained: creating together, inventing games together, extracting their games from within themselves and from one another. I was led to this by the little I had already realised.

The actor always tends to improvise on a given text, to 'textualise' as we say. This is the despair of authors. I have often protested against this abuse by the actor, surely a deplorable one as regards the written play, and the more so in that today's actor always improvises or deforms in the most vulgar sense. But, after all, when he gives in to this penchant, maybe the actor is dimly following an hereditary professional tendency. One could say he is protecting his territory, trying to win back the encroachments made on theatre by the *litterateur* and the writer.

A real troupe, like the one at the Théâtre des Variétés today, or [Molière's] old Palais-Royal troupe, accustomed to playing together, can indulge itself by improvising successfully and even brilliantly on certain texts. An actor like Max Dearly,[6] who is a bit of a clown, constantly inserts *lazzi* of his own in the dialogue, often the best parts of his performance. The Revue artistes, the Music Hall comedians – especially the popular Music Hall productions which communicate very closely with their public – and the circus clowns, all are more or less degenerated improvisers. We can find first-class jokers or improvisers among the populace (on the public squares, in the cafés, in the army barracks, at wedding feasts and in popular celebrations, without mentioning the street hawkers and the charlatans). Many social games (charades, etc.) come out of primitive comedy. It is amusements such as these, improvisation after improvisation, that led Maurice Sand and his friends towards a fleeting renovation of the *commedia dell'arte* in their little theatre in Nohant around 1848.[7]

So, there are some tendencies in the air, faculties, tastes, and even a kind of tradition; here and there some scattered sparks subsist from which we can revive the flame of the ancient art of improvised comedy, providing it finds a favourable milieu.

The habit of improvisation will give back to the actor the suppleness, the elasticity, the true spontaneous life of the word and the gesture, the true feeling of the movement, the true contact with the public, the inspiration, the fire and daring of the jester. And what an education for the poet; what a source for inspiration!

A NEW IMPROVISED COMEDY

Here, from the start, we have to beware of the greatest danger: behaving like sight-seers or dilettantes in love with a lost art form.

There is no question of making historical reconstructions, or of exhuming the old scenarios of the Italian farce or the French medieval mansions in the name of historical curiosity. We shall study the *commedia dell'arte* and the fairground theatre. We shall learn the history and development of improvisation, the manners, the methods and the peculiarities of the actors who practised it. But our goal is to create a new improvised comedy using contemporary types and subjects.

It is a very simple idea which occurred to me suddenly one evening during a conversation with friends.

Choose from among the company, the six or eight actors most suited for this project, the most alert, the most confident and the most compatible with one another, who will henceforth concentrate almost exclusively on improvisation. A true brotherhoood; the jesters of the Vieux Colombier. Each one of them takes on one of the characters of the new comedy. He makes it his *property*. He nourishes it, fattens it up from his own substance, identifies his personality with it, thinks about it continually, lives with it, giving it not only his own constitution, external abilities and physical peculiarities, but his ways of feeling and thinking, his moods, observation and experience, sharing his reading, in short developing and changing along with it.

Not morality characters, symbolising an aspect of the soul, a human passion or a certain social class. But the grand-nephews of Pierrot, Arlecchino, Dr Bolonais, etc., whole characters in their being as in physical appearance (absolutely new portraits and cos-tumes, a little like those of the *commedia*: characters with a wide human and social extension, able to fit their attitudes to an infinity of dramatic combinations, from the crudest farce and pure entertain-ment to the subtlest comedy and the strictest drama). They change expression without changing character or appearance, according to the scenario they are playing, only by a nuance in costume or by adding a prop.

At first I play the role of the poet in front of these jesters. This new thing springs from me. I know its origin and its early develop-ment. In order for them to retain all their freshness, I forbid research by the actors. The lessons of the past and the contributions of tradition filter down to them through me, as much as I feel necessary and salutary to provide. I propose the characters and then the scenario. First the characters, one by one, then the scenarios.

We do exercises repeatedly, but we never take the same scenario more than four or five times. We exercise on any pretext, while out walking, during meal-times, preparing our roles for any eventuality. We become our role, and we confront it with those of our comrades, thus beginning the formation of a collaborative work. Soon, the characters develop entirely without me; they escape from me com-pletely. Scenarios are created one after the other from within them-selves. My only role in relation to them is that of critic. The comedy is ripe; it appears on stage. If it succeeds it will outshine all other genres, and soon there will be a new development when it starts to enrich itself from the outside, by the contributions of the public, who will finish the modelling of the characters we present, and by the contributions of the poets who will borrow their characters from the new comedy to develop or change them according to their own imagination. A genre is born. It will develop, then it will totter and finally die. But it will have given back the freedom of creative imagination, of dramatic fantasy. It will have been truly an authentic creation, a dramatic genre (and not only a pale literary variety of it), and the day when it is replaced, it will be perhaps by something more living and accomplished, by this 'future theatre' everyone is talking about so much without knowing the slightest thing about it. Everything is there.

In any case, this new comedy, as I call it for lack of a better name, will probably last for several generations thanks to the School for Young Actors which will accompany it and which will reap, at least among the older ones, a completely fresh tradition.

Three characters have already come to mind. I do not yet know their proper names, only their generic ones: the Intellectual, the Bureaucrat, the Adolescent.

INITIATION INTO IMPROVISED COMEDY

It seems to me that the best and most direct initiation into improvised comedy will be by observing children at play.

Some children play very badly, never knowing what to do, precisely like some actors who play badly, without élan, joy or fantasy, borrowing everything they do from others, copying one another. But children who play well, who *know how* to play, are models of verve, naturalness and invention. They are masters of improvisation.

I see my three little ones (aged 13, 10 and 7) playing from the time they wake up to when they go to bed, without once dropping the character they have chosen for one another. At meal-times, I have to ask them to put aside their fiction so that I can find my real children again in their natural appearance and voice. This *identification* with a character is the first condition of an improvised creation. Each one is *always the same character*: a certain tone of voice, two or three gestures or attitudes, a rudimentary accessory to the costume, enough to make up the character's outward appearance and to suggest its personality. *Repetition of the same trait.* Then, everything that enriches this first rough outline comes from scrupulous observation of reality – manners, personalities, bad habits, idiosyncrasies, mannerisms – but all slightly magnified and parodied, always distorted in the same way. *Imagination* is added to *imitation* of the traits that are more and more fixed, parodied and almost fantastical.

HOW A CHARACTER IS BORN

By observing children at play, we can witness the birth of types.

These children have a notion of simplicity, rusticity and almost crudeness. That is why, when they observe life, they have a tendency to ridicule everything that smacks of awkwardness, gratuitous refinement, affectation and fashion as well, everything that is not natural and personal.

Hence the character of the little school-girl who mimics and makes faces in a falsetto voice, uses affected phrases and is the parody of the scholarly type. Hence the character of Mme Lim, rich, worldly, recherché in the bad taste of her way of dressing, expressing herself in clichés, affecting a passion for mosquitoes while letting her children suffer – boys dressed up as girls, loaded with lace, etc. Hence the character of M. Lim, a painter, who made a fortune by manufacturing water-colours of 'overly detailed' flowers; the character of Rhympose the 'poet'; the pretentious school teacher, etc. All these characters are from the same stock; they are related. Opposed to them, by contrast, the wild and appealing little boy, loving sports, undisciplined but intelligent and good, the sailor, the pirate, etc.

Another example of creating a character: *by the accumulation of traits* on the same ridiculous face. During the winter of 1915, in the War Ministry, Sergeant Lavarde: blond, ungainly, who spoke oddly through his nose, commenting on all aspects of the war with innate pessimism. With these two traits, *a nasal voice* and *pessimism*, Ghéon[8] and I composed a ludicrous character whom we acted out in turn and whom we made fun of, attributing to him the most preposterously pessimistic opinions concerning military operations.

[All the above from Copeau's unpublished notebook, 'Comédie improvisée', dated January–July 1916, Le Limon, published in *Registres I*, pp. 187–8 and *Registres III*, pp. 323–50]

A FIRST OUTLINE
[*Letter to Roger Martin du Gard*]

To make it clearer, I shall tell you how I think it is possible to create this New Comedy. It can be contained in a few words.

Just as I wish to provide or define for you the instrument of the stage, so I should like to do the same with the instrument of comedy.

This idea or sense of a New Comedy, which I first called improvised comedy (and which certain actors will be capable of improvising some day) took root in my mind – far outside my necessary preoccupations as critic and author – in the theatre itself through contact with actors and acting. It was revealed to me by the experience of the possibilities of the stage. I became more and more convinced of it as my sense of the need for a purging of the stage developed along with my quest for a point at which to start.

As I conceive it, I believe that only I can furnish its *primum mobile* and delineate its first outline. I wish it were possible for me to discuss at length with a few of you who trust in me, to show the nature and nascent possibilities of it as discovered in certain parts of our stage work. I should like to delineate the principal characters, try them out with certain actors, sketch out a few scenarios. Then I would show you on the stage a few very modest experiments and examples, and you could begin to work along those same lines with the same characters, each according to your own personal inspiration and perhaps developing in each one a particular vein, one to be more social and political, another more worldly or family-oriented, or peasant-like or abstractly ludicrous. And perhaps you might create things, necessarily, which would go far beyond in quality and scope the examples I have furnished. But you would have started on the right path, in the vein which is open to development and which I am convinced I alone am able to propose to you.[9]

You will wonder how far I have proceeded with the rudiments. Unfortunately, as always, my work is interrupted by too many occupations and preoccupations. But I can already envisage certain things which seem real and genuine. I am afraid you may think they are rather feeble indications. However that may be, I beg you to keep that between us. All this work must remain a secret among a few of us.

I envisage a certain *Bonhomme*, not so much, in fact not at all because of, Jacques Bonhomme:[10] he just happens to resemble him. The idea came to me one day because, during the war, one spoke of the 'bonhommes'. They were the typical Frenchmen. Nothing more than that for the present, just everything that the name implies, especially the manner of the Frenchman and his way of speaking.

I envisage *Jean Boche* (or Caboche). He once existed in a small part, in the old Franco-Italian comedy. He was not a German, but I make him one because the German is part of our comedy, together with his accent and his mentality, his qualities and his faults. I don't know what he will do, but I know that I shall create a faithful portrait of him.

I envisage an *adolescent boy* whose name I have not come up with yet and whom I imagine with the traits of Suzanne [Bing] because we have often spoken of it together and she has given it some thought. This character is very often quiet. I have one scenario in which he does not utter a word: it is called 'The Comedy of Resemblances'.[11]

I envisage a *Monsieur Paul*, who is the travelling salesman – in everything: politics, religion, Bordeaux wines and several manufactured products.

I envisage a nameless character who would appear only in certain circumstances, who would be *me*, director of the company, the boss. I would be myself, perhaps: I am not sure, it would depend on the circumstances. I would do or say whatever the circumstances inspire in me. I find that beautifully exciting.[12]

We must find characters and situations, movements and reactions, a pre-established form which is inspirational. (When we get that, I tell you, no other work will matter.)

Very important: we must rid ourselves of all *sentiment of realism.* That is not easy. I found that out while creating a character who was, so to speak, the incarnation of realism, or of anti-drama, a comedic kill-joy. You will see what I mean...

From time to time, [this character] will *overflow* into reality, stepping out of the frame. He will be declamatory, a little less generous than the others, lacking in any real emotion, in revolt against his role, the malcontent, the critic (you see how easily one can pass from the general to the particular), unhappy with his fictional character and aspiring after reality. He is a defender of the Old Comedy, which he has seen a lot of, is knowledgeable about, and from which he proposes 'interesting subjects'. The others will call him back to the stage whenever he tries to rush into the auditorium [...]

'What is it you need to say to them?'

'But can't you see they are not taking us seriously?'

He is the one who speaks to the audience, who expounds, who knows all about everything which concerns the audience.

He is remote from the drama, happy to step out of the play and reluctant to return to it. He observes the audience with an opera glass and expounds on what he sees to the actors. He apologises for the play. He is afraid to shock. If he succeeds in establishing himself in the play, in dominating it, we shall have a thesis play. He is in charge of every-day affairs, and he is the only one with the right of access to them.

He is uneasy, nervous, changeable. He follows the current fashions. He reads the latest newspapers (his pockets are stuffed with them), the latest novels (he reads them all). He is a musician. He has friends everywhere. He wonders whether he should not enter politics – 'He is not sure whether he ought not...' He knows people in the audience. Actually, he would like to be in the audience. He understands absolutely nothing about drama. He constantly asks: 'what does it mean?' He has the kind of disarming good sense which causes the creator of the boldest inventions to doubt himself. He is the one I will have a bone to pick with.

A pessimist, like Sergeant Lavarde, and like him, speaking through his nose. He disapproves of the *mise en scène* and frequently repeats: 'There is no scenery.' In order to excuse and to explain them, he takes it upon himself to reveal 'our theories' to the audience, completely misrepresenting them in doing so. Then, I intervene... etc.

This fellow is not borrowed from anywhere. He just came to me like that, and I believe he is a good find. It is a good example, one which will be very useful. Precisely to the extent that he differs from the other characters, he will help create them, and when he is opposed to the spirit of the comedy, he will help define it. And you know when that succeeds, everything will follow naturally: outer traits, movement, stage awareness, individual traits and general meanings, etc. This is one, I believe, we can be confident of; he will come alive all by himself.[13]

The day we are ready, we shall appear before the public with an enthronement of the farce, introducing the characters and explaining how we arrived at that point. It will be a real ceremony.

[Conflation of a letter to the novelist Roger Martin du Gard dated 5 August 1919, published in *Correspondance, Jacques Copeau– Roger Martin du Gard*, ed. Sicard, Gallimard, 1972, vol. 1, pp. 314– 17, and an entry in Copeau's Journal, dated 1 August 1919]

[A CRITIC'S IMPRESSION]

Last Thursday, I saw one of these prologues. I am not insisting on my own great pleasure as critics' tastes prove nothing: but I must say truly that I have rarely seen in Paris an audience in such gleeful high spirits.

Copeau and his company of farcical actors had thought of a way to kill off that excellent actor Romain Bouquet and to look for a substitute to play the role of Argante. Telephone calls were made to the agency's offices, then to a restaurant frequented by actors. Finally, Jouvet appeared, offering to substitute for the deceased at a moment's notice. A banal plot if there ever was one, and in which our merry fellows wove the most surprising pattern of absurdities, follies, buffooneries and satires one can imagine.

Whenever boring sanity would return to calm their antics, Copeau would strain the thread of the comical plot and, immediately, the acrobats would lose their balance, stumbling and falling down, head over heels, in their lampooning. There were six or seven actors on the stage, but in their midst was an invisible and marvellous one who controlled the play, tapping out the beat with satin heels, and who was the subtlest and liveliest of them all: Imagination!

Naturally, so much mischievous vivacity defies comment. One might as well try to define throwing a handful of confetti. It was a veritable burst of laughter, in which the actors' gaiety was joined with that of the audience. Each was amused by the other. All this happened without order, naturally, without grammar or restraint. It is popular theatre par excellence: the legacy of the ancient Jongleurs, *full of daring and good health. It is theatre.*

It lasts as long as it has to, perhaps a half hour. Then, when Copeau, by a skilful turn, calls to the attention of the audience that the comics' farce is really a hoax played out to present the real comedy, we realise that we have completely forgotten about the play, the programme and the author. Fortunately it is Molière. I know of some who could not compare so advantageously to so much good humour.

[Henri Béraud, 'Au Vieux Colombier', *Bonsoir*, 22 June 1920]

THE CLOWNS AT THE MEDRANO CIRCUS

I saw them often during my last stay in Paris, almost every evening, and I was able to observe them closely. There was one, whose name I don't remember, a Portuguese 'Auguste', whom I would perhaps hire for my troupe of jesters.

In addition to the rather numerous troupe of clowns, buffoons and Augustes, there was an English comic juggler who interested me very much. He possessed a remarkable sobriety and distinction. Rather uneven from evening to evening in his mood and disposition. His act, comprised of exercises, *lazzi*, movements around the ring, entrances and exits, was rigorously planned. He always worked with the same precision and conscientiousness. But when he was well-disposed, joyous and keen, I noticed it right away by the excited and playful way he would grab his first prop and wink at it, by the more exquisite freshness of his *lazzi*, by the more incisive quality of his gesture and his voice, by the very slight nuances of his intonation, by subtle variations, by the way everything, on those evenings, would obey him, challenge him to overcome the difficulties, and to take advantage of the least accident discreetly and, at the same time, with authority. One evening, one of his *lazzi* provoked the loud and prolonged laughter of a woman in the balcony. The juggler stopped dead and, standing in profile, took stock of the woman, without moving, his eyebrows raised. And, as she laughed more and more, he continued to stare at her. Then, he resumed his exercise and, that night, everything he did was in keeping with the intimacy that had been created in the hall. The flavour of his act was increased ten-fold.

Andreff's only charm is his youth and his vigour. His improvisations are ordinary.

Auguste, on the contrary, is a sober and enjoyable improviser. He also has charm and distinction in his voice, his features and his appearance. All his *lazzi* are well composed. He adds something fresh to the most traditional farces. There is an elegance in his legs, and a felicity in his mimicry. Perhaps the temperament of an actor.

Ceratto, the stutterer (from the tradition of one of the mummers in the *commedia dell'arte*: Tartaglia, the stammerer), is a 'fantastical clown', the most accomplished actor of them all. Everything about him has a personality: his costumes, his wigs, his whole mimicry, his facial expressions, his walk. On certain evenings, he was admirable. His partner, Dario, does not come up to him, but he has a good clown face.

The *Fratellinis*, 'burlesque clowns', are also excellent. François seems to be the brains of the trio. The sketches are probably his. His white mask is fine, sharp, intelligent. A very small head. Nimble, snappy.

They all have very tasteful costumes. They are all remarkably *conscientious*. Perhaps that comes from the fact that they are the authors of their farces. Once, I saw François Fratellini display an anger mixed with sorrow because the final episode of his act did not come off. When he was applauded he bowed reluctantly, as if excusing himself before his public, embarrassed by the approbation they received, and signified by a facial expression: no that's not it!

In my opinion, the clowns misuse the props. They are never so good as when they do without them during their simplest *lazzi*. For example: the Fratellinis bowing to one another with increasing frenzy.

I love these clowns. The gaiety of their faces, the delight they take in what they are doing, the nimble grace of their trained bodies, and their whole appearance when taking their bows, head held high, eye to eye with their public, arms raised, hands opened, saying 'Voilà!' with little nods of their head which make their eyes blink mischievously.

But, in spite of everything, there is a little of the routine in what they do, and one feels they could be even more extraordinary. The superiority they have over theatre actors is that they are a real brotherhood, a corporation, people working together, unable to do without one another, people with a difficult craft and artisans of a living tradition.

The clowns' humble work: during the intervals they serve refreshments at the bar. The high-wire performers, the acrobats, once their act is over, put on blue aprons and become waiters.

[From unpublished notebook, 'Comédie Improvisée', 1916, op. cit., published in *Registres I*, pp. 319–21]

HAVING A PUBLIC

To the Fratellini brothers

My dear friends,

Last evening, when I returned from holiday and had barely become used to Paris again, a friend who had come to dinner wanted to take me to the theatre. I said: 'Let's go to the Medrano Circus instead...'

After two months' absence, I wanted to see you again. I needed to see you in that ring I like so much: François, with his dancer's ankles, slender hands and eyes piercing through his white mask, dominating the crowds; Uncle Paul – I don't know why I call him that, probably because of his gentleness with children – and Albert, like an East Indian deity.

Since I have known you, I never enter that sweet-smelling and fantastic cave you call your studio without emotion. For me, it preserves the glamour of my childhood attics where my imaginative powers were awakened by the piles of disused and worn-out objects. How many times have I found you in the semi-darkness of this magician's shop. I have seen you outlining your crescent-shaped eyebrows with the sure and light hand of a Chinese. I have seen you half-naked in the midst of your youngsters and your visitors, gravely evoking memories to the sound of a mandolin which one of you was strumming absent-mindedly, or discussing a technical point with other professionals, some of whom were almost old men, but whom you addressed with deference. But when you are at your finest is when you come out of the ring, bathed in perspiration, bawling one another out fraternally in your native tongue – oh little brothers! – because of a *lazzo* that did not come off, or an air that was not properly sung.

So, that evening when I entered the forest of your props, Paul said to me: 'We have a surprise for you. We are going to publish our memoirs. You must write a short preface for us.' It was certainly a surprise, a nice one. But, my dear friends, these *Memoirs* you want me to preface – I have not read them, so I cannot talk about them. I can only talk about you and my friendship for the three of you.

I love and respect you because you are serving, with your personal genius, one of the oldest traditions in the world; because you are practising courageously, simply and with infallible learning, your father's craft and teaching it to your children; because you love this craft more than anything and you live for it completely. In short, my friends, you have earned that rare and magnificent reward: *having a public*. You are popular actors, and all Paris knows you. When you set foot in the ring, the men, women and children of all ages, of all classes, who fill the stands of the Medrano, instantly communicate with one another by the welcome they give you. They are no longer separated from one another. They do not criticise one another. They are at one with you in that circle of light that accompanies your every movement. François, Paul, Albert, is that not a great joy? Sometimes I have seen tears in your eyes.

Always keep that emotion humbly in your work. Never let yourselves be distracted by success from your real beauty. Stay together always, the three of you. It is your supreme trinity. Three great actors knowing how to play together can represent in themselves the entire drama of the universe. Do not hesitate to remain simply *clowns*, the heirs to that divine *commedia dell'arte*. You have already had a real influence on your age. You can have an even greater one, provided you stay as you are. You will have more and more imitators, but you will always be distinguishable by two inimitable traits: your pure style and your gentleness.

What I call your 'pure style' is technical perfection and especially muscular perfection in the service of a spontaneous and sincere feeling. What I call 'gentleness' in everything you do is the smile of your unsullied natures. In past ages, Antiquity, the Middle Ages, the Renaissance, that quality of 'gentleness' was always accorded as supreme praise to the real actor, to the one who, while amusing his contemporaries with his grimace, or enchanting them with his *lazzi*, never allowed his dignity as a man to waste away.

[From the Preface to *Histoire de Trois Clowns*, by Pierre Mariel, *Société Anonyme d'Editions*, 1923]

'CHARLOT'

Charlie Chaplin belongs to the lineage and family of those great characters of the *commedia dell'arte* who, for more than two centuries, have supplied modern theatre with their offspring. In a time when literature has dessicated the theatre, when actors play roles but do not create characters, Charlie, with an instinct perhaps fostered by chance, has resuscitated for us the strongest tradition, the most productive vein. That is why I have allowed myself to tread on a territory which is not my own and to tackle a question which, as soon as it is touched upon, raises the whole problem of contemporary theatre. As this theatre is diminished, how can it regain its grandeur? How can this frivolous theatre recover its meaningfulness? How can this narrow theatre find its universality? How can this literary theatre, low or refined, be restored to the simple, forceful and naive life which would give it back its social *raison d'être* and its popular importance? Simply, this is my profound conviction, by what I call – the renewal of the theatrical personnel; that is to say by the creation of modern character types, precisely defined, extremely well developed and differentiated from one another, not by means of clever plot lines, but by the free play of their powerful individuality... Where Chaplin's art is still weak as a creator of filmed drama is that he is the only one of his kind. The forceful marionette that he has created has no one to play against. His confederates, who are either poor human beings or decent actors playing *realistically* or *accurately*, seem to be mere windbags; they have no consistency. They take on roles but they are not character types. Charlie's character itself suffers from this and is thereby diminished and impoverished. Now, let us suppose that in addition to Charlie's character, others as well developed as his appeared; suppose that one day when the masses, even the least cultured of his crowd of admirers, would be able to *identify* at a glance *all the characters* of the comedy as they can Charlot. Suppose that they recognised them all, loved or hated them, remembered them as Renaissance audiences remembered; loved or hated the flesh and blood creations of Arlecchino, Pantalone, Pulchinella and Brighella. Does it not seem that, in one fell swoop, modern theatre would be transformed, would regain its grandeur and its meaning, and finally, in Shakespeare's words, would become the mirror of the world and the chronicle of the times?

How could such a step backwards be considered an advancement of our art? I reply that progress is not always a step forward and that it can happen that sometimes it finds its way by means of a reaction. How could such a reaction be provoked? I do not have the time to examine that here. It is enough to say that it is not impossible – Chaplin's example is proof. I may add that it is perhaps the great virtue of cinema that it returns dramatic art to its sources and forces it to revive its roots...

[From 'Reflexiones acerca de un comedianté', *La Nación*, Buenos Aires, 7 July 1929, written March 1928]

14

THE CHORUS

During his years as a critic Copeau fulminated against the star-system with its cult of the personality and its predisposition to cabotinage. As a practitioner he became equally fervent in positing an alternative based on collective enterprise rather than individual opportunism: the Greek chorus, the commedia dell'arte *troupe, the circus family, even the brotherhoods of monastic communities, were for him models of how ensemble playing could stem from the sharing of daily life. In Burgundy, as director and mentor of the Copiaus, based in the tiny village of Pernand Vergelesses, between 1925 and 1929, he was able at least to glimpse fulfilment of his ideal:*

Forming a troupe of actors, having them act anywhere, renewing the actor's mind and soul: *that is inimitable.*[1]

The Copiaus, however, despite their social success as a rural community theatre, and their artistic success when playing games in the no-man's land between reality and illusion, were only a fledgling brood. Copeau knew that to attempt to express his full sense of the spiritual and metaphysical implications of Chorus (the French word Choeur *signifying both Choir and Chorus) a mightier instrument would be needed. It is at this point that Copeau's interest in the possibilities of a New Comedy deriving from rediscovered roots in* commedia *and its textual flowering in the works of Molière was withdrawn in favour of another quest: the possibility of a renewal of theatre as a sacred public event through a melding of Greek tragedy (as it had flowered from its dithyrambic roots in the works of Aeschylus) and the extant forms of Catholic ritual. The further Europe plunged into its second cataclysm during his adult life, the more Copeau pondered the viability of such an apocalyptic drama.*

Furthermore he perceived the possibility of old dramatic

techniques being renewed through the new technology of mass-communication. In one of his 1945 talks for radio, pertinently, he said:

> Provided he is prepared by an appropriate study and an adequate number of rehearsals, the actor before the microphone should find ideal conditions in which to reconstitute and reveal that unity, pure harmony and perfect equilibrium of which, as we have said, live theatre was latterly tending to defraud the work of the poet... And here we are inevitably led to wonder whether the microphone could not play in our time a role equivalent to that of the classical mask. That is to say, to help us reconstitute a lost unity, to allow us to attain and to destroy what still remains of realism in our theatrical conceptions, to help us rediscover poetry, together with the great universal subjects of our times. They will not even be conceivable until we have worked clearly and conscientiously to restore every element of the instrument of classical tragedy, notably the chorus.

The normal function of such a chorus would, he considered, be to preserve

> the serenity of philosophy, of contemplation, of prayer, of invocation – that serenity which, on stage, eludes mankind brutalised by destiny, by events, by passion, struggling with one another or with themselves or with the gods. In its words and in its songs, experience, tradition, the wisdom of the ages and of man abound, and the voice of the poet is heard. [...]
>
> It can be a witness to the action, commenting on and explaining it. It can be an instrument for the interludes between the acts. Between the public and the actor, it can take on all the attitudes and use all the intonations from the simple spoken one to declamation, psalmodic chant set to music, and even to song. If this extremely broad range is handled with a keen, lively and agile dramatic sense, it opens up the widest and most nuanced possibility of expressing feelings. By depriving oneself of the chorus, one forgoes the *tragic pulse*, the very soul of tragedy.

In his late essays in this genre, as well as the ancient Greeks, Copeau used once more the model of the Japanese Noh. As Joseph Samson, one of his collaborators, stated:

The chorus in the Miracle du Pain Doré *takes its inspiration from the Noh, and the role of the chorus in the* Petit Pauvre *is inspired by the Greek tragic chorus.*[2]

For the former play, most of the songs were chosen from the monodic and polyphonic repertoire of the fourteenth and fifteenth centuries. Samson, chorus master of Dijon Cathedral, composed a few others to complete the requirements of the text.

The important thing was that the music, closely allied to the heart of the play, constituted its very pulse, as irrepressible as the instinctive reactions of joy and fear.[3]

A TERM FROM ANTIQUITY

A chorus... Are we never to be allowed to form a beautiful chorus? I propose giving this term from Antiquity to the ideal troupe of actors, made up of various people whose sole ambition is to do their share with perfection. Nothing is more exciting than forming such a company. I once pursued this feeling to its furthest limit, when I found myself checked by the meagreness of my resources. For all that, I sometimes tried to go beyond that limit. If I had had the means, I think I would have hired 200 actors, each one for a specific reason and for a subtle gift that I felt they had. I had a hard time refusing the neophytes who daily thronged around my door, begging me to put them to work. For, in truth, most actors want nothing else but to work well. I don't think there is another profession where one is ready to make so many sacrifices to the quality of one's work.

[From: 'Confidences d'Auteurs', lecture to the Societé des Annales, 3 February 1933, op. cit.]

THE COPIAUS

A new dramatic form, one that is clear and alive, provided with all the means of expression that comprise theatre, addressing itself to everyone, expressing the forms, ideas, sentiments, conflicts and personalities of modern life – that, I think, is what our times are asking for. That is what we have aspired to realise with truthfulness for a long time.

That is why we started by trying to restore an innocence to the stage. We rid it of its false prestige and of a few of its futile aspects. We set up that bare platform that was supposed to be transfigured by the poet's imagination, but he has not worked very much with us up to now. Either he retains his old habits, which hamper us, or his ambitions that make him abandon us.

We have tried to teach and to bring up the actor in such a way that the style of the new work, which has eluded us for so long, would emerge in his whole being and be postulated both in him and in his acting. It was from these early indications that there came a new generation of actors and directors. They are courageously trying to favour the production of literary works that are still scarce and altogether uncertain in their orientation.

As for us, persuaded that our compromises with the times would produce nothing fertile, tired of standing still and having rejected the 'boulevard' theatre since 1913, we resolved to reject the so-called 'avant-garde' theatre, which is already infected by counterfeits and lies. At the end of 1924, we decided to risk everything. We wanted this 'renovation' that we had tried for so long to define and to understand, to at least mean something for ourselves. We started over again. We turned backwards in order to check what we knew, learn what we did not know, experiment with what we vaguely felt, no longer proceeding without our sense of vocation, doing something that was not true, but building, moderately but purely.

It is in this spirit that the 'Copiaus' are working.

Their education was based on a conscientious examination of the principles of their craft and on a personal investigation of the elements of dramatic creation. Their teachers guided them towards those innermost discoveries that are necessary to the possession of any technique. Their sense of discipline consists of avoiding nothing, of never pretending, of never expressing or even thinking of anything that they cannot personally and authentically think and express. They applied themselves to finding principles within themselves, to implanting in their bodies, hearts and minds a direct experience of the laws of theatre and the feeling for their necessity. Thus, they were brought back to a naive state that is not an artificial or literary attitude, but is their natural position before a world of possibilities where nothing is corrupted by habits of imitation, nor perverted by an acquired virtuosity... That is where they stand, and they aspire no further at the moment. Far from priding themselves on their sufficiency, they remain at the starting point. In my opinion, this is a positive conquest. Appia said of them: 'I respect these youngsters.'

Based on their early exercises and first village entertainments, the 'Copiaus' have recently gone on to stage productions, very simple but more highly finished, in which we can see the modesty of an almost primitive conception, the aspiration to express everything by their playing, and the remarkable diversity and stability of their technique. Dialogues, declamation, song, mimed action, dance, inter- pretation of things, people, natural phenomena – all that is linked by the rhythm of playing in these choral performances where we also see emerge from behind the mask, the first outlines of 'characters' and the first attempts at improvisation.

It is time for the 'Copiaus' to be known for what they have made of themselves, judged by the hopes they justify. It is time for the public to become their teacher. For certain things in our craft, only the public can teach us. It is time for these young people to take their risks, and for them to do it *alone*. Although their name has given them early recognition, they are now obliged to go it alone. I believe they have earned this freedom and this test.

[From an open letter to the Swiss press, dated May 1928, prior to the Copiaus' tour there of *L'Illusion*, 5–14 June 1928, M-H D]

L'ILLUSION

This is not, properly speaking, either a drama or a comedy. It is a theatre game. Instead of making its interest rely on the development of a character or a plot, we are trying to arouse it by a variety of feats, tones and movements. It is an attempt at an entertainment or, as they say today, pure theatre. Nothing is pursued to the end. Everything remains in suspense, as in a rough sketch where we sought to be free without extravagance.

The theme of *L'Illusion* is borrowed from Corneille, in whose play, *l'Illusion comique*, we see a magician conjuring up for King Prindamant the adventures of his son in the form of a play which turns into a comedy. But we have called on Corneille here only for his subject matter and two or three words of secret homage. The Cervantès of the *Interludes* can also be accredited with a word, and the name of a character, Taguada.

The comedy itself, which unfolds in three acts before the eyes of the father, Beseigne, is very freely adapted from Fernandas de Rojas

(1492). We have borrowed his story of the young lovers led astray by the terrible Celestina, as well as her whole personality. However, we have reduced Rojas' immense portrait in twenty-one acts to three rather short ones, and have completely reshaped the peripeteia.

Every one of the Vieux Colombier's new comrades has usefully collaborated in the realisation of this entertainment, either by contributing an idea for its composition, or by conceiving a dance step, a mimicry, a game, a mask, casting and painting it, creating a backdrop, fabricating a green sward, a prop, a section of staircase, a lighting fixture.

[From the Copiaus' programme for their first tour of *L'Illusion*, October 1926]

He brought us work which we could see, almost embarrassingly, came from his soul: under the guise of a game, he was staging a blend of his memories and his present anxiety; he was portraying that youthfulness he saw around him, threatened and excited by the same dangerous life that had so magnificently intoxicated him; and what youth! His own children were among his dearest pupils. By accepting the risk of playing the roles he assigned us, we knew very well that they were like so many illusions to ourselves, caught up in the reality of the drama we were experiencing at that time, along with the master of Pernand.

But if the play was thus nurtured by the drama of a man who wanted his work to be intimately linked to his life, and the stage personage to be as close as possible to the inner personage, it was none the less meant to be performed before a public; it was to be an outward proof of the evolution of the most important theatre practitioner of his time, whose self-imposed exile had aroused both sarcasm and curiosity.

[From an article by Michel Saint-Denis in the programme of Jean Dasté's 1950 revival of *L'Illusion* at the Comédie Saint-Etienne]

Prologue

The Actor [Copeau]: (*alone*) At the precise moment when the curtain goes up, you have to be ready, Actor. That means that your appearance, your feelings, your memory, should have been swallowed up by the appearance, feelings and memory of another being who is attempting to become more present within you than yourself. You are not quite ready until you have been completely replaced.

Now, I imagine that in this struggle, the Actor who was at first subdued by his character, does, at the last minute, gain control.

I imagine that the curtain goes up and the actor is not ready. Not having had time to lower his mask, he is taken by surprise. He finds himself unmasked in front of the audience. I have often dreamed of such an accident.

What does the actor do? Is he going to run off and hide in the wings? Is he going to pretend to improvise his character's gestures, conspicuously passing from being himself to being in character, openly imposing the illusion? Or, on the contrary, is he going to step forward, taking advantage of the situation, and appear as he is?

I am well aware that no one will believe he is speaking sincerely, for he is expected to be acting, and people will assume that he is. He has to act. Now, that particular evening, he does not feel like acting. We say of a spring that it winds down. As for me, I am not acting any more. I am wound down.

The Actress appears. [Bing] *She goes gently towards the Actor and touches him on the shoulder.*

Actress: Are you ready, Actor?

Actor: I felt you behind me, like a rosy angel reading into a silent heart. I was saying to myself: what does she want of me?

Actress: You were dreaming, Actor?

Actor: I was trying to invent something... Nothing is more obscure than the deep tunnel into which the creative mind descends, nor more solid than the rock at which it chips away without knowing its density... Is it in order to bring me sweetness and light that you have put on your veils again, Viola?[4] They are as pure as our most lovely achievement. You have kept them intact. When I touch them, I feel the same emotion which used to bring tears to my eyes whenever I heard you speak to the Duke of Illyria in Shakespeare's comedy.

Actress: All we have left is the sound of a voice, the shade of a fabric, the perfection of an attitude successfully inhabited by the soul.

172

Actor: It is in this way that our craft becomes a little heroic: everything is immediately consumed, like fire and life.

Actress: And we remain cast off.

Actor: It's a good thing to be cast off. It's good no longer to be anything and to wait, little by little, bit by bit, for the freshness to arise in us.

Actress: If we remain silent too long, if we remain too long in the contemplation of our thoughts, shall we retain the power of some day giving birth to the Illusion? I am only an actress. I don't care very much for reality. I don't like myself very much. I don't wish to be invaded by everything I am. My passions, my desires, my jealousy, my deceits: give me back Comedy so its fire will consume them and purify me.

On this last line Maiène enters.

Actor: I was trying to invent something... a manner of acting, full of thwarted movements, of young faces, of love and music, and for you, a character overflowing with poetry which would make you love as I love you. But I am haunted by nothing but sombre images...

Maiène approaches the Actor

Maiène: Good morning.

Actor: (*kissing her*) Good morning, my child.

Michel [Saint Denis]: (*entering*) Good morning.

Actor: Good morning, youth.

Villard: (*entering*) Are you ready, Actor? The young people are waiting.

Actor: What do these young people want of me?

Michel: That you give them the signal.

Villard: That you let them spring forth.

Maiène: That you believe in them!

Actress: That you make of their vigour, their impetuous ignorance and goodwill, something pure, difficult, simple and well-tuned.

Michel: We want to act.

Actor: There you are, the three... four (*Paul Storm enters*) of you, and the fifth one who utters not a word, to represent the Universe!

Actress: A poor instrument stimulates the invention.

Maiène: Three strings are good enough for inspired rhythm.

Michel: For a rudimentary form to restore the face and energy of comedy.

Villard: We'll know how to dance, like children and savages.

Storm: Yes.

Michel: How to leap up on a *tréteau*, to learn its length and breadth with our legs.

Storm: Yes.

Villard: Let's amuse the people in the public squares with our antics.

Storm: Yes.

Michel: We have no need of theatre.

Storm: No.

Villard: Nor well-written plays.

Storm: No.

Michel: Nor of newspaper articles.

Storm: No.

Maiène: In order to be what we are.

Actress: Actors who live by Comedy, free and poor, from morning to night, kneading the dough of their craft with their own hands.

Actor: My young companions, my young companions, are you going to give me back the courage necessary for forming a world each day out of nothing, and hanging it above reality, a world which falls apart even as it is being created? Will you have the strength, the constancy, the saintly humility?... I had folded up my hope. My memories had faded away. Even the loveliest of them... Why do you come to make my head swim, like birds in a garden in the month of May?

Actress: We shall create a sanctuary sheltered from fame.

Maiène: Far from jealous ones.

Villard: Far from liars.

Michel: Far from thieves.

Actress: We shall change climate every year.

Michel: Towards the East, first off, where we have friends.

Villard: We shall go to Italy, seeking the echoes of the actors of the *commedia dell'arte*.

Maiène: To Russia, to greet the great masters at work.

Actress: To Japan, to pluck the flower of the Noh and the teachings of the marionettes of Osaka.

Michel: First, let's go from village to village.

Maiène: To sing the harvest.

Villard: To dance over the grape-gatherings.

Maiène: Our baggage on our backs.

Villard: Our props in our hands.
Michel: And the dove on our shoulder.
Storm: Yes.
Actress: Let us be off, my children.

*The actors put on their travelling cloaks and take up their props.
Little Peter enters.*

Little Peter [Jean Dasté]: The actors... is this where they are?
All: It is here.
Little Peter: My name is Little Peter and I have run away. I have
been wandering for two days. My father is a labourer. His name
is Besaigne.[5] He never changes countenance all year long. He is a
hard man who barely speaks except to scold me at dinner-time
for everything I've done during the day. He wants nothing to do
with anything he doesn't know or do. He says that is life and I'll
never amount to anything. So I want to try comedy. Maybe I can
be of service. I know how to weave wicker-baskets, trim a whip,
carve a flute from an elder branch. I can imitate bird-calls and the
wind in the trees pretty well. I can dance a *bourrée* and a
perdrielle, and I am twenty years old.
Actress: Let us welcome this wild pigeon into our dove-cote.
All: Enter, Little Peter!
Maiène: Put on the cloak. (*She gives him an actor's cloak*)
Villard: Put on the head-band.
Michel: Carry the rolled-up carpet on your shoulder.
Actress: And may your apprenticeship begin with the love one
puts into a humble task. Let's be off!

*Everyone gets ready, putting on his cloak, taking up his load,
while singing the song of the doves. All exit singing. The curtain
goes up.*

> We have taken two doves
>   From a tile at San Miniato.
>
> We put two doves face to face
>   Above our lintel!
>
> We have brought two doves
>   A-voyaging beyond the seas.

175

We have made a nest for two doves
In the dark façade of an old castle.

We still have our two doves
Half-way up a smiling hillside.

Our children will see our two doves
Nibbling the wicker of their cradle.

So when we are acting, our two doves
Flutter over our *tréteau*.

So when we die, our two doves
Will perch upon our tomb.

[From *L'Illusion*, an adaptation of Corneille's *l'Illusion comique* and de Rojas' *La Celestina*; prologue, three acts, three interludes, epilogue (MS in FC, August 1926, 68 pp.); première given in Basle, Switzerland, 3 October 1926, by the 'Copiaus'; revived by Jean Dasté, Comédie de Saint-Etienne, 1950]

NOAH'S ARK

It is not easy for me now, through anecdotes, properly to retrace those years of our life in Burgundy which knew, despite some reversals, so many sunlit hours, happy days, hard work and success. I would have had to show you the Copiaus at work, in their big wine-store, at the foot of a marvellous French hillside, or again in the village inn, fraternising with the burly folk from the vineyards, or again on the road in summer or in winter, in moonlight or through frost, in their emblazoned wagon, coming back from playing Molière under canvas or on the platform of a village hall, in front of a truly popular audience, a mixture of workmen, bourgeois and gentry, who, as fresh as the farce itself, wouldn't need to be prompted to laugh in the right places. Above all I should describe to you the festivals at Dijon, Beaune or Nuits-Saint-Georges, those *Célébrations de la vigne et du vin* which spread my companions' reputation throughout the province...

In front of hundreds, even thousands, of wine-growers assembled from every part of the neighbouring slopes, my Copiaus, four to the right, four to the left with the leader in the middle, in their well-established choral formation, standing firmly, foreheads raised, their voices clear and strong, chanted pindarics in honour of the little suntanned queens who had been elected by each commune, for the *Paulée*, the wine-harvest festival, to lead the processions and preside over the celebrations.

Then, once this first part of the ceremony was over, at nightfall, my comrades would leave the hall, in their brightly coloured costumes, flowers in their hats, and mingle with the people in the streets, recognised, greeted, fêted and entertained, right up to the hour when the hall filled up again, more alive and turbulent, where we would light our lanterns for a new divertissement whose hero was called Jean de Bourgignon.[6] [...]

Contest between vineyards, amorous dialogues, bacchic choruses, proverbs and songs, dances of tending the vines and making wine. Old Noah would come and interrupt them. Here is Old Noah speaking:

I have been drinking, I am drinking and I will drink. They say it's good for nothing? There's nothing it can't console. If you have business worries, drink a glass of white. If your wife is unfaithful, drink a glass of red. If she does it again, you do it again as well. It cures the lot. If you've got toothache, drink Romanée, if you've got rheumatism, drink Nuits-Saint-Georges. Men like to see women drink Bordeaux, which makes you pine, but women like to see men drink Burgundy, which makes you a hero. It was medicine to Louis XIV and counsellor to Napoleon. And now it's used to toast the Republic...

Thus our plays were virtually improvised, according to circumstances, the season, the place, the audience. They were healthy, vigorous, almost completely free of the dust of the theatre. They gave a bold if incomplete impression, poor but sincere, of freer, more lofty forms. They often attained, *naturally*, that acclaim from the audience, those instants of perfect communion between stage and auditorium which are the summation of theatre, and which so many aesthetes and theoreticians seek to attain by more sophisticated means.

[From *Souvenirs du Vieux Colombier*, op. cit., pp. 114–18]

THE GREEK EXAMPLE

Let us remember once again the spirit and the conditions of the Greek theatre 400 years before Christ. The populace is massed in the auditorium. Thirty thousand spectators assembled, but assembled in a chosen place where everything has been prepared and calculated so that no one misses a gesture of the action or a word of the sublime text.

And facing these tiers is the barest stage that ever existed. On it, a very small number of characters: three, four, at the most six, but colossal in stature and apparel, as well as in dramatic content.

The theatre-going populace is here represented, in the semi-circle of the orchestra, by a chorus, not as numerous, but so musical, so rigorously trained and responsive to the flute that leads it, that it can express through dance, song and declamation all the reactions necessary to make a configuration of the great sentiments and attitudes of a people's collective identity: the waiting, the worrying, the doubt, horror, insurgency or jubilation.

It is on that essential instrument, which has not one superfluous note; it is with those reduced yet formidable means, which were the same for poets; it is in that austere and incorruptible style that the drama of men, heroes and gods was played out. It was equal to the greatest themes which the theatre of all times has tackled – those of fatality, faith, revolt, justice, war and the anguish of peoples.

Contemporary authors have shown their inability to treat those themes without diminishing them. Modern drama no longer has enough vigour to display itself under the open sky. Its actors are lost on an empty stage. They cannot get along without the little props which were unknown to the antique stage. Spectators without endurance are no longer accustomed to stone seats.

And yet, all those who denounced the failure of our theatre and the narrowness of our vision, all those who have dreamed of a radical renaissance of our theatre, have begun by invoking the Greek example.

[From *Le Théâtre Populaire*, op. cit., pp. 45–6]

EASTER SUNDAY

Assemble the dramatic chorus. Their presence, constant attendance, gives to the drama its universal and religious value, even when the chorus does not intervene, or intervenes solely to provide it with a décor, an echo, a brief commentary on time or place. On the one side, there is God, His angels, saints, martyrs, the elect of His faithful servants: His blessed nature. On the other, there is Satan with his demons, the beautiful and the deformed, his misled heroes, conquerors and seers, the damned, his knowledge and his inventions. *Personality* of the elements of the chorus.

There are interchanges from one chorus to the other – some elements of which are temporarily charged with confronting one another more closely and distinctly in the orchestra or on the sub/ lower stage.

The main stage is very elevated and has its own accesses to an invisible space from which emerge the masques or characters, who can choose to share in the choral episodes without taking part in them.

(The décor is no longer a dead thing, but a living and active one, no longer behind the actor but before and above him, on a lower level and alongside him, between the actor and the public, solely controlled by the chorus, an integral part of it, and which carries it in and out by means of a path which is determined by the architect.

Only the celebrant moves about at will in all parts of the edifice.)

[From *Journal*, Florence, 17 April 1938]

A SENSE OF THE TRAGIC

A German, Friedrich Wilhelm Foerster,[7] has written that one must turn back to St John's Book of Revelations in order to understand and to judge thoroughly the present era.

According to him, there are times when conflicts are dormant, and when the eternal conflict between the higher and lower powers abates. Then the times return when the accumulated centuries-old conflicts must be settled... At these times when the spirit of evil hurls its defiance, God in turn launches a call to His earthly servants to support the struggle.

Foerster describes this antagonism as resembling the famous scene figured on the altar of Zeus at Pergamos where the Titans confront the gods.

In these words and evocation, I find a sense of the Tragic which has been forgotten or unknown in our times.

If, for over two centuries, the art of the theatre has lost its splendour, has become so small and insignificant, and if it reaches only superficially those who would still like to give it some attention, it is because the notions of good and evil, just and unjust, worth and demerit, along with a coherent notion of man and of divinity, have become more and more indecisive and vague, to the point of playing almost no part in dramatic conception, not even mentioned on the stage.

In the state of neutrality, even anarchy, by which, little by little, we seem to have become enthralled, Tragedy, bereft of the fundamental concepts which rendered it intelligible, has lost its structure. It is like a mountain made formless by a landslide, like a land whose watershed was destroyed by some inner cataclysm.

Today, it seems that the current calamities are inviting us to rediscover the sense of the tragic.

All of us Europeans are now plunged in the midst of events whose enormity, complexity, inner contradictions, deepest origins and future consequences form an accumulation which we might be tempted to believe or to say is unthinkable.

Nevertheless, we want to understand this conflict; it is not sufficient to endure it. By an effort of the intellect, we want, even provisionally, to give it structure and style. That is almost like saying that, consciously or subconsciously, we are trying to reduce it to the form of tragedy.

Quite naturally, we evoke ancient Tragedy because, in its simplicity, grandeur and incomparable power, it is perhaps the only form of human art in which the trajectory of destiny is legibly inscribed for us, from its point of origin to its last extremity, within a very short period of time. The subject I am treating, or rather outlining before you, that of unreason in force, of punishment meted out by the gods to the hero who becomes guilty of injustice by transgressing his human measure, is a Greek subject. The ancient tragic writers returned to it constantly. Even in those of their works where it was not the essential theme, they introduced moral judgements which echoed it.

In Greek tragedy, the Chorus engages in dialogue with the tyrant, at times wisely, at others hypocritically and sometimes cowardly. It endures the excesses of the master, as in a storm, heads bowed. But it is the Chorus, finally and always, which adjudicates the failure and which condemns the man who has over-reached himself by his unholy pretensions.

On today's European stage we observe the appearance of the

Protagonists, each with his mask and his attributes: the Pope, the King, the Heads of State, and the Army, the Dictators and their Followers.

The Chorus consists of the numberless workers and soldiers who, all over the world, in all the warring countries, and even in others, forge arms in the factories, mount guard on the frontiers of land, sea and air.

[From 'Puissance et déraison, ou la démesure dans la tragédie grecque', lecture in Brussels, 15 January 1940, prior to a reading of *The Persians*; reprinted as 'La Démesure', in CRB, XI (1955), pp.100–10]

15

TOWARDS A POPULAR THEATRE

As Copeau envisaged it, a new popular theatre would have its roots in the Greek dithyramb (which had been the core study of the first syllabus of the Vieux Colombier School) and the medieval Mystery (which was used as the subsequent research base). But, as a twentieth-century phenomenon, such a theatre would need foundations in a very different social context. As Leonard C. Pronko puts it:

> What the French call 'Théâtre Populaire'... does not mean 'popular theatre' in the sense of frothy comedies which would have a broad appeal to the most frivolous public. Théâtre populaire is theatre for the people, le peuple, the working man, the masses. And as such it should appeal to those who would agitate for social reform, as well as to those who simply want to be amused by a colourful spectacle.[1]

> In this sense, Copeau argued, it did not suffice merely to entertain a popular audience (as he had seen the Fratellini Brothers do), or to create a new stock character, even one gaining world-wide appeal such as Chaplin's little tramp. One possibility was for companies to follow the example of the Copiaus and put down roots in provincial communities; on the other hand, in a seminal article entitled 'Le Théâtre Populaire' (written in 1941), he argued for a centralised effort towards a new kind of national theatre.[2]

A POPULAR DRAMATIC FORM

For my part I believe, and I am happy to say this to one who shows evidence of advanced tendencies, that if it is true that a new dramatic form is to appear in the future, it will be a very simple, direct form, saying only what it has to say, clearly, to everyone, and concerned with their real-life preoccupations. In a word, it will be a popular dramatic form.

That is why I cannot bring myself to understand the state of mind of those who, worried about today's problems and determined to turn away from that blasé and worn-out portion of the inattentive public, think they can educate it by giving works which are refined, obscure and so often of a complication that hides an indigence of thought.

[From a letter to a dramatist, 11 August 1921, on his manuscript for a play, M-H D]

CHARLIE CHAPLIN

I was in Paris recently. A total mediocrity reigns in the theatre. It is producing little by little a mediocrity in the demands of the public, which is even more disconcerting. And I am not talking about the critics, who no doubt in order to apologise for their existence and to maintain their position, strive to find pleasure and even some merit in the most puny productions. Often one hears that a new play is 'rather good', or 'curious' or 'amusing'. (Such is today's vocabulary of taste.) One's hopes are raised and one rushes to see it. Stupefaction. Discriminating taste no longer exists. This is a serious symptom.

But the latest Charlie Chaplin film is announced: *The Circus*, and everyone rushes to see it; yes, *everyone*, elite and masses alike. The principle of 'popular theatre' is realised by an admirable actor, on the screen. Not the least bit of literature, not the least theory. Only this absolute and miraculous phenomenon: the entire universe in love with an actor and a universal reconciliation before his acting. I do not know whether Chaplin is the greatest actor in the world, as is said rather too often these days. I do not think he is equal to Shakespeare, as I heard asserted the other day by a young dramatist who believes that mankind is divided into two groups: those who love Chaplin and those who do not. But the really staggering fact is – the popularity of Charlie, or Charlot as we call him in France, which came to my wonder-struck attention a few years ago.

It was in Paris, thanks to my friend, Waldo Frank, an American writer, that I met Charlie. We spent the evening together, and I had intended to introduce him to three other friends, the charming Fratellinis. As we took our seats at the Medrano Circus, the entrance of the clowns was taking place in the ring. You remember, those poor wretched little clowns who bark along with the trained dogs, jump along behind the equestrienne, picking up the horse dung, helping to roll out the carpets and serving beer during the intervals – those sad little clowns whom Chaplin portrayed so well in one of the early scenes of his new film. They wandered round the ring singing snatches of songs. Then, suddenly, they recognised Chaplin and I cannot say with what exquisite graciousness and tender smiles, without interrupting their sad badinage, each one passed before him to greet him: 'Hello Charlie!... Good evening Charlie!' And Charlie would answer them with a modest and embarrassed nod. But, at the interval, it was something else. How my companion had been recognised, how the news of his presence had spread, I do not know. But now I saw the whole crowd get up, from top to bottom of the stands and, with one movement, 3000 people surged into the ring and crowded round the little actor until he was almost smothered. The police had to intervene to extricate him. We went out into the street, the crowd went out with us. We quickened our pace, they did too. We began to run, they ran ahead of us and turned back to surround us. Women with children in their arms would hold them out to be petted. Charlie, a little pale, constantly repeated in a weak voice: 'They are charming... charming... aren't they?' To escape the ovations he had to hail a taxi. I understood later that crowds frighten him. And I had this thought, a quite simple one, but which does not occur to one at first, that this idol of the crowds is never in contact with them, that he gives up his image to them but never himself or his sensitivities. His work is done in the studio, performed in contemplation. That would explain why, as Charlie matures, not only does he not become deformed but he asserts himself with more measure, style and distinction. 'Never could I have ever acted on the stage,' he explained to me. 'The only thing I like to do is to play charades with a few friends.' I saw him playing with a child, the entire evening, making delightful grimaces which he knew how to adapt for children and which were much less those of a professional actor than of a tactful improviser.

Whence comes the immense popularity of Charlie Chaplin? How come that, while still very young, he formed an audience larger than any other artist, and that in working for this audience both popular and cultured, appreciative and impulsive, not only does he not demean himself but he constantly raises the level of his art to a classic abstraction? Does it only come from his technical mastery, or from the charm of his personality, or from the universal character of his means of expression? From all that, undoubtedly, but only in part. All his qualities, his art, his naturalness, his inventions, his style, his comic strength and his power of emotion, reach this supreme degree, receive that complete adherence which fixes them in the mind and heart of millions of all ages and nations, only by virtue of one thing: *Charlie is a character*. He has created a character which lives in him and for which he lives. He has impressed himself vividly on the imagination of the masses forever. He lives, thinks, acts, suffers *for the benefit* of this character which he nurtures daily with his own essence and his own artistry. He is so attached to his creation that he can no longer do anything that does not augment and embellish it. Thus it is understandable why, to a certain extent, the young dramatist I mentioned was able to compare Chaplin to Shakespeare. It is a naive remark, but it expresses rather well the enthusiastic response to a true, living creation. Charlie is neither poet nor dramatist, neither acrobat nor actor. Technically he is all those things, but none of those terms defines his art. Can we say that he is comical, farcical or tragic? Each time, we run the risk of being wrong by one or two fine points. We have to say that Charlie is Charlie. And when his name is spoken, without needing to recall any one situation or plot, an extremely lively image, full of humanity, forms before our eyes. When Charlie dies his character will continue to live. What am I saying? He may have an influence on future dramatic forms which we do not yet suspect. I knew Chaplin at a time when he himself did not suspect the force of his character. He was thinking of casting off his old clothes, his cane and his little hat! What a dreadful catastrophe if the only actor of our time who has risen to such a glorious synthesis had abandoned it to return to the crumbling contemporary theatre so demeaned by anecdotes and lost in self-analysis. Can you imagine Pierrot refusing to be Pierrot, or Harlequin throwing away his multi-coloured tunic and leather mask?

[*La Nación*, Buenos Aires, 7 July 1929, written March 1928, op. cit.]

THE THEATRE OF IDEAS

Thoughts on the substance of contemporary drama and on the poverty of action, morals and roles in our contemporary theatre.

The drama that will interest the multitude needs heroes, in and by whom world tragedy is played. The theatre *of* ideas will not be, any more than Shakespeare's, a drama *with* ideas. In order for the form that will embrace such a substance to develop, I believe more than ever that it is necessary to break the existent form and return first of all to primitive forms.

[From *Journal*, 29 August 1920, published in *Registres I*, p. 186]

THE POPULAR THEATRE

There was a time when an entire people would prepare itself through meditation and self-purification to await an annual theatrical celebration presided over by a god. All the rites, meant to inspire man's feeling of civic dignity, would serve as a preface and accompaniment to the contest of the tragic poets. The youth would call on their oldest native divinities to witness their oath of manhood.

The forms of the performances were so powerful that they touched the spectator to the very core. The assembled citizens were so united in body and soul, and this union of mind taken so seriously by the city's leaders, that they often ruled out a work as being offensive, too exalting or too depressing for the Athenian masses.

The subject matter of these tragedies was sometimes the commemoration of a great national victory, as in Aeschylus' *The Persians*, or the restoration of moral laws, as in Sophocles' *Antigone*, or the evocation of the horrors of war, as in Euripides' *The Trojan Women*.

The philosophy which emerged from these examples was a humane one, respectful of the fate which did not spare the gods, severe towards the tyrants and heroes whose pride, rashness or self-intoxication pushed them to transgress the limits of their human condition.

Comedy, born in intoxication, does not suffer from any restrictions in its audacities, whether in subject matter, plot or language. It is the reverse of tragedy and often parodies it. Its topics include the portrayal of the everyday life of the Attic peasant, the satire of mores and of political passions, the mockery of industries profiting from war, and praise for the benefits of peace, in short, the burning reality of the day. However, it is escorted by dances and songs, wrapped in a shining poetry which transfigures everything: 'Seeking an indestructible shelter, the Graces encountered the heart of Aristo-phanes.' This was Plato's epitaph on the tomb of the great satirist.

There was a time when crowds even larger than those of the Greeks, more ignorant perhaps but none the less just as faithful and imbued with the solemnity of the circumstances, would take to the primitive highways, heedless of a less favourable climate, in order to stand for hours and sometimes days attending the performance being presented by the population of an emotion-filled city, by its clergy and laity, soldiers, officials, artists, artisans, merchants, young and old.

Why did these spectacles hold such a far-flung attraction for an entire region?

Because they produced images and expressed ideas based on popular forms and sources from which an entire people could learn and receive spiritual nourishment.

What was being presented to these people?

They were shown the life, suffering and death of a God become man in order to save humanity. Too uncultured to understand theological ideas, they opened their hearts to the spectacle from which they expected enlightenment.

They were shown ignoramuses jeering, unbelievers deserting, villains persecuting, and in their guilt they would kneel and strike their breasts in contrition.

They were shown common folk responding to the preaching of love and, like them, in communion with them, they were uplifted.

The miracles of Notre Dame taught Hope and Charity, and in clear terms presented the precariousness of man's destiny. Good and Evil are not only named and defined, they are shown and personified. The confrontation between nature and grace, the dispute between the sinner and the saved, are expressed in dramatic fashion by the battle of the angels with the demons.

Before our eyes, we have the incarnation of forces which daily exert themselves to influence man's will in its smallest efforts, to set traps for him, to warn him, to trouble him or to save him, to solicit his poor freedom both from above and below. The demons pull down and the angels raise up.

The Virgin Mary, mother of God since eternity, and of man since the Crucifixion, adds the power of her love to this often unequal duel. Through her constant intercession and her tireless supplication that the justice of God be merciful, she prepares for the pardon of a great crime at the cost of a small prayer. For she believes that a prayer, no matter how small, is an indication that man is trying to put his trust in God in order better to obey His will, that is, to evoke the powers that purify, preserve, direct, enlighten and construct, to the confusion of those which defile, lead astray, paralyse, blind and destroy.

These two examples from the distant past, antiquity and the Middle Ages, are the indispensable preface to all development of popular theatre.

They illustrate two forms of dramatic presentation which originate in the moral life of the people and which also influence it.

Both of these forms imply a strong conception of humanity, its origins, its condition and its relationship with the beyond. [...]

We are often asked, what will be the drama of the future? As though it were up to us to decide. As though that future form depended only on us, on our work, on our intelligence and our conceptions.

There is no drama of the future. Drama is essentially a fact of the present, a contemporary phenomenon, a proposition whose destiny depends upon the reception and the response given to it. The greatest geniuses of the theatre, those whose immortal works still touch us in performance or in reading – Aeschylus, Aristophanes, Shakespeare, Lope de Vega, Calderon, Molière – worked for the people of their day. Several of them were, to a large extent, improvisers. Their genius, however exceptional, appealed to the taste of the public, whether the taste of an elite or that of the masses.

If, in 1910, 1914 or even in 1920, someone had asked the master of the Russian theatre, Constantin Stanislavsky: what will be the theatre of the future? I think he would have refused to answer, or if he had, he would have run the risk of being greatly mistaken. For, on the eve of war, the old society was coming to an end and Russian theatre was entering into a twilight. During the post-war period, Soviet society was in the midst of evolutionary chaos. But, when I questioned Stanislavsky a few years later, this same representative of the old regime and elitist culture answered that the new Russia had become the promised land for theatrical activity. He added that, by popular demand, the theatres had been obliged to add several matinées to their regular evening performances, that numerous new theatres were being constructed, and finally, that he was directing the organisation of a great theatre academy which would be enriched and regulated by all past experiments.

In October 1934, at the Volta Congress held in Rome's Italian

Academy, Alexander Tairov's report on the state of Russian theatre emphasized its debt to the great October revolution: 'It instilled an ideological discipline into our theatre by banishing moral indifference and opportunism from the stage once and for all. It chased away from our audiences the spectator who would come to the theatre in order to stimulate the digestion of his dinner. It introduced a new public to our theatres, the one which made the October revolution and is now looking to the theatre for answers to its problems, a public which is building a new society and which also communicates its creative energy to the theatre.'

These words came from the official representative of the USSR.

As for myself, before this same assemblage, I ended my communication with these words:

'The question is not in knowing whether today's theatre will draw its appeal from this or that experimentation, its strength from the authority of one director or another: I think we must ask ourselves whether it will be Marxist or Christian. For it must be living, that is to say, popular. To be living, it must give man reasons to believe, to hope, to grow.' [...]

The theatre must find its meaning, its sense.

A poetic sense. But we must not confuse poetry with an empty and laborious fantasy, nor with a certain kind of ornate, decadent literature.

A dramatic sense, through action and through its dénouements, through the opposition of passions and convictions.

A human or tragic sense, through the creation of personalities and types, the invention of characters, the manifestation of heroes.

A satirical sense. I mean nothing negative by this, but a vigorous opposition, an *élan* of the spirit, a healthy laugh. And not those genre paintings where some pallid love-intrigue is there to attenuate and make bearable the slight pinprick given in passing to the fashions and foibles of the day, but a joyous device built for battle and not afraid to show its sharp teeth, nor to get a bit intoxicated, in the manner of Aristophanes.

A social and a universal sense, which would correspond to the life of the times (the life of the city and the life of the world), which would try to consider its preoccupations, to pose and clarify its problems, to crystallise its ideas and its passions.

Each of these genres has its style. And it is by employing clearly defined genres, well-characterised, pure genres, that the theatre will find once more its sense of style. [...]

189

[We have seen] a great nation pushed aside and toppled in a few hours, literally overcome. Its youth uprooted from the soil, cut off from the nation. Those who called themselves its leaders, felled, in exile or in prison. Everything which made up its way of life and its way of thinking called into question.

It is enough, I believe, for those who are least disposed to reflection to realise that there was, after all, something which was not being run as it should.

But it is not a matter of savagely turning on all of our past, of indolently taking the opposite position, of being slavishly ready to accept from alien hands all that we were lacking in order to be wise and strong.

What we must do now is to find, in that vast rubble of living thought and national ideas, the roots, however weak or mutilated they may be, that we had planted with our own hands and which it is our duty to save, to cultivate, and to make grow green again.

We must rebuild our own ideal ourselves. But to begin with we must try not to be too ambitious. It is upon sincerity, upon truth, that everything must stand. It is up to us to see clearly and deeply, up to us to guide ourselves by the purest of laws and to call upon the best men.

After living with the theatre, studying its origins and its various developments, I am convinced that it does not progress like practical and scientific knowledge, by leaving behind it old truths in order to go beyond them towards ones which will take their place, until they, in turn, are corrected or replaced. In art an inner strength is renewed as it was by the giant in the myth – by a periodic return to primal sources, to the maternal lap.

If we wish to create healthy, natural, living works, essential and durable, we must become attached to this *renewing of inner strength*. It will give meaning to all our efforts. It will become one with the unanimous aspiration of our country, with the unique duty of all Frenchmen today: the remaking of France.

There is no alternative, no choice possible. What we need is a Theatre of the Nation.

It is not a class theatre, a theatre which makes claims for any particular group. It will be a theatre of reunion and regeneration.

A reform of such breadth cannot take place undirected. It can be directed and made fertile only by and under the aegis of a strict authority, provided that that authority is well informed.

Competent people are not lacking, nor are honest intentions. But we must be able to discern them, to promote them, to discipline them, in the name of impartiality, knowledge and love for the sake of simplicity, sincerity and greatness.

In order to transcend differences and petty individual disagreements for the benefit of a professional community, it would be desirable for the State no longer to content itself with information gained through a 'commission' which is often incompetent and sometimes subject to dubious influences, but to make a direct contact with the creative forces themselves.

The first step in this direction would be the organisation of a study centre, where a small group might gather, men old enough to speak with experience, young enough to rethink the future of the theatre according to new methods, for new needs.

These needs are not unknown. They are not even mysterious. They have been felt by artists before, and sometimes expressed. They had not yet been liberated from the hesitancy with which they were feeling their way, but they were already alive. These needs have become even more obvious today, more pressing than ever. We must examine them, define them, propose programmes and put them to the test.

The most important of all these needs is the creation and organisation, first of all and as the basis of everything else, of a centre of *theatrical culture*. A big school, generously subsidised by the state, where all forms of dramatic invention and performance would be studied and practised; where each section would be headed by the most qualified person, regardless of official titles or political recommendations; where the whole would be harmoniously stimulated by a dominant spirit. [...]

Today, in France, we can see already the stirrings of a new genre of dramatic activity which could become numerous, varied and useful.

I mean these young companies which, in the past few years, have multiplied themselves like the cells of a living tissue and which the Popular Front government of the 1930s had begun to encourage with its subsidies to perform before workers' audiences.

For the most part they were thrown out of occupied France by the military defeat. This was an excellent start, this break with Paris. They retain their connections there, but move about in non-urban areas. Thus we have the beginning of the decentralisation we had so long been calling for and which is one of our theatre's vital needs.

The necessity of travelling, often by road, requires them to travel light, that is to reduce their baggage. The result is that the sobriety of the *mise en scène* is accepted as one of their characteristics, requiring them to be received by their audience for what remains essential: the pleasure in the works performed and the vitality of the acting.

There are many of these companies. I am told there are too many and that they compete with one another, but that is only a temporary inconvenience. In order to operate more effectively, they will have to organise themselves and accept a rigorous discipline. [...]

We shall have to study this development more closely in order to understand it. As it stands, it has begun already to invade our country, to penetrate it, to conquer our cities and to spread out into the countryside. These travelling companies at least present to their newly recruited audiences the spectacle of their youth, good health, ardour, discipline and courage. Is that not something completely new?

They complain about a lack of repertoire. We do not have a popular repertoire, as has been noted by all who have wanted to lay the foundations for a new theatre. [...]

These young companies are much better placed in this respect than their predecessors, not having retained as many literary superstitions.

What were the writers of the early 1900s trying to do?

They were attempting to renew, to refurbish the theatre through its literary, ideological and human substance, but using the same form. They had not envisaged a recasting of the means of expression corresponding to the thing which they proposed to express. The dramatic form was not questioned. They simply took over the form as they found it, as they received it from their predecessors. By saying that they had no repertory, they meant that they needed well-made plays, plays built according to the bourgeois canon of the nineteenth century. They grafted their popular movement onto the Boulevard Theatre of 1889 and the *Théâtre-Libre* of 1897. So, of course...

The young today are infinitely freer in their conceptions. They have in front of them a field which is incomparably wider, more varied, more elastic. They address themselves to a public which is fresher than the Parisian public, and, being less well-informed, is also much less limited. They are free from the discipline of routine, pedantic and unimaginative criticism. They are more or less dis-encumbered from Naturalism. That is the chief service that the art theatre movement of 1920–40 has done them. They benefit from a technical liberation which was no easy task. Lyricism is not taboo. The development of mime does not frighten them. They know what play is, what it means to establish a sense of play among themselves, and even between themselves and the public. They have established a contact with the classics. Molière is alive for them. They are not unaware of the theatre of the Far East. They have had some contact with the *commedia dell'arte*. They have great confidence in the actor and make no attempt to produce illusion by a change of scenery. They have rediscovered poetry.

Henri Ghéon's *Compagnons* and those who followed them – the Scouts and the Routiers,[3] the Jeunesse Ouvrière Catholique, the Vieux Colombier students who entertained the Burgundian wine-growers near Beaune from 1925 to 1930 – all know that little is needed to hold an audience and gain its confidence provided that the entertainment's approach is frank and lively and strikes a note of honesty and sincerity.

Thus I see no inconvenience in the fact that the travelling companies of France cannot find a ready-made repertoire. On the contrary, the more it will be impossible for them to use the one they might be tempted to adopt as a last resort, the more they will be convinced of the need to construct their own repertoire, adapted to their means, circumstances and functions, and the more we can expect from them a profound renewal.

Within the limitations of our climate, we should increase the number of large-scale and inspirational celebrations in the open air. For, in order to become strong, our art does not find a more healthy constraint or a more stirring lesson than those which will be imposed by the masterpieces of French architecture and landscape. However, we must watch carefully that the architecture and landscape is not profaned, or spoiled, as has happened in such choice areas as Orange.[4]

By spreading the taste and habit of dramatic celebration in all our provinces, we shall be obliged to respect the variety of France, to produce a natural, non-ideological *oeuvre* by developing what already exists in each place, by using local resources and traditions, inspired from history, folklore and the calendar, and by protecting and inspiring, whenever possible under the inspiration and guidance of local artists, the choral groups, dance schools, amateur groups and professional and athletic associations. [...]

As admirable as these open-air celebrations may be, as nobly as they fulfil the desires for popular leisure time by their communal expression, they will never be anything more than occasional.

Their solemnity will thus be all the greater, and their periodic return at the appropriate season will revive the nation's expectations, emotions and joys, thereby making it ready to appreciate them completely.

A national, political or religious feeling for great events or commemorative dates will always hold a sufficiently strong attraction among the populace for these festivals to be organised almost spontaneously in any given historical or circumstantial locale. It will simply be the task of the poets, musicians and artists to organise them. [...]

The totalitarian states have encouraged grandiose and spectacular displays in their need to obtain an inner propulsion from their masses. Those who have attended the multitudinous *mises en scène* that Mr. Hitler has proliferated throughout his empire as nothing more than pretexts to fan the flames of the National Socialist faith, agree in praising the grandiose éclat and thrill which they produce. Their quality is based on the enthusiasm of the animators and on the natural degree of emotion and military discipline of the supernumaries.

However, theatre should not, even if it tends toward the mystical, take its example from these spectacular displays for which it is not fitted. It should avoid confusing what falls within the domain of processions, parades and festivals with what is in the essence of drama.

Theatre *for* the masses is not necessarily theatre *of* the masses.

In my opinion, theatre of the masses is a formal contradiction to the economy of means required by the concentrated playing of a dramatic force.

I believe that the more the theatre intends to appeal effectively to a wide public, to remain vivid in its memory, to influence its life on the deepest levels, the more it will have to be simplified and purified, reducing its elements numerically in order to develop their force. [...]

Nothing more clearly denounces the impotence of our era than our fear of taking on a primitive language.

It would be deplorable, even absurd, and certainly a hopeless situation, if the people coming to the theatre today should only accept the worn-out forms which the writers of the past century used and fiddled with time and again without getting anything new or valuable from them.

Neither the pseudo-medieval and pseudo-Elizabethan forms of the romantics, nor the pseudo-Classic and pseudo-Antique ones of the professors.

Let us continue to perform the masterpieces of our heritage in as faithful a style as possible. Let us continue to study them and venerate them as prototypes which cannot be surpassed.

But if the popular theatre is to undergo a healthy birth and live its own life, it must live through this entire developmental experience for itself. It must take its point of departure from the soil, drink at the source, discover and gradually assimilate the laws of dramatic creation, composition and performance. In other words it must re-invent its form according to its own needs and its own powers, according to the nature and capabilities of its public, and not create through great effort, and following ancient recipes, false antique dramas, false classical tragedies, false Shakespearian dramas.

Let its tragedy begin with choral chants. Let its comedy begin with gatherings and festivals, embellished with songs and local farces, inspired by the images of characters known in the area. [...] At least they will have grown out of the people for whom they were made, they will have been renewed, refreshed at the very source, and will have developed organically, naturally. They will be truly new because they will be truly living.

[From *Le Théâtre Populaire*, op. cit., pp. 4–8, 15–17, 18–19, 30–3, 39–43, 44–5, 55–6]

16

SACRED DRAMA

In his last major productions Copeau sought to synthesise his idea of the dramatic chorus with that of a socially regenerative popular theatre. Since he now lacked a permanent company, the work was occasional, but on suitably large canvases. For example, the outdoor performances he directed for the Maggio Fiorentino in 1933 (Santa Uliva) and 1935 (Savonarola), and finally Le Miracle du Pain Doré *(1943) in the courtyard of the Hospice de Beaune. To which must be added Orazio Costa's 1950 production of Copeau's last written text for the theatre,* Le Petit Pauvre: *a dramatisation of the life of St Francis of Assisi, written at various times between 1930 and 1948, which further explores the dramaturgical possibilities of interaction between choir, chorus and celebrant.*

The critic Eric Bentley viewed Copeau's conception of mass theatre as a kind of theatre Mass with a suspicion that cast a shadow not only on his religious convictions, but also his political ones:

Copeau's conversion came, I believe, in the later twenties. Religion seems to have occupied a larger and larger place in his mind: Catholicism and, it would seem, the sort of right-wing social philosophy that often goes with it. The latest publication of Copeau's that I've seen is a pamphlet published in 1941, entitled Le Théâtre Populaire. He says that at this date (the first year of the Occupation) he feels that for the first time his words in favour of a great theatre may not be spoken into a vacuum, and this because the new situation is conferring on the French an improved sense of reality. In the pages that follow we learn, if largely in obiter dicta, that a strong state is good for the theatre, that there is danger in too much liberty, that the liberal, secular outlook has tended to destroy all that is good.[1]

The letter to Jean Schlumberger which begins this section, written in 1919 on Copeau's return from New York, reveals, however, a much earlier, completely a-political, origin to Copeau's sense of a religious mission. Since he was already nominally a Catholic, his was, anyway, a return rather than a conversion, but none the less fervent for that. In view of the gradual drying up of his public work during the thirties and forties, parts of this personal testimony read almost as prophecies intending self-fulfilment. In the solitude of the theatre of his mind, at least, he was then able to draw together the threads of his theatrical vision in a last attempt himself to become the 'Poet' for whose coming he had prepared. Richard Hayes, the American editor of Le Petit Pauvre offers the alternative perspective to that of Bentley:

> Behind all his labours lay the dream, romantic yet built on the real anguish of all nostalgia, of a theatre of communion, through which – as in the analogous litany of the church – the discords and divisions of men would be reconciled, the rites of their nature, and the bond to what lies beyond that nature, celebrated.[2]

The superficiality of Bentley's much-quoted remarks could be attenuated by the lack of biographical information available to him at the time of writing (1950). The proper explanation of Copeau's use of religious vocabulary can be found in the writings of many other intellectuals of his generation, struggling, as they saw it, to free themselves from the outworn creeds of the positivistic and materialistic society of the nineteenth century.

As a lycée student of philosophy, reared in the atmosphere of Bergson's emphasis on intuition and élan vital, of Nietzsche's Dionysian affirmation and elitism, Copeau found his ideal role in Plato's philosopher-king. His letters to a fellow student are studded with his youthful idealism: 'My dream is to be one day useful to society, to my country, to the human Ideal, to sacrifice myself a little for those in need of honest words'; 'The Poet has a duty – "to seek among the stars the path which reveals to us the hand of God".[3]

Another revelation came from his reading of a then little-known work, appreciated only by a 'happy few': André Gide's Nourritures terrestres, urging his readers to 'suppress in yourself the idea of merit – one of the mind's greatest stumbling blocks', and to take as their motto, 'ASSUME AS MUCH HUMANITY AS POSSIBLE...'[4]

Copeau asked in a speech to the New York Drama League (26 March 1918):

What is it we want? In a word, we want to return the theatre to its religious character, its sacred rites, its original purity. Thus, first of all, we must chase the money-lenders out of the temple, or else raise a new temple alongside those sacrilegious dens called commercial theatres. This problem is at the heart of all the others. The economic problem is dominating the artistic problem.

Finally, we have included in this section an appreciation by Copeau of the Gregorian chant as sung in the Abbey of Solesmes, where he went on retreat at regular intervals from his home in Pernand Vergelesses. In his diary for 4 May 1930 he wrote: 'Worked on *St Francis*, which impels me towards a mystical and detached attitude. The most profound influences on me – Molière, Greek Tragedy, the Japanese Noh, Solesmes.'

A RELIGIOUS CONCEPTION OF ART

My dear Jean,
I assure you that for you as well as for me, the problems appear both in a 'theatrical' and a 'monetary' aspect. All my efforts are towards *liberating* the instrument of our work, and I shall even try to adapt to the present conditions. However, in this matter, I have experience which you do not have, and which allows me to see things which you do not. I beg you not to take me for a chimerical thinker who must be humoured over certain things. Is having a vision being chimerical? From my bourgeois heredity, I possess a sense of reality down to the last detail. But it is true that I will abandon nothing I hold to be true. It is true that I have ambition and that the pettiness of our modern life disgusts and irritates me. I am aware of what I could do if everything was as I wish it. I admit openly that I have a *religious* conception of my art. Will you smile if I tell you that it is only in *churches* that I feel a peace descending on me, and that my spirit rises towards that for which it thirsts? Maybe it is a church that I want to build, a poor weak man lost in the masses of the twentieth century. I came to this in a natural, pro- gressive and fatalistic manner. That is why I say we shall do nothing until we have reared a new generation for this new religion. Beauty must return among us. If I am only a false prophet, if my era does not need me, I shall go off into solitude to atone for a dream that was too beautiful, or to strengthen for myself alone the visions of

my mind. For I want to live for my truth. I want to live truly. I no longer want to settle for lies, approximations or parodies. You know that I have been condemning the modern theatre for the past twenty years. And little by little a great image is forming in my mind that I could begin to shape if only it were possible some day to work freely (which I have never done).

I know, my dear Jean, you have already proved it sufficiently, that I can count on you, that you will do everything you can to help me. I should like to convince you that it is no longer a question of what it was in 1913–14; we are confronting something very solemn, it has now become necessary to give all we have. I believe we are alone on the path we have chosen. And we are no stronger, no more numerous that we were in 1918. We are fewer and less strong.

I dream of a real community, a true sharing of work – something that we have never really known – a total use of that beautiful friendship which you rightly praised above all, an anonymous sharing and communion of all our forces, with only the single *work* in common as our aim. I am not asking you to serve *me*, but to serve the work. This is the sense in which I could say that I no longer wanted collaborators but servants,[5] a phrase which caused me to be criticised, although it is merely the most innocent expression of my faith. I have no other ambition but to define the goal, to forge the means of attaining it and to utilise all energies to the fullest. [...]

Au revoir, my dear Jean. Don't think your old friend has gone crazy. He has spent two years fighting against all kinds of vulgarity, on the stony soil of New York, enduring all the stains and the jibes. He has come through, purified by this hell.

We can revive and win at the cost of our lives, but we must be very persuaded of the *reality* of our mission. Some have already called me, derisively or insultingly, an apostle. If I am not that, I am nothing. Do you understand that I want to live, think and act *according to my plan*?

Your JC

[From a letter to Jean Schlumberger, 2 August 1919, published in *Revue* d'histoire du théâtre 4, 1963:376]

IDEAL CONDITIONS

Whenever anyone wishes to laugh at the Vieux Colombier, they talk about its being a parody of religious feeling. It's a chapel, they say, a brotherhood where high priests pontificate and say mass, it's a cult, etc.

These jibes do not frighten us. What is *religious* is everything which brings men together. Nothing great is accomplished without faith, and it is precisely that semi-religious consciousness of our art and our mission which constitutes the best in our ideal. What we want is to appeal to the public, to that public which needs something more than life can offer and comes to find it in the theatre, to those who only know the anguish of modern life. We want to make the theatre, the most decried of all the arts, worthy of this appeal and of its cultural and edifying role. [...]

We must plough up the soil and begin at the beginning.

[Notes for a speech before the Order of the Eastern Star, of the Theosophic Society of France, on 'Les conditions idéales d'un théâtre futur', 10 April 1921, M-H D]

SACRED THEATRE

Master of the Ceremonies: it cannot be said that he plays no part in the action. He initiates and guides it, step by step, by hand signals. He possesses the knowledge and prevision of it, is imbued with it and remains in close touch with it. He adds to it, since he receives and transmits the kiss of peace and places the host in the monstrance. However, he does not enter into the action; this is in order for him to be able to control and possess it. (A little like the role I play: setting out others, who will go further, on new paths which I have discovered, but was never able to explore sufficiently.)

Choirs – The entrances and exits, the genuflexions, the various movements suffice to animate the orchestra – and to embellish it with a living décor. If the choir carries standards, banners, crosses (garlands, trees or other accessories), if the choristers bow to one another, turn, cover themselves with a cowl, bow to the lectern to read their text, walk, rise, sit, this is enough to envelop by a living décor the actors who are playing on a raised platform behind them.

The movements executed behind the choir while it is in action give complete freedom to the changes of scenery while allowing the continuity of the action upon a fixed stage. This is what I have been seeking for a long time.

[From 'Notes towards a scenography of sacred theatre', written in the Abbey of Solesmes, 7 September 1930, M-H D]

LE MIRACLE DU PAIN DORE[6]

Back at Pernand since Friday evening, it is only this morning that I have found the time and the motivation to write a few notes on those two great days at Beaune, the 21st and the 22nd [July 1943]. Great, above all, thanks to the harmony and favour they received from Heaven. They were actually encircled by storms; that did not, however, affect the ceremonies themselves which unfolded exactly as planned. Great as an expression of love; that of the nursing women who welcomed, surrounded, pampered us, at once great ladies and pious domestic servants; that of the patients, the healthier of whom followed our rehearsals. And, as for those who were bedridden, they were visited by the actors in costume after the dress-rehearsal; they stretched their arms outwards towards the angels and towards the Holy Virgin. Great, as an expression of my love, too, which was given without measure; and that of the actors who did their utmost; that of the Choir assembled in the gallery; of Samson[7] who excelled himself at this festival; of the clergy, some of whom wept; of the organisers who are already speaking of repeating these pageants. [...]

It was really, I believe, the model for a religious celebration, as beautiful as *Santa Uliva* in Florence, in the same line, but with more resonance and perhaps more discipline. This time we really 'got away from theatre'. There must be a follow-up: I am thinking of the twelfth centenary of the death of Saint Benedict which may be celebrated at Solesmes in four years' time. [...]

Tonight, unable to sleep, I have considered at length, with a supernatural lucidity, the great significance of that fortnight's work, crowned by two days of exceptional performances. I have profoundly understood the truth of the Portuguese proverb evoked by Claudel in *Le Soulier de Satin*: that God writes straight things in zigzag lines, and the *etiam* and *peccata*. I have admired the persistence of the intentions of Providence in my life, from a certain moment on. How it tore me from the Vieux Colombier and led me to Solesmes, and then made all my attempts to return to profane theatre fail, including the short-lived rupture with the Comédie-Française which brought me to Pernand, made me write *Le Petit Pauvre* and led me into the courtyard of the Hôtel-Dieu in Beaune to celebrate, in the midst of the faithful and of the Sisters of the Faith, almost at the bedside of the impoverished invalids, *Le Miracle du Pain Doré*. There I really got away from theatre and from all purely aesthetic considerations. There I found a sympathetic milieu: the affection of the charitable sisters of mercy, the co-operation of a modest company which had not been formed by me, but brought up by Jean,[8] whom I myself had raised; the collaboration of those whose work has for so long been harmonised with mine: to whom I had been faithful and who have remained faithful to me: Maiène, Jean, Barsacq;[9] the emotion of my son Pascal and that of my son Bernard [Bing]; the spiritual presence of my dear old Suzanne; the new friendship and fertile understanding of Louis-Noël Latour[10] and Joseph Samson; the total approbation of Agnès[11] whose eternal fidelity and steadfastness prepared and made it all possible, and the encouragement and transcendant thoughts of my saintly little Edi. The atmosphere was really that of the miracle. So much so that, the other morning, seeing the veil of a nun floating down the Pernand road, I thought for a few moments, and Maiène and Catherine[12] thought with me, that it was Mother Francis [Edi] come to rejoin us.

[From *Journal* entries, 26 July and 1 August 1943, M-H D]

The Little Poor Man

Through the impetus, and thanks to the courageous and persevering efforts of Gianna and Guiseppe Gazzini, the Istituto del Dramma Popolar was founded in San Miniato.[13] Learning that one of the many churches there was dedicated to Saint Genest, patron of actors, they decided to inaugurate a Festa del Teatro on his day when, for a four or five day period, a drama of religious inspiration would be performed each year. For the fourth year of its existence, the Istituto del Dramma Popolar called on the Piccolo Teatro di Roma and on Orazio Costa, who proposed Jacques Copeau's Le Petit Pauvre. Thus, by founding an annual celebration with a specific aim, before a public aware of the type of spectacle to be presented, the Istituto was meeting the true conditions of the renaissance of a popular theatre.

Orazio Costa, who studied with Copeau for one year and remains his disciple, had studied at the Academy of Dramatic Art in Rome, founded by Silvio d'Amico in the spirit and according to the principles of Jacques Copeau's Vieux Colombier School. In turn, Costa is training his students to make up the company of Rome's Piccolo Teatro.

Thus it was that, during those unforgettable evenings of San Miniato's Festa del Teatro, we had the moving experience of seeing, through a play written by Jacques Copeau, the realisation, perhaps in more modest circumstances than those he had envisaged, but in an identical spirit, of that contact, that communion between a company formed by a school, inspired with the same spirit, and an aware public – the meeting between 'two dramatic purposes, that of the actor inspired by a poet and that of people coming together eager to hear the poet's word.'

It was to Orazio Costa's credit that he aroused and held his company in that state of fervour and jubilation which lifted the play to the same plane as that of the public's anticipation, thus creating a spiritual exaltation which carried the play from beginning to end and held both public and actors enthralled. It was also to Costa's credit, to that of his teaching and his fidelity to the idea of the school, that he had in hand for the realisation of his lovely mise en scène, *such a supple instrument, so receptive to his least instructions that both actors and director seemed to understand one another instinctively through a common vocabulary and in a perfect harmony, resulting in an impression of improvisation and freedom. Each of the actors seemed so naturally fitted to the assigned roles, filled with such an inner glow and so united to their actions, that it is impossible to praise anyone individually for that state of grace created by the five performances.*

[From notes by Marie-Hélène Dasté for the programme of a production of *Le Petit Pauvre*, performed in Vezelay, Beaune and Pernand, 5, 6, 7 July 1988]

THE MELODY OF SOLESMES

I can bear witness to the peace which it pours into the soul, to the joy which it communicates: aerial, transparent, soothing and powerful, balanced and absolutely lacking in material substance. [...] Coming from the depths of time, the anonymous chant, having no consciousness of its own, reaches only to God. In the service of prayer, as the ancient legislator [Aristotle] ruled it in the service of poetry, this melody is simply speech raised to its highest level of potency, 'the Word operating at once on the sensory and the intellectual faculties'.[14]

Here, the rhythmical development which amplifies or extends the

Word, is simply its vibration, its spiritual prolongation. The dilated soul of the Word. And of what a word! Father, Lord, God, Jesus, Angel, Virgin, Love, Humility, Consolation, Germination, Resurrection, Alleluya... Primitive art, the holiness of primitive art is there in the fullness of an expression which is not detached, not loosened from its internal meaning. Flexibility seeking simply exactitude in human sentiment. A freedom which loves nothing more than the divinity of breathing.

Those of us who make it our work to interpret feeling through words know what this expression means: the *radiance* of a text. To examine, take up, transpose a written text, through sound, rhythm and modulation, so that the sense multiplies of its own accord without distortion, so that it wells up inside the measure, so that it finds its deepest point of departure inside us, and, in the listener, its most meaningful point of arrival: we know what a precarious business this is, how limited the means of achieving it are, without overstepping the bounds of propriety and naturalness. And though emotion sometimes enables us to encounter such a tone, we know that the sincerest study will not be enough to enable us to render it at will... Gregorian prayer has annotated the inflexions of the heart. The voice can be beautiful or not, the diction and the movement can be perfect or otherwise. The attitude of the soul will at least know how to find itself without artifice.

Saint Benedict himself says in his *Rule*, that 'our soul must be in accord with our voice'. One would love to be able to grasp the secret of such accord.

The truths of the Catholic faith are so well interlocked that, in order to speak properly of the 'chant that belongs to the Roman Church', as Pius X called it, and of the perfection to which the Benedictines brought it, one ought to depict the Benedictine way of life itself and to give a picture of the Peace of Solesmes.

[From *Revue Universelle*, 1 December 1931, pp. 638–40]

17

AN APPEAL TO
THE YOUNG

One of the constants in Copeau's thinking about theatre was that youth should have its day. His endings (and there were several of them) would, hopefully, be someone else's starting points. His own career as a dramatic practitioner had begun with an appeal to the young to join him in his indignant reaction to the mindless theatricality which the new century had inherited from the old. The poster announcing the opening of the Vieux Colombier in 1913 began:

APPEAL

To the young, in order to react against all baseness of mercantile theatre and to defend the freest and most sincere manifestation of a new dramatic art...

In 1928, established in the house in Pernand-Vergelesses, his study on the first floor looking out over the wine-store where the young Copiaus were rehearsing, he wrote:

The day when I feel my tread weaken upon the boards, the day when I have no voice left, when I will finally retreat among these three hills where the view stretches right to the line of the Jura, at that moment I would like something of me to carry on in the world, something more robust, younger and greater than I, about which I might be allowed to say: that's what I worked for.[1]

MAKE WAY FOR THE YOUNG!

We have no more ardent desire than to see France's theatrical vitality manifest itself through the ideas, efforts and productions of the younger generation. It is time for the avant-garde to regroup itself, not to work on new ideas, for at the moment there do not seem to be any on the horizon, but at least to develop and enrich with renewed energy the inventions and methods which were germinating in the teachings of their elders. It will soon be twenty-five years since André Antoine, upon finishing his career at the Odéon, recognised the birth of the Vieux Colombier and, in pointing this out to his audience, repeated the words of Henri Becque about the beginnings of the Théâtre Libre: 'Forward! Pass over our bodies!'

It is now our turn to invite the young to go on the attack, even brutally, from the captured positions. We have ourselves prepared this attack. The creators have the luck of arming themselves with the troops they have trained. It was from the first Vieux Colombier that came the Dullins, the Jouvets, Delacre's Théâtre du Marais in Brussels,[2] Ghéon's Compagnons de Notre-Dame and his numerous imitators, those of the Flemish People's Theatre, and a great number of young dramatic organisations throughout Europe, America and even Asia. From the second Vieux Colombier, that is its school in Pernand, came the Compagnie des Quinze whose influence is widely felt in England, the Comédiens Routiers and their emulators, and to a certain degree, the elements of a renaissance in university theatres. These are all attempts of unequal quality and varied import-ance, but they have contributed to stirring up the public, awakening it, orienting it and to launching certain ideas. These ideas have reached into areas where the question of popular leisure-time activities is being actively discussed. The use of such leisure-time is often thoughtless and absurd. The rising tide of life is full of impurities and *arrivisme*. However, when the ministry in power proposes to favour, in the French provinces, the peregrinations of a small, ardent, selfless little company able to bring good quality entertainment to the peasants and the workers, it will be able to address itself to two of our young comrades, André Barsacq and Jean Dasté, two good workers from the Vieux Colombier and the Compagnie des Quinze, who will soon set out on the road with the Compagnie des Quatre Saisons that they have just founded.

For a few years now, Paris has been welcoming a young actor whom we know well from having seen his debut and followed his efforts along a path that is familiar to us. This path began in Charles Dullin's Atelier, and his name is Jean-Louis Barrault.[3] He started in the cinema rather than in the theatre, and his fame spread quickly on the screen. This allowed him to put some money in his pockets, which were not particularly full. Our friend Barrault, through his youthful energy, new convictions and with encouragement from friends, formed a company and mounted a play, Cervantes' *Numancia*, which has been running successfully. It is a success which belongs primarily to the great Spaniard and, perhaps, also to the analogy it presents to the tragic events in Spain. But it must be especially due to the magnificent ardour of his company and to the talent of Jean-Louis Barrault, who can be said to be already a remarkable director.

As we delved deeper into the problems and practice of the *mise en scène*, and as our attention was drawn even more to acting technique, we were surprised and disgusted to find routine, inadequacy and lack of a serious education. So then we thought of giving the actor a total education, not only by improving his mind and stimulating his imagination, but also by increasing and multiplying his physical pliancy through gymnastics, mimicry, rhythm and dance. Without intending in any way to diminish the importance of words in a dramatic action, we concluded that for them to be right, sincere, eloquent and dramatic, it was necessary that the articulated speech, the enunciated words, result from thought felt by the actor in his whole body, and from the flowering of both his inner attitude and the bodily expression which translated it. Hence, the primordial importance given to mimicry in our exercises, which we made the basis for the training of the actor, for he must be above all else on the stage, the one who acts, the personality in motion. We pursued this method rather extensively so that the student-actor could succeed in being able to embody any emotion, feeling, or even thought by attitudes, gestures and movements without the need for words. For a long time our school was nothing else in its principles and researches but a school for physical interpretation. And this embodiment, renewed by the most ancient and even primitive forms, took its vocabulary, not only from the human repertory but also became imbued with that of the animal world and all of nature, by examining the trees and branches, running water, the passing of clouds and even fire. It is obvious that these didactic explorations, meant to give the actor a new 'poetics', did not represent for us anything but a restorative method, a step in his education, and not an end in itself. But for the young minds, the experience was new and so important that many were led to think they possessed a complete art, and that this training confirmed them in the area of their discoveries at the edges of drama and dance. I fought against this error for which I was, in part, responsible, but with no success. These young actors dreamed of nothing but the Japanese Noh and Cambodian dances. They envied the technique of the Jooss Ballet, of Meyerhold's or Tairov's Russian troupes, and that of the Russian inspired Palestinians. Music contaminated more and more of the plays, or, lacking music, the 'tom-tom'.

One could, to a certain extent, criticise these excesses in the Compagnie des Quinze when it left my control. One could, more properly, criticise them in Jean-Louis Barrault, who comes from the same school and who was inspired by the same tendency, but who took its consequences even further because of his more perfect technique. His art is entirely figurative. He has respect for the author's text and for the main lines of the action, but he does not miss a chance to develop this action or to add on some original episodes. His natural tendency is to 'show everything', as in the cinema – more than in the cinema, that is, with more continuity. This results in monotony because the technical means cannot be renewed endlessly; also in excessive stretching out because the plastic gestures end up by going beyond what they want to signify; in tension because the means are used to their extreme limit; in dryness because the abuse of technique brings on the exhaustion and even the abolishing of emotion.

In spite of that, the spectacle is very attractive. Between the chattering and the repetition, a few quality discoveries emerge. These discoveries will certainly be developed when the young artist will have abandoned his caprices and be able to have less systematic conceptions. He will have to understand that the art he is practising at present with such mastery and brio is a dead-end art, a means and not an end, one more method among others, a part of our dramatic art meant to enrich it but not to replace it, precisely in the same way as the 'noises' and the 'spoken chorus' (also born in the Vieux Colombier) are being used today in certain circles in such a sterile and excessive manner.

In any case, these attempts attest to the theatre's vitality, to its search for new and rejuvenated ways which will be found if it can meet up with its poet, i.e. he who has something to say and who, in order to say it, will one day take advantage of all the methods previously partially explored.

[From 'Lugar a los Jovenes!', *La Nación*, 22 August 1937, reprinted in *Registres I*, pp. 112–16]

FINAL ADVICE TO THE YOUNG

You are addressed on all sides; you are beseeched, flattered, solicited, bribed, molested and exhorted, perhaps more than you are guided.

I see many of you suffering from not knowing where to begin, how to find a balance, or what way to start working. Students complain that they receive only vague instructions and lack the basics. And their teachers, their elders and their leaders are sorry to find only an inconsistent clay to mould, minds which are not sufficiently docile.

How I should like to help you! How I should like to find the words to answer your questions, to enlighten your minds and to warm your hearts!

I think you are placed between two dangers: the one of blindly and radically repudiating what was said and done before you, and the other of awaiting future salvation from some other effort than the one you will be able to make on your own. Contempt and disgust for old disciplines is no less perilous than hesitation and laziness in forming new ones.

I am neither a sociologist nor a qualified moralist. I am only a sincere worker, a friendly adviser who does not claim to give advice except from his own personal experience. For this reason, I can tell you two things. The first is that no great change is valid, no great renewal is durable, until it is linked to a living tradition, a profound native spirit.

The second is that, in order to bear fruit that is neither artificial nor ephemeral, a renewal of this kind must begin with the human being. Without falling back, without egoism, with as much modesty as ardour, it is primarily with yourselves that you should begin, with lucidity, simplicity, seriousness, application and courage. Try to be men, whatever your desires and aspirations, the career you choose to follow, or the technique you intend to master. Do not let yourselves get dried up, nor debauched, but apply yourselves with a will to making a beautiful, solid, happy, courageous and adaptable human harmony prevail in your character. You see, my friends, it is especially and uniquely important, in the midst of such confusion, to sign a pact with your soul, and to hold firmly to it. Do not smile too much at the gravity of my words. Everything today is of an exceptional and implacable gravity. You have no choice. Each one of you must, in your secret soul, be a hero... and a saint for yourself.

You are probably saying that this takes us a long way from theatre and devotion to theatre. Far from theatre perhaps, but not from the devotion I think is needed, and will be for a long time yet, if we intend to make a new spirit prevail. My language has hardly changed in thirty-one years, and has often been ridiculed. Indeed, I have been able to observe too often that theatrical mores have not changed very much. Even today I see theatre threatened by the same evils, the same abuses and the same treacheries it suffered from when I declared war on them a quarter of a century ago. We still find arrogant stars, sordid intrigues and base literature in the theatre, and I am afraid there always will be. Thus, it is another reason for increasing the numbers of its defenders and for closing ranks; another reason for trying to purify it, even if, and especially if, we do not flatter ourselves that we completely succeed.

Let us make an effort to acquire the craft and not let ourselves be devoured by it. Actors, authors, critics, public: let us prepare a phalanx of energetic theatre people with a healthy and elevated taste, full of fervour, gaiety and severity. [...]

Therefore, respect for work, assiduousness and diligence, punctuality at rehearsals, attention to minute details in preparation; in short, respect for the public for whom the work is being done. Faith in art, in work, in the public, and, above all, *faith in the young.*

[From 'Dévotion à l'Art Dramatique', lecture at the Théâtre Récamier, Paris, 16 May 1944, published in *Registres I*, pp. 108–10]

APPENDICES

APPENDIX A: ANDRE ANTOINE (1857–1943)

In one of his talks for radio, recorded in May and June 1945, Copeau paid this posthumous tribute to the founder of the Théâtre-Libre:

'It was when I was barely out of short trousers that I used to sneak out of the house to go and spend the few sous I had carefully saved from my pocket money to attend the theatre, choosing plays a bit haphazardly.

'One day I found myself at the Gymnase Theatre where they we giving Jules Lemaitre's *L'Age Difficile*.[1] The curtain went up on a garden scene. Around a metal table, several characters were drinking coffee. One of them, a grey-beard who was not sharing in the general conversation, was sipping his coffee while smoking a cigarette. Everything he did fascinated me and riveted my attention: the way he was smoking that cigarette, holding it between his thumb and index finger, flicking the ash; the way his heavy-lidded eyes would blink through the smoke, frowning and arching his brows at the same time; and finally, the way that he incorporated this mime action to augment the silent action of following the conversation. I understood the importance of this precise and lively miming in an actor's interpretation to attract the attention of a spectator.

'The one who taught me this lesson was André Antoine [...]. This was my first encounter with a master whom I am honoured to call a friend.

'Another memory of Antoine goes back to 1913. It was about the time of his last years at the Odéon. I was then preparing to inaugurate the Vieux Colombier with a few young actors, thus becoming Antoine's neighbour. [...] At the end of a speech to his subscribers, presenting the new season, he generously brought to their attention the existence of our enterprise, which for our company of young beginners was the equivalent of a veritable baptism.'

[First printed in *Registres I*, pp. 69–73]

'He said: "You will be offered there the most interesting and important productions. I ask all my subscribers and friends of the theatre to become closely involved in this enterprise. It is absolutely desirable and necessary that a new enterprise, comparable in principle to that of the former Théâtre-Libre, come into existence and prosper. There have been already several tentative attempts. This one is serious and seems to be well directed by people with ideas." '

[Reported in *Le Figaro*, 26 September 1913, reprinted in *Registres III*, p. 105]

'I recall how moved I was, thankful for this generosity. He was taking us seriously; he was seriously encouraging those who had been following him to pay attention to us. And this little speech ended with an exhortation which was quite meritorious from the lips of an old wounded lion: "I have only one thing to recommend you – addressing himself to us – about the same thing that Henri Becque advised us when we started: Forward youth, and proceed over our bodies!" '

[From *Registres I*, op. cit.]

Thereupon, Copeau wrote an open letter to Antoine, published in *Gil Blas*, 29 September 1913:

'I heard your lecture and admired the lively remarks, the freedom of mind, the frankness of attitude and, in a word, the *sincerity* which you have always been known for. It is to your credit that you turn to the young and move them to emulate your example and your energy. There is no danger that they will mistrust your advice and encouragement, for you have not aged; you are still one of us. In reaching out to take your hand, we are conscious that this binds us to a beautiful tradition of labour and courage. [...]
  'To be sure, we are not in agreement with you on more than one

point. However, like you, we believe in the cult of our art and have an intense love for our craft, the same love we can feel in your every word and which moves us deeply. When you spoke last Thursday of your admiration for the great artists of your time, describing how you would follow Mounet-Sully in the street, and of having got hired as an extra at the Comédie-Française in order to be able to observe him more closely on stage, I could not help recalling somewhat similar memories: but they were about you. [...] You developed in me, during my early years, that great love for theatre which remained all my life. Your teachings were the foundation from which arose my first hopes and assurances. [...]

'But you also said, speaking about us, "These people do not like me." You are mistaken, Sir. The further we stray from your aesthetic principles, the more we insist on affirming our moral solidarity with you. Undoubtedly, the theatre we wish to create does not resemble yours. But, if we succeed, it will be because of the same qualities which made your strength. If we seek an example to follow, yours is the only one that exists. If we do not find complete satisfaction in your teachings, you are nevertheless our only living master, the only man of action today who has brought honour to contemporary theatre and marked it with his imprint. We admire you, Sir, because in having imposed an aesthetic formula which has temporarily renewed the French stage, you have not ceased to be nobly worried over the novelties and efforts of a new generation. We admire you especially because you are Antoine: sincere, loyal and courageous; because you despise false talents and are not fooled by false authorities, and because you are always attracted, through a natural tendency, to what is young, living and generous. We admire you because you have always been a good workman, enamoured of his work, unstinting in his efforts.

'Lastly, Sir, you are what is so rare today, *someone who knows what he is doing*. We shall all be proud in our little theatre of the Vieux Colombier, which will begin its struggles in a few days, if our work, though it may not meet with your approval, at least receives your esteem. Since you have become the *patron* Sir, there is no other. As for myself, I have already found the way to stimulate my actors and to instill in them a salutary stage-fright for our opening night. I told them: "Antoine will be in the audience".'

[Reprinted in *Registres III*, pp. 105–7]

Later, in his notes for the first lecture at New York's Little Theatre, 12 March 1917, Copeau gives further explanation of why he did not 'find complete satisfaction' in Antoine's teachings:

'Causes of the decadence and failure in dramatic art:

'The Théâtre-Libre, a literary movement.

'Antoine's personality linked to this movement that he provoked and of which he became the prisoner.

'Narrowness of the realistic concept, excluding all fantasy, all poetry.

'It is pessimistic and thereby dessicating, limited, the vision of mediocrity. It ends quickly in sterile nastiness, in a superficial tableau with pretensions of sincerity. It soon became no longer that healthy realism that we find in the heart of the well-balanced works of our classical art, but a sickness of vision, a kind of *realistic romanticism*. It fell prey to using tricks of the trade and mannerism, to bias and stereotypes. [...]

'Antoine did not educate his actors. He imposed his style on them. The whole Théâtre-Libre is in Antoine, his body, his hands etc. He does not like the actor; he brutalises him. He created realistic *cabotins* like those who come from the conservatoire.'

[First published in *Registres IV*, App. B, p. 499]

'Antoine fell before his time. I have never understood why he did not ever rise up again. Something had broken within him. [...] Yet he continued for many years to "loiter" around the theatre, writing articles, reading manuscripts and, particularly, going to the cinema. He had a passion for the cinema in his last years, and went almost every night. He found in films the fulfilment of all his dreams. Although I do not share this passion in the least, I understand it in Antoine. I understand how this height of realism could have fired his imagination. He who had searched for, and loved above all in the theatre, the truth and naturalness of material objects, could see his dream realised on the screen: the water flowing, the fire flaming, the wind-blown trees...'

[From *Registres I, op. cit.*]

During the post-World War I seasons of the Vieux Colombier, Antoine regularly wrote reviews for the daily newspaper

L'Information. One of his first articles (5 April 1920) reaffirmed the generous tone of his pre-war declaration, now speaking of Copeau's School as well as his Theatre:

'The Vieux Colombier is the most truly artistic corner of Paris: the other evening I truly felt that the future lies there. M. Copeau is completing the forging of the really new and unexpected instrument which we need for another stage renewal; and if he reveals his work to us, it will be over his house that the star will rise.'

Upon publication of *Mes Souvenirs sur le Théâtre-Libre* in 1921, Antoine sent Copeau a copy with the following dedication: 'To the one who is coming, from the one who is leaving, his work done.'

At the end of his radio homage to Antoine, Copeau recalled:

'I should like to mention yet another image of my old master. It concerns the last years of his life [...]. I would visit him rather often, early in the morning, and find him already working at his desk. I think it was then that we had our best and most intimate conversations. Both still alert, as dissimilar as possible in stature, appearance and ideas, but sharing the same love of theatre, almost identical experiences and disappointments; so much so that Antoine would end by exclaiming: "It's true all the same that we resemble one another!"

'And it was true, by Heaven! Thus, after these encounters, I often regretted that we had never succeeded in forming a true friendship. It is so difficult in the theatre!

'As Antoine aged, I felt him detaching himself, retiring within, and disappearing into the distance. It seems to me that he misjudged a period that was no longer his, with a semblance of bitterness.'

[From *Registres I*, op. cit.]

APPENDIX B: CONSTANTIN STANISLAVSKY
(1863–1938)

Copeau's first acquaintance with the work of Stanislavsky came from a reading of Jacques Rouché's *L'Art Théâtral moderne* (1910), and from his 1915 conversations with Gordon Craig. It was mainly a reading of Alexander Bakshy's *The Path of the Modern Russian Stage* (1916) which revealed to him the essence of the innovations made by the Moscow Art Theatre. Eager to study them at first hand, Copeau wrote to the Russian director about his projected lecture tour to America and his ambitious plan to return to France via Japan and Russia, offering to give lectures and dramatic readings to Stanislavsky's company:

'It seems to me, although I am a newcomer in the practice of our theatrical art, and far from believing that my research is in the least comparable to your work and experience, that something good, alive and interesting could come out of our meeting. Those who have sincerely devoted themselves with an unshakable passion, to an absolutely pure dramatic art, are so few in the world that they have a duty to do all they can to meet and know one another.'

[From a letter, 10 November 1916, M-H D]]

Stanislavsky's reply, written on 30 December, was forwarded to New York, where Copeau did not receive it until 1 March 1917:

'Sir, I received your letter after much delay, at the very moment when our precious collaborator, Mr Sulerzhitsky, known in Paris for his *mise en scène* of *The Bluebird*, was dying. Mr Sulerzhitsky died yesterday after a long and painful illness, and today I can finally answer your letter. First of all, I express my thanks for your having written to me directly and amicably. Now that international interests bind us, your request is particularly dear to me. I know of your fine work, but although I have been to Paris often, unfortunately I was not able to attend your performances to see your lovely creations. In the summer, when I can leave Russia, your theatre is closed.

'I should very much like to see you and talk with you. If possible, I should like also to work with you in our art. I am still thinking about the founding of an International Studio which would unite all the most interesting workers in the world of theatre. But, let us get down to business.

'The months of April and May in Russia are bad for the theatre. During the war, thanks to the comings and goings of society, the Russian theatres have been working steadily, but unfortunately, the aristocracy, which is interested in French theatre, leaves for the country, and the majority of the Russian public does not like or very well understand French lectures and readings. Based on recent experiences, that is on the lectures of Lugné-Poë and Antoine, I sincerely regret that I cannot promise you material success. At the time of the lectures made by Lugné-Poë and Suzanne Desprès, attended by our actors, there was some profit and a certain moral and political success, but that was at the time of the [Franco-Russian] Alliance, and in the midst of winter, when all the theatres are full. In spite of these successes, it was impossible for us to arrange a second lecture, for we could not have covered the cost.

'For more details, maybe you could consult with Lugné-Poë, if he is in Paris. Up until 17–30 May 1917, our theatre will be giving performances, even two on Sundays and holidays, so that the stage will not be free for you during the week-days and the day-time. Under these conditions your success will be even less. Maybe we will be able to find another building, although it is difficult to be sure of it in advance. For all these arrangements and for the organisation of your lectures, our theatre will do the utmost to assist you. In a word, we are at your entire disposal, but we cannot guarantee you any material success. This is all the more painful for me to write that my letter may cool your intentions, and that you may give up your trip to Moscow, which would deprive me of the great pleasure of receiving you here, of making your acquaintance, and of speaking of art with you.

Sincerely, C. Stanislavsky' [M-H D]

Copeau replied on 4 April 1917, shortly after the Czar's abdication and the start of the Russian revolution. In the light of these events, it was no longer possible to fulfil his plans for a visit, but he was moved to express his fraternal enthusiasm for the Russian people and for Stanislavsky's project of an International Studio, adding that he hoped to bring the Vieux Colombier to Russia after the war.

Their first meeting did not occur until December 1922, when the Moscow Art Theatre came to Paris for the first of two visits. Copeau and Stanislavsky met often during the month, privately as well as at official ceremonies. The students of the Vieux Colombier School were required to attend the Russian performances, and Stanislavsky himself came at least once to Copeau's theatre:

'This evening,' wrote Copeau in his *Journal* on 14 December, 'S. came to see *Twelfth Night*. After the performance we talked together for an hour. It is restful to listen to this old magician. With him, one goes naturally to the heart of things; actor training concerns him most. His idea is that theatre cannot be saved unless a community of all the world figures is formed to work together. He seems a little bitter over the incomprehension of his actors and students. Why, he asks, do men who are seeking one another out, and can come to an understanding, remain separate from one another, continuing to be dedicated in their respective countries to people who do not, or scarcely, want any part of them? It would be unfortunate if *I* cannot entrust or transmit to someone what my long experience has taught me, no matter whether he be French or English...'

A week later, the entire company of Russian actors was received and honoured on the Vieux Colombier stage after the evening's performance, and Copeau glowingly referred to Stanislavsky as a 'father in the midst of his children'.

In 1934 Copeau readily agreed to write a Preface to the French translation of *My Life in Art*:

'It was in New York, in 1927, that I made my first acquaintance with this book, in its American version. But I read it much later, because, having opened it on the ship on my way home, I shut it again at once, startled by some of the sentences in it.

'I had left the stage three years before, and I could not endure hearing a voice so true, reciting an experience so very much like my own, which had led me into a blind alley. It reminded me that my own resources were perhaps no longer employable. [...]

'If this narration had appeared a few years earlier, and if I had been lucky enough to have read the book before meeting the founder of the Moscow Art Theatre, it would have helped me immensely to come closer to him. Yes, and if he himself had during those few talks in Paris wished to take me into his confidence as regards his experience, I would have been better prepared, with the help of his clearer and more enlightened spirit, to settle problems which alienated me from my companions. [...]

'Dear Constantin Stanislavsky, I have never had a guide in my art. I have never known that living, familiar and redoubtable presence, rude and tender, which every day, giving of itself to us, has won the right to demand our best. The thought that could have come to me, as it has to many others, to question this privilege, to be irritated by its constraints, to misunderstand it, is the only thing that attenuates my regret of never having served under some elder. But among the people whose words instructed me, whose example sustained me, it is you, dear Constantin Stanislavsky, whom I should like to name as my dear teacher. Perhaps you will reject this title, you who wrote at the end of your book: "I know that I know nothing..."

'Then I will say that I love you for your modesty, for your grandeur, for your fearlessness.'

APPENDIX C: CHARLES DULLIN (1885–1949)

One of Copeau's most famous disciples, Dullin was to found his own school and theatre, l'Atelier, soon after leaving the Vieux Colombier in 1919. He had begun his career in Paris playing in popular melodramas when, one day, he was called to audition for one of his most brilliant roles, in Copeau's adaptation of Dostoievsky's *Brothers Karamazov* in 1911. Copeau later recalled the event:

'When it came to casting the difficult role of Smerdiakov, the epileptic and murderous valet, Durec[1] and I were not in agreement. I was holding out for another, more experienced actor. Durec claimed he had a young actor who was made for the role and he urged me to try him out, so I consented.

'I can recall the cell-like office backstage. The door opened, and I saw appear a puny figure with an odd smile and an anxious look. When I told him he was being considered for an important role, he looked at me intensely and said simply: "If it's the role of Smerdiakov, I think I can do it." He got the role and, at the premiére, Charles Dullin – for it was he – received his first great triumph. It was then that a great friendship was born. We used to walk for hours after the performances, exchanging ideas full of hopes and confidence. And it was from these exchanges that was to emerge, a little later, the first plans for the Vieux Colombier.'

['Souvenirs pour la radio', May-June 1945, op. cit.; published in *Registres III*, p. 30]

Dullin himself had this recollection of that fateful audition:

'With my part in my pocket, I returned to my friends to announce the good news, but I did not stay long because I was in a hurry to be alone, to savour my good fortune. At moments like those, the intoxication one gets from art is very close to that one gets from love.

'I spent the rest of the night working; my experience as an actor in melodrama had made me quick to enter into a part and, therefore, I had hoped to be able at the very first rehearsal to show mettle enough for the tryout to result in a final casting.

'Early in the morning, I went out to buy a copy of Dostoesvsky's novel which I wanted to re-read without delay. The first rehearsal gave me neither disappointment nor encouragement... from the second rehearsal on, I began to gain some confidence.

'Despite the encouraging words I heard, I was not satisfied with myself. I could see the character right enough, but I felt I was playing him too much from the outside; the little quirks from my own nature, my physical appearance, might fool others, but not me.

'I wrote a long essay about Smerdiakov,[2] dense and crammed with generalities, in which I minutely analysed the character. Everything I had to do was covered, from his walk to the trembling of his lips as the epileptic fit came on, all of which only confused me the more and, for a while, even cancelled out my spontaneity and naturalness. Because I rehearsed with a great deal of sincerity and gusto, the director and the author tended to take advantage of this vehemence. Yet I felt it was getting me away from my model. Fortunately, a few impressions that I experienced brought home to me what I had been seeking in vain through extended analysis. At one point it was a bit of stage business that the director suggested which suddenly projected me into that second state, so necessary to the actor. Another time, the natural tone in which I said one speech re-oriented my whole approach and got me beyond ordinary theatrical conventions. My character was beginning to speak; what I had so meticulously tried to expound in that long study of mine was, little by little, unconsciously translating itself in a living manner. Copeau's intelligent criticism helped admirably in my efforts, and I felt myself daily more possessed by my character [...]

'I can honestly say that since that time, both as an actor and a director, I have tried never to allow critical sense and intelligence to gain the upper hand over instinct, although I have not always succeeded.

'This experience had allowed me, at a relatively early age, to find my bearings. From that moment on, I became aware also of the reforms that were needed: to throw off the yoke of naturalism, to borrow from melodrama what was authentic in it from a theatrical point of view, to place the poet at the very core of all inspiration, and to return instinct to its proper importance, the actor's most wondrous gift.

'Copeau had befriended me and helped me to make rapid strides; we got on together admirably. I never had a single professional disagreement with him; his critical sense, which was so right, and his imagination, had the most beneficial effect on me. The founding of the Vieux Colombier, the summer rehearsals at Le Limon, and the 1913–14 season are unforgettable memories.'

[From *Souvenirs et Notes de travail d'un acteur*, Lieutier, 1946, pp. 38–42]

As Dullin was more familiar with theatrical circles than Copeau, it was he who recruited from among his acquaintances many of the actors to be auditioned in his basement apartment in Montmartre. 'The candidates were first received in the street,' Copeau recalled, 'and when their time came, they had to descend a ladder to meet me. In this way, before hearing them, I had the opportunity of observing them as they came down the steps.'

[From 'Souvenirs pour la radio', op. cit.; published in *Registres III*, p. 78]

The rehearsals at Le Limon did not always go smoothly, but Copeau's friendship and confidence in his company did allow such expressions of opinion as the following letter from Dullin:

'Cher patron,
'First, I have a great and true affection for you and I do not wish to add to your worries; also, I am fully devoted and loyal. [...]
'I have a great admiration for you, and I have an <u>absolute confidence in what you are saying</u>, but you are allowing and encouraging a certain manner of acting which is completely counter to what you have so often told me. [...] I have seen you being severe, too severe [as a critic] towards certain actors, and now you have become a director, you are falling into the same faults and accepting things that no one else would accept elsewhere in Paris. I have told you that you were encouraging their way of acting, since you say nothing to them. When you yourself are acting (<u>proportionately speaking</u>), you seem purposely to avoid giving your roles the <u>life</u> which I think the theatre requires, and often you maintain the <u>tone</u> of your readings.
'Is that what you want? Am I in the wrong, or is it you that, <u>when</u>

listening to the actors, allow yourself to be entranced by the text, making up in your own mind for their deficiencies and not seeking a finished product. I am explaining myself rather badly, but you will understand well enough. At first, I thought it was a kind of work-out and that you were not looking for anything else, but we have been rehearsing for two weeks and the same thing is still going on. Consequently, we have come to the point of reciting a series of dead lines. [...]

'You told me yesterday: when one has something to say, one says it. Done. I am, and will remain, your affectionate and devoted friend.

Charles Dullin'

[From a letter dated July 1913, published in *Registres III*, pp. 92–3]

The triumphal first season ended in June 1914, accompanied by war clouds in the Balkans, but this did not dampen the ardour of the young company. In July 1914, Dullin wrote:

'Have you yet finalised the programme [for next season]? Now I am also convinced of our success. Please believe me when I say that if I sometimes lost my temper, it was through an excess of zeal and love for the success of the cause. We were all a little brutal, and if we had not been so, it is quite probable that we should not have done all this work. On the whole, I think you can be proud of your company and that things will be even better next season.

'As for myself, whatever I say, you can completely count on my dedication, and never doubt my sincere attachment to you and to the theatre.'

[*Registres III*, p. 219]

A few weeks later, this selfless enthusiasm was put to the test when Dullin enlisted in the army and was sent almost immediately to the front to participate in the defence of Paris in the first battle of the Marne. Soon embittered by his experiences, he nevertheless urged Copeau to uphold the spirit and ideals of their creation:

'Give me your news and stay where you are, for in spite of all the courage and desire to do the right thing, this is an impossible apprenticeship at our age...

'Do not give in too much to your enthusiasm. There will be enough dead and wounded, and the new France will need men of your calibre. [...]

'Do you have any news from our comrades from the Vieux Colombier? I think there will be a few missing from the first rehearsals.'

[Letter, October 1914, in *Registres III*, p. 237]

'I should desire above all that you <u>do not join up</u>. If you only knew how little your dedication and enthusiasm would weigh in the balance, and how much it would be impossible for you to serve according to your intellectual capacity and real worth! No, preserve yourself for other battles... We can disappear, the Vieux Colombier will be reborn with you. But if you get yourself killed... it would be the death of our work.'

[Letter, January 1915, in *Registres III*, p. 345]

Dullin's talents were not completely wasted, however, as he was asked to form an amateur group of actors just behind the front lines. This occasioned the exchange of a series of long letters with Copeau and Jouvet in which they discussed improvisation techniques and the creation of a new form of comedy.[3]

Finally, four months after the departure of the Vieux Colombier Company for New York in 1917, Dullin received exemption from further duty in order to join them. The details of his engagement and subsequent dismissal after one year are related in *Registres IV*.

Upon his return to Paris, Dullin joined the company of Firmin Gémier[4] who put him in charge of classes for actor training. It was then that, influenced by his Vieux Colombier experience, he decided to form a school of his own, l'Atelier, 'Ecole nouvelle du comédien', and published his own manifesto in August 1921:

'The Atelier is not a theatrical enterprise but a laboratory for dramatic experiment. We have chosen this name because it seemed to correspond to our idea of an ideal corporative organisation in which the strongest personalities would submit themselves to the needs of ensemble collaboration; in which the artist would have a thorough knowledge of his instrument, like a good horseman his horse, or a mechanic his engine.

'Amateurism, dilettantism are as dangerous as *cabotinage*. Theatre is a complete art, sufficient unto itself; such is the legacy left us by the great masters who preceded us.

'Its aesthetics must vary with each era, its forms of expression must always maintain the attraction and freshness of innovation, especially when they are borrowed from the classics, for theatre is like life, multifarious, fluid and mysterious, while its basic elements remain eternally the same.

'To collaborate in this work, we need resolute and combative men, simple and devoted women; for this our educational task becomes involved with a spiritual direction that is very difficult in these pitiless times when men are judged by the contents of their wallet. Our school exerts all its forces, still quite young and inexperienced, to this regeneration of the actor. Our productions will be only the results of our immediate research. If they shock by their imperfection, we believe they may interest through their instruction, of which others may later make more successful use. We are merely taking on again the harness abandoned by modern actors more avid for gain than for true beauty.'

[Reprinted from Dullin's theatre programme, in *Correspondance*, no. 16, May 1930]

These first experiments were encouraged by Copeau, who invited the youthful company to perform them at the Vieux Colombier. One of Dullin's young collaborators, Antonin Artaud, later made a comparison between them, based on a partial appreciation of Copeau's intentions:

'Jacques Copeau's idea of a theatre consists in subjugating the *mise en scène* to the text, of making it come forth from the text by means of an intelligent twisting of the very text itself. For Jacques Copeau, it is the text and the words which count above all. Thus, he has a Shakespearean concept of gesture, movement, attitudes and décor. In short, this is the submission of theatre to the language of written literature. Nothing more, that was it: afterwards the French theatre followed his lead. [...]

'Charles Dullin was one of the last actors in France to possess a real, searing intensity in his actions, and his playing sometimes brought to mind an image of a pneumatic drill penetrating the toughest of walls.'

[Lecture in Mexico City, 18 March 1936, reprinted in *Antonin Artaud, Oeuvres Complètes*, vol. viii, Gallimard, 1971, p. 215]

In 1949, a few weeks before his own death, Dullin dictated these words to Marie-Hélène Dasté on the death of his beloved *patron*:

'Your father knew that I never missed a cue [...]. Today, if I am not present among you, it is for a serious reason, the most annoying of all, illness. [...]

'From the start, our relationship was truly one of disciple and master and not that of actor and director. It was impossible, with such temperamental and plain-spoken personalities as ours, for this relationship not to be interrupted by a few stormy passages. More than once we lost our tempers, but I think that is what makes my testimony the more valuable. In our work, we never quarrelled; his instructions were so clear and lucid that only uncomprehending actors could dispute them.

'That is because Copeau had an admirable gift for making a text come alive. He knew how to unravel it, highlight its central idea and produce a dramatic explosion. [...]

'Copeau had a horror of fakery, of ostentation, and his sincerity was his true *raison d'être* and also his torment. Copeau was an artist.

[Dictated 25 October 1949; Dullin died 11 December; M-H D]

APPENDIX D: LOUIS JOUVET (1887–1951)

Jouvet shared a close relationship with Copeau, at once personal and professional, both having married girls from the same small Danish village and becoming fathers, as well as by their mutually idealistic approach to theatre. At the age of twenty, Jouvet became a certified pharmacist, but was more attracted to the theatre. In the same year, 1907, he helped to found an amateur company whose manifesto foreshadowed that of Copeau six years later:

'An Appeal to Youth
The Group of Action in Art wishes to imbue more beauty, clarity and tenderness in all forms of human endeavours. Our task is great, and we are a mutual society of illusionaries, a Union of Idealists.'

For three years, the Group gave performances of modern and classical plays in whatever small theatres they could find, one of which, the Athénée Saint-Germain, was soon to become the Vieux Colombier.

Engaged at the Théâtre des Arts in 1911, Jouvet attracted the attention of Copeau, who chose him for a role in the revival of *The Brothers Karamazov*. Before long, the triumvirate of Copeau, Jouvet and Dullin joined forces for the founding of the Vieux Colombier. Jouvet's organisational talents earned him the position of stage manager, in addition to his acting roles. From the trenches in the early years of the war he, like Dullin, engaged Copeau in a forward looking correspondence, particularly on the subjects of new improvised comedy and the related subject of actor-training:

'What struck me with the classics was the barrenness and aridity of certain texts at first glance! – the difficulty they present in approaching them and trying to play them; the imagination does not flow freely, we are paralysed before them. This seems to me to be due to a number of complex reasons, where we can see, first of all, the influence of schooling, the <u>classrooms</u> and <u>all the literary criticism</u> that has been laid on the text, already very literary etc. [...] All those critics have embalmed, dried up and mummified the text. And then, there is <u>the influence of the contemporary actors, of those we have seen before</u>, who leave you with the memory of all sorts of stage business and inflections, difficult to get rid of, and finally the <u>deplorable effect of memory</u> – of the text that is familiar, re-hashed, worn out, shabby, which has lost its savour and spontaneity, reduced to repetitiousness, declamation and twaddle. [...]

'I have noticed that the actor <u>becomes aware of the action and what he is playing</u> – he is so accustomed by memory that <u>he loses the scene</u>; he has only the text left; and I blamed that on the <u>mechanical</u> and <u>arid</u> aspects of certain problems. Declamation is typical of this.

'Don't you think that certain texts could be revitalised, regenerated by an exercise which would consist of reducing them <u>to outlines, resumés or skeletal actions: which the actor should first improvise, animate and clothe by himself.</u> This would then return the actor to himself *vis-à-vis* those texts full of prior influences, and maybe we could more easily renew the classics in this way? At least, the director would no longer have to deal with mechanised actors, and maybe, instead of having to whip up his imagination and inventiveness, instead of trying to polish up each and all of the actors and skimming the text in order to clarify it, he would have only to correct and direct actors who are already <u>alive</u>.

'If this work method does not seem useful or effective to you, maybe it would be good for the <u>young ones</u>, [who would be] raised far from the Théâtre-Français or the Odéon, far from textual analysis, <u>maybe even from the text itself!</u> [...] What do you think of this Rousseauesque idea of giving the beginners only a copy, <u>an altered and substantial text drawn from such and such a classic,</u> then, later, as a final initiation, give them the <u>real text</u> in all its splendour and perfection?'

[From a letter written 31 January 1916, quoted in *Registres III*, pp. 332–5]

Copeau transcribed this letter into his notebook on the 'comédie improvisée', op. cit., and commented:

'I find these observations so right and new, so fruitful, that I do not hesitate to accept them as one of the main chapters in the method to be applied in the training of the beginners. I have summarised the essential points in my notes on the creation of the School. This idea of renewal, of revitalisation, was truly at the heart of my thinking when I first turned towards improvisation. But the application of the method to the classical repertory, as a procedure for regeneration, belongs to Jouvet.

'Since then, I had the opportunity of explaining these ideas to Mme Lara of the Comédie-Française, and I was a little surprised to hear her say that it was the method used by Worms.[1] But, as a matter of fact, in his work with his students, Worms was using this method which we ourselves have often practised empirically. It consists of momentarily withholding the text from the student while furnishing him with a similar text with different words, or by saying: how would you say this to <u>yourself</u>? This is the search for something <u>natural</u>, sometimes at the cost of the dignity of the text.

'The method that Jouvet proposes goes much further. It puts the text out of the reach of memory and habit. And, so as not to strain the actor in his work, it invites him to make an initial try, a first outline of his interpretation, like the painter who first distributes his colours and divides the volumes into rough sketches before starting the definitive composition on his canvas. This problem must be resolved: work (or research) and the realisation [of a performance] should not work on the same materials.'

The idea for reviving the medieval '*tréteau*' was also discussed in detail in this correspondence. Jouvet was also studying stage architecture which subsequently enabled him and Copeau to engage in a lengthy exchange of letters with the American architect responsible for the reconstruction of the Garrick Theatre some 3000 miles away. And for the re-opening of the Vieux Colombier in Paris in 1919, it was the close collaboration of Jouvet and Copeau which resulted in the construction of the solid concrete stage with its fixed architectural features. Jouvet also designed a system of octagonal luminaires with different colour glasses rotating round a fixed-focus lamp: the first automated colour-change system in France.

His abrupt separation from Copeau in 1922 was the inevitable decision of the devoted apprentice desirous of making his own way. Although initially bitter, Copeau proved his admiration for his former student's qualities by turning over to him the company and repertory of the Vieux Colombier upon its closure in 1924:

'I hope that this example we are giving today, of co-ordinated efforts and solidarity in independence, may be followed by all those who, like us, have their hearts set on a sincere dramatic renewal. I would hope that, putting all detestable egoism aside, rising above personal success and often false originality for the sake of a common cause, all good labourers in the theatre would unite their talents and forces one day, not only to show the right path, but to reach and capture the great majority of the public.'

[Letter to Jouvet, 23 September 1924, in programme of the Comédie des Champs Elysées]

In honour of Copeau's seventieth birthday, Jouvet declared what was to become his final tribute:

'What homage does one give to a life and an activity which were a perpetual homage to theatre? All praise is insufficient. The most proper homage is the wonder we felt over the praise for Molière and Shakespeare which Copeau taught us, and the way he praised them.
'In the genealogy of French theatre, Jacques Copeau is in the

centre. As he linked, either contradictorily or directly, the Meiningens, Antoine, Stanislavsky, Appia and Craig, so he is now the link in our professional life.

'He dominated the contemporary theatre exchanges of the Vieux Colombier. He dominates those who followed him. Today, he presides.

'There is not an author or an actor who is not heir to his work and who is not indebted to him.

'Even those productions furthest from his own repertoire come from him.

'As for me, I owe him the most precious friendship of my youth.

'Like a few privileged men of my generation, I owe him everything.'

[*Les Nouvelles Littéraires*, 10, February 1949]

APPENDIX E: MICHEL SAINT-DENIS (1897–1971)

Copeau's nephew was the general secretary of the Vieux Colombier 1920–4, and was one of those who chose to join the School-cum-company when the Parisian theatre closed down. During his later, international career as a director and teacher, Saint-Denis never forgot his years of apprenticeship and, towards the end of his life, began to classify his uncle's papers for publication – a task which has been carried on into the Gallimard/*NRF* series of *Registres* in French and the present volume in English. We have taken the following texts from some of the extant correspondence between Copeau and Saint-Denis [M-H D] and from the latter's notes for an Introduction to such a publication.

'When I was growing up, Copeau was for me a sort of hero. He lived in Paris amid an exciting milieu of great literary and artistic people, and through his affection for me, I was able to meet many of them. My cousin, Marie-Hélène, five years younger than I, was one of my best friends, and we both shared a great enthusiasm for this enchanted world. I remember acompanying my uncle to various theatres when he was a drama critic. In 1911, he allowed me to attend rehearsals for his *Brothers Karamazov*, where I first saw Jouvet and Dullin. I myself nurtured a desire to write, and when the Vieux Colombier opened, I would attend as many performances as I could after school. At the start of the war, I remember when

Copeau returned to Le Limon after his visit with Craig, and the question of my career came up during dinner. It was then, for the first time, that I said I wanted to be an actor.'

But in July 1916, Saint-Denis was conscripted into the army; before leaving for the front, he wrote this impassioned note:

'Dear old uncle,
'What remains of our long conversation last Sunday is the thirst to know more, to understand more deeply. I can perceive the details well enough, but it is the whole picture that I should like to grasp, from the inside, its broad general concepts. You never told me about the series of experiences and indignities that led you to conceive this magnificent work, and it seems that it would be helpful to me. I too should like to feel the spirit of the work itself, not in its development, but in the abstract, and to share in this spirit. Raise me up to as complete an understanding as possible. Since I possess the faith and the *élan*, what more do I need? Am I not worthy of receiving your confidence? Teach me, little by little. Give me the orientation that I need. Let me be the dough in your hands. I should like to feel that you are shaping and tranforming me with your fingers. During the next three years that will separate me from direct action by your side, prepare me. [...]
Your Michel.' [10 July 1916]

Whenever possible, on leave in Paris, Saint-Denis was with his uncle, continuing those precious conversations. He was able to spend a few days helping to prepare the American tour, and later report his observations of the few theatrical events in Paris. Once demobilised, he wrote: 'Again, if you can find comfort in this, say to yourself that I am here, starting my life, waiting for your encouragement and anxious to work. I am waiting for you to make a start in my life.' [10 December 1918; published in *Registres IV*, p. 365]

From New York, Copeau replied:

'My dear boy,
'I hope that in a not too distant future, I shall have with me for the great work I am planning, and which has barely begun, only those I

love, trained by me, and who will devote themselves in full consciousness.

'Upon my return, I hope to find you ready. I shall ask much of
you. Do not let yourself be too joyful yet. <u>Do not flag</u>. Many
months will pass before you enter the life for which you are
waiting.' [29 January 1919]

And a few months later:

'You will have to be able, and there is where I shall put you to the
test, to concern yourself with the most humble, even tedious jobs.
In order to do that, you must shield yourself against the need for
<u>entertainment</u> that I find in almost all who tarnish their gifts. They
turn immediately to play and reject all need for effort. [...] If I
myself am worth anything, believe me it is above all because I
found myself, through force of circumstances, continually thwarted
in my upbringing. I have never done completely or exclusively what
I pleased. I have always pursued the same goal, yet I never followed
my natural inclination. That is why, though still young, I have such
a long past behind me. To such an extent that now, when I should
let myself go, I find it difficult to do what is most natural. I have
always done everything with all my heart. I can shell peas and take
care of a child; I can sweep the floor and arrange flowers. Automatically, I put as much of myself into a humble, material task as in
the highest artistic expression of which I am capable. [...] I should
like to stimulate this in those who follow me. I think it was this
kind of radiant consciousness, this transfiguration of matter by an
applied mind, that was the eminent virtue of the ancient workmen.
The very paving stones of a Gothic cathedral have a soul, as much
as the most beautiful sculptured figure in the portal or the choir...
Today you hear that the complications and feverish pace of modern
life do not allow us to work this way, and that the superior man
should only do what he cannot turn over to an assistant or even a
machine. Perhaps that is why today's superior men do not create
superior or lasting works, or at least beautiful ones. For the beauty
of a work is like God's breath on His creation.' [...] [Spring 1919]

Following his uncle's advice, Saint-Denis proceeded to learn all he
could about theatre from the ground up, sharing all the details of
the work during the first post-war season of the Vieux Colombier.

'My dear Patron,

'I have had the time now to think over what the last season meant for me. I thought about our talks. Obviously, the resolutions we made were not all precisely carried out. I believe, however, that I learned much in my contact with the stage. If, for me, my role and my craft might have seemed to be a little unrewarding, a little aimless, a little vague, at least I can believe that I have made a step towards working more freely on the stage. I have only just learned what it is, but it is enough for me to think about a better methodology founded on basic understanding. I still have to <u>practise</u> the craft very precisely, to practise it every day, strictly; I mean stage managing. I have to know about staging from the inside out. We shall talk about that. This was my inadequacy: it was <u>impossible</u> for me to direct rehearsals. I felt helpless, incapable of improving myself by an effort of intelligence and perseverance. There are many reasons for that. My helplessness came mostly from my ignorance of production and from the obscurity that prevented me from seeing the goal; consequently, it took away all my will to produce, through the lack of an overall conception. You know all that, and what work is still ahead for me so that my collaboration will be more satisfactory on this point. But I feel a great passion in me that says I must succeed. Personally, I could have felt disheartened, but I never felt I had gone astray, nor that I was not following my vocation.

Your Michel' [1 August 1921]

With his debut as an actor in a small role during the theatre's last season, Saint-Denis felt himself ready to assist Copeau closely when the company left for Burgundy. It was he who organised 'Les Copiaus', writing the first scenarios, and when Copeau took over the direction, Saint-Denis continued to write, direct and participate in the work of the school in Pernand. 'It was in Burgundy that I really learned the craft of acting and directing. I wrote two plays, but I was especially interested in the creation of a character named Knie, for which I made the mask with my own hands. When I left Burgundy in 1929, I felt I had learned the basic elements of theatre. The decade with Copeau had been remarkably rich for me.'

When Saint-Denis founded his own company, La Compagnie des Quinze, the following year, Copeau loaned them the stage of the Vieux Colombier and wrote a letter for the first programme, the premiere of André Obey's *Noé* (Noah):

'A new theatre company is setting itself up at the Vieux Colombier, on the stage where I worked for six years. It bears the arms of the two doves. No longer the ones we selected long ago from the pavement of San Miniato. These birds have changed position and have modernised their appearance a little. They are not from the same brood, but they are from the same cage. In this symbolic form, the *Quinze* bears witness to an affiliation. The question is, what is the nature of this affiliation? What is the precise link between the *Quinze* and the founder of the Vieux Colombier?

'Here is the answer: I opened a school in 1920 in order to train new actors, but especially to try out some methods which were meant, eventually, partially to renew stage work by extending the range of dramatic interpretation. I selected for this school the participation of young people who were willing rather than talented. Some very young people came enthusiastically. Some of them found themselves bound by the pleasure of the work, a professional attachment, and by the bonds created in time through a communal life. [...]

'Michel Saint-Denis did not belong to the school at the beginning. He shared its work from 1925, but right after the war he came to my side. As secretary-general at first, then as general stage-manager, Michel extended his activities to all aspects of theatre. In Burgundy, from 1924–9, he became little by little the captain of the young team, directing several plays and, by choice, became an actor, applying himself to a few experiments in improvisation. [...]

'What we have here is a *Company*. Its title is not ceremonial. It is very nearly the company, plus a few new recruits, which, under the nickname of the *Copiaus*, took its repertoire on the road into the villages of Burgundy and to several foreign stages.

'What have I done for this newly-formed company? First, I have made room for it to hatch and then let it soar. I have given them my concrete stage, supplied them with the backing of a few proven friends. [...] Then what? What has been my share of the work or inspiration in the play they are about to present? *Not any*. Nothing. Absolutely nothing.

'I did not attend one single rehearsal; I saw nothing, I said nothing. I await the première like everyone else. If it turns out well, it will prove that I have trained a little company able to stand on its own. That's all. If you think the shoot is hardy, you can say that the branch is not dead. [...]

'The Ark is ready; it is afloat. I am on the bank, waving with a branch that I picked in Pernand: proof of my confidence.

Pernand, 16 December 1930'

Saint-Denis recalled:

'We had worked ten years together. We had developed a lot of possibilities as a company: we were mimes, we were acrobats; some of us could play musical instruments and sing. We could invent characters and improvise. In fact we were a chorus with a few personalities sticking out rather than actors ready to act the usual repertory, classical or modern. [...] As actors we were sincere and resourceful; on the stage we gave the impression of being free, fresh and real. A critic in Paris wrote that we brought "nature" back to the artificial theatre world of that period. We took London by surprise and by storm. [...]

'During that period, 1931–5, I directed all the plays – there were about ten – given by the Compagnie des Quinze, and acted in most of them.

'In 1935, following the success of my company in London and its slow disintegration, I was asked to establish myself there. I drew up the plan of a school. The kind of actor I wanted was not to be found ready-made. Training and experiment seemed to me to be more important than the quick gathering together of a company without either meaning or unity. With the effective support of Tyrone Guthrie, the close collaboration of George Devine, and soon the help and friendship of Laurence Olivier, John Gielgud, Glen Byam Shaw, of Peggy Ashcroft, Edith Evans, Michael Redgrave, Alec Guinness, and of "Motley", I opened my first school, The London Theatre Studio, a private school.'

[From *Theatre: The Rediscovery of Style*, Theatre Arts Books, 1960, pp. 43–4]

After the second world war, Saint-Denis went on to found The Old Vic Theatre School and the Young Vic company, and later The Drama School in Strasbourg, The National Theatre School of Canada, the Stratford Studio of the Royal Shakespeare Company, and the Juilliard School of Drama in New York.

APPENDIX F: ANDRE BARSACQ (1909–73)

A student of architecture, Barsacq began his career with Charles Dullin, who entrusted him with the décor and costumes for the memorable production of Jules Romains' *Volpone* in 1928. He joined Michel Saint-Denis' Compagnie des Quinze in 1931, staging *Noé* and *Le Viol de Lucrèce*. Copeau's esteem for his work led to the request for him to design, in addition to the Florentine productions, three other plays for 'le patron' before joining Jean Dasté as Director of the Théâtre des Quatre Saisons in New York (1937–9). In 1940, Barsacq assumed directorship of Dullin's Atelier, where he produced a revival of Copeau's *Les Frères Karamazov* in 1946.

'I had the good fortune of working with Jacques Copeau at the time of his last experiments with outdoor staging, in 1933 and 1935 in Florence, and in 1943 in the courtyards of the Hospice de Beaune, the same hospice where he has just died after a long illness.

'These productions of his, almost unknown to the Parisian public, were nevertheless rare moments in dramatic poetry. Copeau, who was often hindered by the framework of traditional stages, was able to give free reign to his theatrical imagination and scenic invention which, in my opinion, were never more fertile, more extensively pedagogical of a theatrical art finally freed from the constraints of its accumulated habits.

'I can still see my old Master, standing in the middle of the Santa Croce Cloister [...] he is directing the actors. There are more than thirty of them. They are coming alive, slowly forgetting their bewilderment and letting themselves be won over by Jacques Copeau's *élan*. Through the sole magic of art, through the sole virtues of a penetrating sensitivity and a loving concern for old texts, a naive work was blooming, awakening a profound emotion, and acquiring a strange power.

'I worked with "le patron" by his side for the first time about twenty years ago. I discovered what was the import of his initiative, of his teaching and of his example. I discovered the sincerity of effort, the taste for candour and honesty in theatrical expression put to the service of poetry. [...] He taught us flatly to refuse easy solutions, the sleight of hand and deplorable habits which unfortunately still rage in our craft.

'Copeau's example stands for the vocation of beauty, for poetry and radiance in our theatre. Each one of us has received from him a little of this *élan*, this intoxicating joy, this ardour, which he awakened more than thirty-five years ago and which must not die out even after his death.

[From 'Témoinage', *Combat*, 22–3 October 1949]

APPENDIX G: JEAN DASTE (1904–)

In an article for the programme of the *Cahiers de la Maison de la Culture de Grenoble* (3 November 1945), Copeau wrote:

'Everywhere I see students of the Vieux Colombier, or students of its students. None is dearer to me than Jean Dasté. No other has been closer to the heart of the Vieux Colombier. Others, perhaps, have enriched their art more, proved stronger or more original; none with more love, fidelity and purity: Jean Dasté is like my son.

'This child of the people, at the age when he was starting out in life, murmuring the verses of the French poets, barely suspected his destiny. At fourteen he would go from school to the Châtelet Theatre, checking his school-bag with the porter, in order to rehearse his small role of mustachioed extra in *Michael Strogoff* or *Around the World in Eighty Days*. But that did not satisfy the hunger of his soul. The most cherished dreams of this young man were realised thanks to a young Russian colleague who told him of the marvels being performed at the Vieux Colombier. So he did not hesitate when his teacher, Jean d'Yd, also advised him to apply to the Vieux Colombier.

'Two years in the School in Paris, five years in Burgundy with the "Copiaus", three years in the Compagnie des Quinze, then the Compagnie des Quatre Saisons with André Barsacq, and the Saison Nouvelle Company, comprised various steps by which he perfected his craft. They allowed the man to become mature without becoming stagnant. He became the director of a company, earning the devotion of his colleagues by his humane qualities, his goodness, his generosity, and also his knowlege of his art and the quality of his mind, all without needing to impose himself by any offensive authoritarianism.

'Jean Dasté is a good workman. Everything in his life seems to have prepared him for the role he will now play. He is of the people, thus he knows, understands and loves them. He has had a professional education closely linked to his moral development. He has participated in many of the great events of the day and has been knocked about a bit. For several months he experienced the prisons of the Gestapo. And now he is here, on the verge of bringing to the Art of the Theatre what it lacks most: the experience of a good journeyman, the conscience of an honest man.'

Elsewhere, Dasté writes of his own debt to Copeau:
'It was at the Vieux Colombier School that I rediscovered the joy of acting. There were twelve of us, and most of the day was spent in inventing, improvising very freely, discovering characters and expressing feelings or emotions by the use of masks. [...]

'Jacques Copeau would come to see us, and we would show him our more or less finished exercises. Our research interested him very much. He would advise and encourage us, communicating his fervour for the theatre, speaking of the beauty of the actor's craft and also about its complexity; he would tell us about the great periods in the life of the theatre... It was in the Vieux Colombier School that I discovered the theatre I loved. [...]

'At the School, we did daily exercises with masks. In this way, Copeau wanted us to return to the spontaneity and talent for inventiveness and disguise that children have. When the face is masked or hidden, one is less timid, feels freer, more daring, and insincerity is quickly apparent. The first dramatic exercises I did with the mask were, for me, the discovery of a mysterious world. In the beginning, at the School, Copeau obliged us during certain exercises to hide our faces with a stocking over our heads, in order to help us liberate our bodies from all facial grimaces. The mask demands both a simplification and an extension of gestures; something forces you to go the limit of a feeling being expressed. If you are supple, if you have done acrobatics or dancing, the gesture takes on a greater dimension.

'Begun as a school exercise, a research, the mask allows us to see a world which could give an actor a whole new life. One thinks of the magic masks from Africa and Polynesia, of what the *commedia dell'arte* must have been on the planks of the public squares. We left behind us altogether the naturalistic way of acting, and yet the characters possessed a greater reality and a greater vitality. One must project oneself with passion, intensity, and always with a certain joy, which amounts to "freedom".

'Copeau believed he could see there the beginnings of some character parts, and this confirmed his desire to create a comedy of fixed characters taken from "types" in the modern world. (The creation of representative characters is part of the work being done today by Ariane Mnouchkine and the Théâtre du Soleil.)

'We not only did research with characteristic comic masks; we also would make masks with plain human traits we called neutral masks: two long openings for the eyes, allowing the spark of a true gaze to pierce through.

'We would make up very simple exercises with various themes: waiting, discovery, fear, anguish. Thanks to the mask we were penetrating further into a strange and mysterious world. One group made up the families of sailors, watching from the shore for the arrival of a boat. It has been shipwrecked; we wait; we realise that the sailors will not return. We are all carried away by a great emotion. It is the chorus. The force of this masked group astonished Copeau as well as all those who attended this exercise.'

[From *Voyage d'un comédien*, Stock, 1977]

'The profound aspiration of an actor, consciously or subconsciously, is to be other than what he is in daily life; "becoming" another allows him to live an intense human reality and to penetrate an unknown world.

'I have always kept the memory of a first "projection of the self"; we were playing Copeau's *L'Illusion* [...]. I was 22 years old and full of fire; I wanted to do too much and was never able to do it well. Always tense, never master of myself, voice a little hoarse, I articulated badly and spoke too fast, in the sincere belief I was living the part. I was playing the role of Calixte and, in the principal scene, I had to express the violent and blunt passion of the young man, followed by his despair at having been cruelly rejected. One evening, on tour, something happened within me: during my great love scene, without having prepared more than usual, I suddenly felt myself in control of my voice, my elocution and my gestures, as if in spite of myself. I was able to protract a movement, a silence, an intonation. I found myself in another "time", another space, another dimension. At the end of the scene, full of an immense joy, I went into the wings, all fired up. Jacques Copeau was waiting for me, took me in his arms, embraced me, and said: "Tonight you acted".

'All my life, thanks to my craft, I have always aimed to relive such moments. It feels as if one is being carried away by "something", not knowing how one will speak or act in that moment; however, one is absolutely in control, certain of not deviating from the truth of the character. The projection of the self is the "reality" the actor is looking for.'

[From *Qui êtes-vous?*, Jean Dasté, Lyons, La Manufacture, 1987]

From Grenoble, where he created a drama centre which included a school for actors, Dasté was named director of the Comédie de Saint-Etienne (1947–71), the first Centre Dramatique established under the post-war programme of decentralisation. In supposed retirement, he often gives poetry readings throughout France, most recently in the theatre of his daughter, Catherine, in Ivry.

APPENDIX H: JEAN DORCY (1895–1978)

Jean Dorcy is best remembered as the founder (in 1947) of Danse et Culture, a school of dance training whose pupils included Marcel Marceau and Yvette Chauviré.

'Before arriving at the Vieux Colombier School, I was what is known as a young actor. Neither better nor worse than other young actors. I had, like them, and from master to master, followed the path of the traditional training. I could tell my right arm from my left foot, and I knew how to play with my tie, my handkerchief and my key-chain. That was all my tangible equipment. I would have laughed if anyone had spoken to me of gymnastics. [...]
    'The Vieux Colombier School, first situated on the rue du Cherche-Midi, then in the very courtyard of the theatre, was a sacred place. No one, not even a member of the company, had the right to enter the school.[...]
    'The Vieux Colombier School consisted of seven girls and six boys [in 1922–3], leading the life of day-boarders and accepting a severe discipline.
    'Work clothes: gymnast's costume or overalls.
    'Start at 9 a.m., stop at 6 p.m. The two pupils on weekly duty, a boy and a girl, would arrive an hour earlier to do the chores: sweeping, washing up, cleaning tables.
    'Teachers: Jacques Copeau and Suzanne Bing (directors), Georges Chennevière, Albert Marque, Daniel Lazarus, Lucienne Lamballe, the Fratellinis. In my second year I was put in charge of acrobatics and the Hébert method of calisthenics. What I learned at the

Medrano Circus with the Fratellinis, I would teach to the other pupils.

'Subjects: theory of theatre, dramatic instinct, history of Greek civilisation, grammar, singing, music, sculpture, classic dance, acrobatics, calisthenics.

'All this was no visionary programme; it was quite truly practised with continuity. Each evening, the pupils would take home lessons and homework.

'It is important to note the consideration given to physical training, although it is not what makes up traditional actor-training. [...]

'For three and a half years, I received in all only sixty minutes of lessons from Jacques Copeau. I make an exception for his lessons in the theory of theatre (besides, I was the only pupil of the School allowed to attend this class which was reserved for the actors; Jouvet, Carette, Valentine Tessier shone by their pertinent remarks). At that time I considered this lack of classes from "le patron" all the more monstrous in that I admired his mastery. It is only now that I can understand: Copeau was taking care not to make orators of us. In addition he was afraid of developing our gift for imitation, which is nothing but a gift for mimicry.

'Jacques Copeau saw the direction our work was taking and, like us, he was unaware of how far it would go. He did not even try to influence our work. It was important for the director of the Vieux Colombier to observe our research from afar, as from an aeroplane, which is what he did.

'With the intuition of genius, Copeau sensed how close we were still to children's games, and he encouraged our inclinations, allowing us to invent and to develop our little dramas. It was in this laboratory that the mask was born.

'If one reflects that once the face is hidden, only the body is left to express our thoughts and make them understood, then one can appreciate the importance of this tool. [...]

'We had to find this instrument, the mask. In the beginning we fumbled about. We first covered our faces with a handkerchief. Then, from cloth, we moved on to cardboard, raffia, etc., in short all pliable materials. Finally, with the help of our sculpture teacher, Albert Marque, we found the desirable material as well as the necessary modifications to the form of this new instrument. Without Albert Marque we should have continued to make masks "small and pretty". A good mask must always be neutral: its expression depends on your movements. One of us, Yvonne Galli, had a talent for making them.

'After the material side came the exercises, the themes: these required months of constant research. We baptised our mask efforts: mime. We used to say "shoe" and not "put on" the mask. Why? As the mask must stick to the face, the muscular sensation of something that shoes – at least that is how I can explain it – was better then the sensation of putting something on. Hence the expression "shoeing the mask".

'Thus, this newest and most recent chapter of contemporary dramaturgy, the *Mask*, came out of the Vieux Colombier School.'

[From *A la rencontre de la Mime*, Jean Dorcy, Neuilly, Les Cahiers de Danse et de la Culture, 1958, trans. Robert Speller Jr and Marcel Marceau, *The Mime*, Speller, New York, 1961]

APPENDIX I: ETIENNE DECROUX (1898–)

Considered as the originator of contemporary mime, Decroux has given lecture-demonstrations throughout Europe and North America. He founded his first school in 1930, and was instrumental in establishing mime studies in several universities and theatre companies. Among his most famous pupils are Jean-Louis Barrault, Marcel Marceau and Alvin Epstein.

'It was in 1923, at Jacques Copeau's Vieux Colombier School, that bodily mime was first revealed to me. The essence of this art was there; it only remained to enrich it with divisional rules, to extend its intent, to limit it. [...]

'We obligatorily attended all the classes. To tell the truth, it never occurred to us that they could be optional. Even better! During my first year, Jacques Copeau did not give one single lesson. It was to the instructors, I think, that he gave them. [...]

'Bodily mime at the School was called the mask. Contrary to Chinese masks, ours was inexpressive. The body was as naked as decency would permit. An indispensable requirement, for once the face was cancelled out, the body needed all its members to replace it.

'We mimed modest actions: a man being bothered by a fly, trying to shoo it off; a woman, disappointed by a fortune-teller's prediction, strangles her; a trade; a series of machine-like movements.

'The exercise resembled slow-motion in the movies, except that where that is a slowing-down of fragments of reality, ours was the slow producing of a gesture in synthesis with many others. This already perceptible exercise was beautiful.

We would reproduce sounds of the streets, the home, nature, animal cries; all with the mouth, hands and feet. After a quick consultation – three minutes maximum – the pupils would make up a scenario and perform it on the spot. Only they knew what could or could not be expected of this type of exercise; they thus had to be their own dramatist. At the end of the 1923–4 season, they gave a performance before an invited audience.

'Being still in my first year of studies I was not allowed to participate.

'From my comfortable seat I saw an extraordinary performance. It was mime and sounds; the whole thing without a word, make-up or costume, without lighting effects, props, furniture or décor. The unfolding of the action was sufficiently skilful to represent several hours in a few seconds and several locations in only one. Simultaneously, we could see the battlefield and civilian life, the sea and the town. The characters moved from one to the other in a completely believable manner.

The exercise was moving, comprehensible, plastic and musical.

This was in June 1924.

The productions which are considered astonishing today [1939] do not surpass in any way what was done that day, and are often not as good. [...]

One of the studies at this school consisted of acting out short plays, many of them moving, without words, face unmasked, body almost naked. In this study of the mime, Jacques Copeau saw it as only part of spoken theatre, thus making sure the body did not betray the voice and so that when the actor had to remain still during the action, there was no disillusion.

'It was not long before I thought that this causal order of the two arts should be inverted: instead of seeing the mime as one of the preparations for spoken theatre, I saw the latter as one of the preparations for mime, it having been revealed, in action, as the most difficult.'

[From *Paroles sur le Mime*, Gallimard, 1963, pp. 13–19, 33, 87]

APPENDIX J: GIORGIO STREHLER (1921–)

Strehler's association with the Piccolo Teatro in Milan, of which he was co-founder with Paolo Grassi, began in 1947 and has continued, with a break of four years from 1968–72, into the 1980s. Among his outstanding productions have been two of Goldoni's *The Servant of Two Masters* which may be argued to complete the process of reconstruction and re-animation of *commedia dell'arte* begun by Copeau.

'The youth of today no longer want masters. They feel that they do not need any. They do not want to "owe anything to anyone". That is perhaps one of the first signs that, henceforth, I belong to a different world, a different "historic phase". But masters are necessary; with "methods" and relationships that differ from those of the past, but they are necessary. I have had three of them.

'The first is Jacques Copeau. I did not know him personally, but he is nevertheless one of my masters. I owe him much; I owe him something fundamental in my education as a man of the theatre, and which is not easy to define today. Let us try: Copeau, the severe, Jansenist moral vision of theatre. Copeau, the feeling of unity in theatre, the unity between the written word and its performance; actors, scenographers, musicians and authors forming a whole, even down to the least stage-hand. Theatre, a place where each one can, knows and must do the work of the others, some very well, others less well. Theatre as a "moral responsibility", like a fierce and exclusive love. The feeling of a fraternity among theatre people, not made up only of joy. An aching religious feeling of theatricality. Copeau firmly believed, not in an easy or ritual dogma, but in a kind of battle, almost cruel, between himself and the Other. So much has been said of his giving up the theatre and of the reasons for it! As for me, today I believe that, beyond what some of his students have told me, Copeau abandoned the theatre simply because he should have asked, in order to make theatre as he wanted it, something that God alone can ask of men.

'I am not a believer. But I do believe in this demanding "commitment" to life and to others; I believe in this unitarian theatre, in this theatre which is a wrenching of one's self and an absolute giving. I believe in the theatre which is done "on stage" for others and with their help. My vision of theatre is not "joyous" either, but attentive, severe, exclusive, painful in its search for order, honesty and truth – including laughter.'

[From *Per un teatro umano*, Giorgio Strehler, Milan, Feltrinelli, 1974]

APPENDIX K: MARIE-HELENE DASTE (1902–)

Marie-Hélène acted small parts and made some costumes during the Vieux-Colombier's seasons in Paris, as well as participating in the work of the School alongside Suzanne Bing and Louis Jouvet. She became an active member of 'Les Copiaus' in Burgundy, where she married fellow-pupil Jean Dasté. Together with Michel Saint-Denis they founded the 'Compagnie des Quinze'. After its dissolution in 1935, she pursued her career as an actress and costume-designer with Dullin, Baty and Jouvet. She joined her husband's company in Saint-Etienne after the war, then became one of the first members of the Renaud-Barrault Company in 1947, until her retirement in 1982. She states, simply,

> 'I am a child of the theatre, daughter of a great and authentic man of the theatre, whose teachings have made me an actress and a costume designer.' ['A propos du costume', M.-H. Dasté, *Théâtre*, Premier Cahier, Ed. du Pavois, 1945]

Here she recalls her childhood impressions of the first rehearsals of the Vieux Colombier company in the garden at Le Limon in the summer of 1913:

'This feverish activity delighted the children of the house. Through-out the summer they could be seen peering through the wire fence which they were forbidden to cross, avidly observing these adults on the other side who also seemed to be playing marvellous games.

'We would see Blanche Albane collapsing to the ground while our friends Jouvet and Dullin rushed to her side – and our papa? He seemed to be playing a nasty role in this game that we did not understand very well! Later we learned that these were rehearsals for *A Woman Killed with Kindness*, in which our father played the role of Wendoll, the seducer. In the evenings, put to bed early and not being able to fall asleep, we were fascinated by the tree outside our window. It was lit up as if by a flare from the light of the window beneath us, where our father and his collaborators were working on a translation of *Twelfth Night*. Their outbursts of laughter became quite fantastic for us as we became attracted to approach the window stealthily. We would see a kind of shadow ballet on the garden foliage and we could overhear entire scenes from Shakespeare's comedy. Then, our father, coming to the window to shake out his pipe, would look up towards us: "What's going on up there? Get back to bed!" There was a silence, followed by a scrambling to our beds, only to fall asleep as soon as possible so the night would pass quickly and we could awaken to another day when the festivities would resume in the garden where everybody was playing – adults and children alike.'

[From 'Le Ballet des Ombres', Marie-Hélène Dasté, *Nouvelles Littéraires*, 29 October 1959; reprinted in *Registres III*, p. 98]

Throughout the darkest years of World War I, when the Vieux Colombier was closed, Copeau maintained close contact with his actors in the armed forces in an attempt to keep alive what he termed 'the spirit of the Vieux Colombier'. The following excerpts from letters to and from the newly-married Jouvet reveal their mutual preoccupation with the coming generation as inheritors of their ideal:

August 1915

'My dear Jouvet,
'Maiène thanks you very much for your lovely letter which gave her great pleasure. You see, I have plans for this little girl. As soon as she is fifteen or sixteen, I shall make a real apprentice of her so she can learn etching and all about the art of drawing. In addition, I shall have her learn thoroughly about cutting and dress-making, dress materials, dyeing, and other things connected with costume and ornamentation. Thus, in eight or ten years, we shall have someone with us who will be *competent*. [...]'

22 August 1915

'Dear Patron,
'What you tell me about Maiène enthuses me more than I can say, as it is a task I should have liked, and one which I am planning for the son which will be born [...]! I shall make a good illuminator of him – patient, calm, gentle – with a regular standard of living, on a steadfast plane of joy – who will love the 'material' he uses with a scientific knowledge of it. [...] It is too bad there is such a great difference in ages between Maiène and 'Jean-Paul'.[1] [...]'

25 August 1915

'My dear Jouvet,
'My boy, my boy, your lovely letter brought tears to my eyes. Yes, I

wept gently as I thought of your friendship, your fervour, your gaiety, and of all that draws us slowly together, more and more. [...] You must feel I belong to you as you belong to me. Yes, a total communion – of the heart and of the whole being, for such an ardent work, as sacred as that of the medieval artists (and, like them, without pretention). My ambition for our work *has no limits*.

'In turn, my heart was pierced with joy by what you tell me of your future son. You are already dedicating him, ordaining him! [...] You promise your son. I offer my daughter.'

Two years later, preparing for the Vieux Colombier tour of America, Copeau wrote to his nephew, Michel Saint-Denis, then twenty years old and called up for military duty:

'August 1917

'Dear Michel,

'The other day my three children were here, and from the first day we could feel how much their presence has already charged the atmosphere. Later, there will be a veritable troupe of children; it will be the true source of all inspiration. Maïène is already quite grown up and serious; without saying much about it, I think she is already taking her future work to heart.' [...]

'August 1917

'Dear Uncle,

'You say that Maïène is already taking her future work to heart. I felt that in the long letter she wrote to me when she said: "There are three hundred costumes to be made before leaving [for New York], and they are making the material themselves by painting on cloth; it is wonderful. I am happy to be grown up so I can do all that."' [...]

[From excerpts from letters in *Registres III*, pp. 268–9 and *Registres IV*, pp. 138–9]

After the war, writing of his plans to his friend and long-time supporter Jean Schlumberger, Copeau explained the importance of his daughter's presence by his side:

'2 August 1919

'Dear Jean,

'*Vocation* signifies something very great and very difficult. The petty vanities of literary figures must be set aside. We must not wander round and round important things. We must constantly aspire to grandeur and be self-sacrificing. And I know that a generation can be raised in this religion, because my daughter is already completely devoted to it. She is able to do whatever I ask of her, and quite often I listen to what she is saying as a warning. Her judgements of my work go to the very heart of my inspiration. Sometimes, it happens that I say things which she alone understands. Ties of blood and mind, a multiplication of forces. Creation through love. These are not vain words. [...] On opening night in New York, my three children were beside me on the stage, in their street clothes, and I took Pascal in my arms to crown the bust of Molière. I assure you it was not theatre, but it was the only real thing in the whole performance.

[From letter to Schlumberger, op. cit.]

APPENDIX L: CATHERINE DASTE (1929–)

Interviewed by Gilles Costaz for the magazine *Acteurs*, just after her appointment as director of the Théâtre des Quartiers d'Ivry in the suburbs of Paris, Catherine Dasté (Copeau's grandchild, daughter of Marie-Hélène and Jean Dasté) gave the following account of her career to date:

'As a child, I was both fascinated and ill at ease. I remember my mother dragging me backstage at Dullin's Atelier. I didn't like it. When she would visit the Fratellinis backstage, I would say: "Why are you bringing me to see these men when they are no longer funny?" And I would tell her she was not beautiful without make-up. I thought to myself: *I* shall have children and I shall take care of bringing them up. This feeling of distrust lasted until I was seventeen. At that time I saw a Noh play marvellously produced by my mother, *Ce que murmure la Sumida*, and I acquired the taste for theatre. I went every night instead of preparing for my high school diploma – which I received nevertheless.

'[At that time I only wanted] to act. I had wanted to write when I was younger. But I never gave a thought to directing. Of course, my parents approved. As for my grandfather, I was afraid to tell him my decision. So, I arranged to speak to him in passing one day and I fled without leaving him time to question me. He did keep in touch with my early beginnings, and he died while I was in my first year at the Old Vic.

'My parents sent me to London because they thought it was the only good school. It had been founded and directed by Michel Saint-Denis in the spirit of the Vieux Colombier, but everything was in English! It was really a very complete schooling.

'After the two-year course, I joined the company at Saint-Etienne where my father had me act in the season's four productions. My first role was in Rojas' *Celestina*, in my grandfather's adaptation. I played the juvenile leads. I was very happy with my father; I simply felt a little bewildered by the style of work, acting with actors whose training was based on text. As for myself, I had learned improvisation, masks and physical training. Then I married and quickly had three children. I kept my promise and took care of bringing them up.

'[My husband, Gordon Allwright] was the first to return to the theatre, to direct the Tréteaux de Saint-Etienne, which my father had founded alongside the Comédie de Saint-Etienne. They wanted to put on a production for children, the first in a Centre Dramatique in France. I participated in it...

'That was in 1960. *Les Musiques magiques*... I was back in the theatre, but I wanted to reconcile my children's education and my artistic life, and this form of theatre allowed me to do it more easily.

'Thus [I founded the Compagnie de la Pomme Verte] in 1968, when Patrice Chéreau and Claude Sévenier asked me to settle in Sartouville, in the suburbs of Paris. [...]

'Sometimes my mother was our set designer. She designed our costumes, but she did not act. I don't like family rehearsals very much! However, it is something to belong to the Copeau family, which is like a gypsy family, and it is always important for me to please my mother, head of the Copeau dynasty. I feel the need to have my parents' blessing.

'My father always used to tell me: "A man of the theatre must always be able to pack his bags and leave, he never settles down." That struck me, and I'm convinced it's our case. Besides, it's what I did. Because of that, I feel both enthusiastic and detached. In the Copeau family we have a rich sense of inheritance, which prevents us from prizing a career or honours and which prevents us from being ambitious.

'[So] I left empty-handed, without lighting equipment or a tape-recorder and with no guarantee of subsidy; I had to repeat all the phases of applying for grants and so on, but it all went fairly quickly; with the election of the Left, we were accepted "unofficially". The name of the company [Folié-Méricourt] is that of the street where we settled, which pleased us.

'I wanted three things. First of all, to work in the theatre.

'Second, to establish links between the various arts. In the different fields of art, everyone is enclosed within his speciality. Bonds must be established with the poets, musicians, painters, cineasts. It's very difficult. At first it worked. Afterwards, people stopped making progress.

'Third, to be open to forms of theatre other than those I like. [...]

'Now, finally, I have a locale! Ivry is almost Paris, with its own identity, a local audience which we shall have to cultivate.'

In October 1989, the Ivry company visited Pernand Vergelesses to celebrate the Fête du Vin by performing a number of shows.

NOTES

INTRODUCTION

1 Copeau's choice of title can be traced to his great admiration for Molière, whose company history had been faithfully recorded by one of his actors, Charles Varlet LaGrange, under the same title of 'Registres'.

2 Published to date by Gallimard:
Registres I. Appels, notes by Claude Sicard, 1974, 360pp.;
Registres II. Molière, edited by André Cabanais, 1976, 365pp.;
Registres III. Les Registres du Vieux Colombier. I, notes by Norman Paul, 1979, 464pp.;
Registres IV. Les Registres du Vieux Colombier. II. America, notes by Norman Paul, 1984, 625pp.

The final volumes, *Registres V and VI*, are in preparation; Copeau's *Journal*, edited by Claude Sicard, is announced for publication at the same time as this anthology.

3 From *Souvenirs du Vieux Colombier*, Nouvelles Editions Latines, 1931, p.92.

4 *L'Ecole du Vieux Colombier*, Cahier no. 2, November 1921, *NRF*, 50pp.

1 THE CHILD AT PLAY

1 Translation of 'Un Essai de rénovation dramatique: le Théâtre du Vieux Colombier', *NRF*, September 1913; also known as 'manifesto'. 'Un Essai' has consistently been mistranslated as 'An Essay'. 'Attempt' is the correct and more revealing reading. Since we have quoted from it extensively in the present volume, we have not reprinted it in its entirety. The most recent reprint in French is in *Registres I*, pp. 19–32; an English translation by Richard Hiatt is available in *Educational Theatre Journal*, XIX (December) 1967: pp. 447–54.

2 Quoted in *Antoine and the Théâtre Libre*, S. M. Waxman, Cambridge, Mass., 1926, p. 128.

3 The first of several ensuing publications on Copeau's project for the school, 'Une école de comédiens', appeared in *La Semaine Littéraire*, Geneva, XXIV, 1166 (6 May) 1916: pp. 224–7.

4 From *The Birth of Tragedy* (1871). Copeau's interest in Nietzsche's works dated from his lycée studies and were shared by Gide and other members of the *NRF* group.

5 Founded in 1923 by two former students of Stanislavsky; Richard Boleslavsky and Maria Ouspenskaya, teachers of Lee Strasberg and Harold Clurman. Clurman (1901–81), co-founder of the Group Theatre, recalled later (*The Fervent Years*, New York, Knopf, 1945, pp. 16–17): 'Copeau's presence in New York acted as a catalytic agent in bringing Strasberg and myself together with the thought of forming a theatre of our own. [...] There was a moral cast to Copeau's appproach to the theatre, which might have been discomfiting to a dilettante, but which was good for us. ... It was a sense of the theatre in relation to society.'

6 Maria Montessori (1870–1952), Italian doctor and pedagogue, wrote in *Scientific Pedagogy* 1909 on her method: 'The great problem in education consists in respecting the personality of the child and in making him a free being.' Her first school was founded in Italy in 1907.

7 Pascal, Hedvig (Edi) and Marie-Hélène (Maiène). The latter recalls:

> He took us out on walks, followed by our pet dog, Filou – and he would soon take out his pocket notebook to jot down what we would tell him. We were not at all pleased. We would keep silent about what we did not want to tell, and embroider for his purpose what we did tell, which in any case was our own affair.
>
> On the other hand, he knew very well how to inspire us without seeming to, and to encourage whatever gifts we had without forcing them.
>
> I remember one day when he came upon me by surprise, as I lay crying on our 'thinking bed' (a divan we used for thinking) in the 'children's room'. That day I had failed in all my attempts to draw or to tell stories, and I was plunged in despair, convinced that it would last forever and that everything was over for good. That same evening, he brought me a brand-new sketch-book, larger than the others, a beautiful box of gleaming watercolours and some paint brushes made of marten bristles.
>
> As of the next day, everything was better than ever.
>
> He would point out the quarries in the area where we could find clay, suggesting that we try to model it. I started immediately by modelling the characters in the story I was writing. [Translated from 'Un Cahier de dessin tout neuf', *Théâtre en Europe*, no. 9, January 1986, p. 16]

8 For a full reading of Copeau's notion of the role of the 'Poet' see Part Two: 'The Poet in the Theatre'.

9 Edi was the nickname of Hedvig Copeau, later Mother Francis of the Benedictine Order in Madagascar. She recalls:

> One day my father made me a magnificent sword out of wood from a packing case – he carved it with his jack-knife, polished it for a long time with rounded pieces of glass. I was crouched by his side, watching over the manufacturing. I did not dare express the impatience that gnawed me; I was anxious to possess the

marvel, however the perfecting process that he was going through never seemed to end. He pared down the edges so well that my dear sword was becoming really sharp. Then he gave me two pennies to go to the tobacconist and purchase a ball of red string which he wound round the hilt in the form of a cross, after having coated it in strong glue. What a joy it was when he armed me with this sword, the like of which I had never owned in my life. Even at meal-times, my parents did not insist that I take it off. At night I hung it over my bed, so that it was the first thing that I looked at when I woke up. [Translated from a note in *Registres IV*, p. 512]

10 A reference to the first series of weekly sessions with children that Copeau undertook with Suzanne Bing and two former students of Jaques-Dalcroze. See 'Educating the Actor', note 8.

2 IDEAS IN COMMON: EDWARD GORDON CRAIG

1 From brochure printed by New York Drama League, 27 March 1918, 14pp. Copeau's chief American critic was the formidable George Jean Nathan, who had just written a scathing article, 'Les Fourberies de Copeau', in *The Smart Set* (February) 1918, reprinted in his *The Popular Theatre*, New York, Knopf, 1918.

2 Presumably a reference to the *Cahiers du Vieux Colombier* which Copeau intended to publish six times a year under the imprint of the *NRF*. In a publicity notice in a Vieux Colombier programme during the 1920 season he wrote: 'The *Cahiers du Vieux Colombier* will illuminate, complete and expand upon the work of the Vieux Colombier Theatre. They will dispel misunderstandings and explain future intentions. They will form a living bond between the artist and his public, an aid to coherence in the heart of that same public.' Pressure of work meant that only two issues were published: *No. 1, Les Amis du Vieux Colombier* (November 1920), *NRF*, 42 pp. and *No. 2, L'Ecole du Vieux Colombier* (November 1921), *NRF* 50pp.

3 In English in the text. Other instances are included in single quotation marks in the present translation.

4 Craig was forty-three at the time of their meeting.

5 G. K. Chesterton, *What's Wrong with the World*, London, Cassell, 1910, p. 40.

6 Ernest Marriott, in a brochure of 1913, *A Living Theatre. The Gordon Craig School. The Arena Goldoni. The Mask. Setting forth the aims and objects of the movement and showing by many illustrations the City of Florence, the Arena.*

7 Vincent d'Indy (1851–1931), founded the Schola Cantorum in 1896, where he taught composition.

3 EDUCATING THE ACTOR

1 'What is *cabotinage*?
    We no longer have a clear idea of what it is, we are so saturated and infected with it. [...] It is a disease which is not only endemic to the theatre. It's the malady of insincerity, or rather of falseness. He who suffers from it ceases to be authentic, to be human. He is discredited, unnatural. Outer reality no longer reaches him. He is no longer aware of his own feelings. Whenever they arise, somehow they become detached from his personality. [...] I am not only speaking of the 'so-called stars', of those phenomena, those poor monsters whose deformities are too obvious to require description. I am speaking of all actors, of the most unimportant of them and of his slightest gesture, of the total mechanisation of the person, of the absolute lack of profound intelligence and true spirituality.' [From an address to the Washington Square Players, New York, 20 April 1917, printed in *Registres I*, pp. 123–4]

2 *An Attempt at Dramatic Renovation*, op. cit.

3 Otto Kahn (1867–1934), a prominent New York banker and generous patron of the arts; founder and director of the Metropolitan Opera Association: sponsor of tours by many of Europe's most famous musical and theatrical artists. Kahn had selected Copeau upon their first meeting in 1917 to direct the failing French Theatre of New York and remained a faithful sponsor of the Vieux Colombier until its closure in 1924.

4 Dullin's own theatre and School, founded in Paris in 1921. See Appendix C.

5 Jessmin Howarth in a letter to Norman H. Paul, dated 19 July 1960. See 'Ideas in Common – Jaques-Dalcroze' for Copeau's assessment of Howarth's work. She later became assistant choreographer at the Paris Opera for three years, returning to New York in 1924 with the Gurdjieff Institute, whose methods she taught throughout the USA and Canada.

6 See Part Three, Chapter 15 'Towards a Popular Theatre'.

7 Elitism was, however, to be only a temporary expedient. For Copeau's later ideas on the theatre and its public see 'Towards a Popular Theatre'.

8 'Creation of the School in Paris.
    First step. Monday, 1st November 1915
    On several occasions, I already had had discussions about creating, at the rue de Vaugirard, a group of children who would prefigure a theatre school. The biggest difficulty was always the recruiting of the children.
    On Monday, 1 November, at 2 p.m., Paulet Thevenaz [a pupil of Dalcroze] presented one of his friends [Mme de Manziarly] to me, a woman of forty, Russian, involved in many charity works and enthusiastic towards the cause of children.
    In order to facilitate recruiting [she] advises not mentioning our real plans and simply opening, on the rue de Vaugirard, every Thursday to begin with, a sort of patronage institution interested in nothing but

entertaining children. Thanks to this slight subterfuge, she takes the responsibility of bringing us a dozen subjects. Later it will be possible to talk with the mothers about the aptitude of their little ones, thereby interesting and deciding a few of them. When spring comes, we can try to bring our little colony out to the country.

I accept this arrangement immediately so that something will exist. [...]

Second Session. Thursday, 18 November 1915

There are twelve children (four boys, eight girls, ages 6 to 14).

The two-hour session (much too long without a break) is broken down this way:

1. Gymnastic technique (Thevenaz)
2. Solfeggio (Lanux)
3. Rhythmic gymnastics (Thevenaz)
4. Games (Thevenaz)

Miss de Lanux' sister and Suzanne Bing attend as assistants.

I note that these first attempts are being made without funds. That is, the help I am receiving is absolutely gratuitous.

During the first session, I limit myself to observing the little pupils and, especially, their teachers. These latter are full of goodwill, gentleness and optimism, as well as having a deep faith. But they are flabby. No vigour. And when I speak to them, they think they have understood and answer: yes, yes, with a distracted and fervent air, even before being spoken to.

They do not understand what is being said.

Only Suzanne Bing understands what I want to do, and gives of herself to me with all her might.

From now on, Bing will take on the 4th part of the lesson, the games. And, every fortnight, when I am there, I shall take them over.

It is there, somewhere between the games and the rhythmic activities, that the initial starting point is to be found for a new method.

What we have done today lacks shape. The basis for everything is discipline. These little ones must be led in a military, but cheerful fashion.' [Entry in Copeau's Notebook, 'L'Ecole du Vieux Colombier', op. cit. There are notes by Copeau and Bing on seven sessions altogether.]

9 The offer to go to America pre-empted the development of this project. It did, however, lie dormant in Copeau's mind and eventually re-emerged in 1924 when he closed the Vieux Colombier Theatre and took his School to Burgundy.

10 'In attendance' were three actresses from the first season: Blanche Albane, Suzanne Bing, Jane Lory; four actors and actresses: Lucienne Bogaert, Madeleine Geoffroy, Jean Sarment, André Chotin, later engaged for the American tour; plus about a dozen 'auditors' and beginners. Albane, Bing and Lory rejoined the Vieux Colombier in 1920; the others pursued their careers in various Parisian theatres, notably Sarment as actor-director and dramatist.

11 Valentine Tessier (1892–1981) engaged in 1913, remained with the

Vieux Colombier until 1924, then joined the Jouvet company, becoming one of France's foremost actresses.

12 For a description of this character see Part Three, Chapter 13, 'Improvised Comedy'. Marcel Millet, actor during the two seasons in New York, later pursued his career in Paris.

13 One of the terms used by Copeau to describe his idea of 'Improvised Comedy'. See Part 3.

4   THE VIEUX COLOMBIER SCHOOL

1 Suzanne Bing (1885–1967), separated from the composer, Edgard Varèse, remained Copeau's principal collaborator throughout all the seasons of the Vieux Colombier, and continued to share in the work of 'Les Copiaus' in Burgundy until 1929. Later Copeau wrote the following letter of recommendation for her:

Suzanne Bing has been, even before the founding of the Vieux Colombier, one of the most faithful and precious of my collaborators. The work she accomplished often surpassed the capabilities, application and strength of ordinary women. She helped me through her faith, her work and her intelligence and her selflessness, and she represents more than anyone the spirit of the Vieux Colombier.

All the roles she acted under my direction, whether in Paris, New York or on numerous tours in France and abroad, carried her unforgettable imprint of sincerity, emotion, imagination and technical perfection. One of her most noteworthy creations was that of Viola in *Twelfth Night*. It was particularly noticed by one of England's great men of the theatre, Harley Granville Barker, who wrote of her that he had never seen a more accomplished actress since Eleonora Duse left the stage. [In *The Observer*, 1 January, 1922]

It was to Suzanne Bing that I turned for help in founding the Vieux Colombier School in 1921. Without her, my plan would probably never have come to fruition. For more than ten years, she took the heaviest share of a thankless task. To a certain extent, she sacrificed her own acting career and pushed herself to the very limit. Through her experiments, constantly performed and developed, she furnished me with the elements of a method of education of young actors.

As an instructor of diction at the Sorbonne and at the Lafayette School, in the leisure time the Vieux Colombier occasionally allows her, Suzanne Bing is today beginning a series of dramatic readings. She is fully qualified by her profound knowledge of the works, the suppleness of her vocal technique, her understanding of *mise en scène*, her human and poetic sensitivity, to attract an elite public who will delight in the high quality and instructiveness of her performances. [M-H D, no date]

2 This was the Children's School founded by Margaret Naumburg (Mrs Waldo Frank) to be known as the Walden School from 1918. She later wrote to Copeau that it was thanks to him she had discovered the importance of improvisation in children's games and had incorporated it in her curriculum. [*The Child and the World*, New York, Harcourt & Brace, 1928, pp. 304–5]

3 Jules Romains (1885–1927), founder of *Unamisme*, author of *Dr Knock* (1923) and the *roman fleuve*, *Hommes de Bonne Volonté* (1932–47).

4 Copeau's daughter, Marie-Hélène. See Appendix K.

5 Georges Chennevière (1884–1927), poet and friend of Jules Romains.

6 The staff were recruited from among the friends and collaborators of the Vieux Colombier and the *NRF*. Of those not mentioned elswhere in this anthology, Romain Bouquet, André Bacqué, Georges Vitray and Line Noro were members of the Vieux Colombier company: Marthe Esquerré, designer and teacher; Louis Brochard, Daniel Lazarus, Garcia Mansilla, Jane Bathori-Engel, singers and musicians; Lucienne Lamballe, ballerina at the Paris Opera; Emile-Albert Marque, sculptor; Ruppert and Suzanne de Coster, designers.

7 In 1913–14 Copeau had asked Henri Ghéon to organise two series of twelve matinées, each preceded by a lecture. Copeau approached Romains to organise more poetry recitals in 1922: ten Thursday matinées of readings were given by actors from the company and pupils from the School between December 1922 and May 1923, covering the whole history of French poetry from Villon to Cendrars.

8 Swinburne's *Atalanta in Calydon* was the work that first brought him celebrity. His third play, in classical Greek form, with choruses, it must have attracted Copeau's attention in his quest for renewal of the choric mode (see Part Three, Chapter 14, 'The Chorus').

9 All of these authors or literary critics belonged to the *NRF* group and many of their Vieux Colombier lectures were subsequently published.

10 A play by André Gide, published in 1903, but not performed until June 1922 at the Vieux Colombier.

11 Copeau is relying heavily here on Arthur Waley's introduction to the *Noh Plays of Japan*, first published in 1921.

12 In 1930 Copeau was able to witness the work of a traditional Japanese company for the first time. Afterwards he wrote:

> Tojukiro Tsutsui, I am told, is the Japanese equivalent of a provincial company. His 'Kabuki' repertoire is facilely adapted to please a foreign tour and does not represent at all that which is the purest and most elevated in Japanese drama. Tsutsui comes here from the US, where he undertook the production of enormous stage settings and allowed himself to be rather ill-advised. In addition, under the guise of modernism, he introduces into his art a dangerous naturalistic tendency, injecting between the powerful plays of his repertoire a few 'sketches' of a rather doubtful taste. But with all that, in spite of and perhaps because of that, we see in Tsutsui's productions, in his staging principles, in the natural solemnity of his performances, in his own interpretation and that

of his actors, the living outline of an incomparable artistic tradition. Neither the action nor the interpretation is indecisive or ordinary. His continuity is absolute, like that of life, but is sculpted in a way that makes it stand out appealingly. There is not a shadow of affectation or of pretence which is not sustained by the talent of the actor, absorbed into the action with a naturalness so that even the most towering rages do not trouble us. The least actor, even when he has only three or four lines, never makes a mistake in his bearing, his demeanour, his tone of voice or in the pitch of his cue-line. He is entirely in control of both his muscles and his legs, as well as of the slightest facial expression. His immobility and his silence possess an expressive intensity which never leaves the spectators indifferent, and constantly holds their attention without provoking it in a tactless or gratuitous manner. The most insignificant actress, when she has to make a hurried, running entrance, preserves the rhythm, never taking more than the required number of steps, in descending order, with her resonant sandals, and never going beyond the precise place on stage where she should stop. Many more examples could be cited, describing in detail each of the gestures and details of the drama, but I prefer to condense my praise of these actors into a few words: they are saturated with drama, music, dance and speech. They interpret the drama religiously.

In order to judge the worth of these actors, they must be seen in the wings, behind the scenes, while the play is going on. That is where I was best able to observe their personality and the nature and quality of their talent. Touchingly, I realised that they recognised me as one of their own. I saw by their knowing smiles that they understood me from the moment when, one evening, at the Théâtre Pigalle, I stood on the stage, leaning against the little collection of drums which accompany their movements and voices. From that position I watched for a long time the demeanour of the actors as they exited and prepared to go on stage. What order! What silence! What modest conviction! What passionate reserve! No artificially-induced excitement or preparatory contortions, nor any of those insolent grimaces, those bravura expressions, that know-it-all pretence which most of our Western actors take on as soon as they come off stage, congratulating themselves on having finished their part and making fun of the character they have just played. Here, on the face of the least important actor, one sees only the obedience, the fervour, the habit and the power of concentration. They are all imbued with their role and nurse the inner preparation of its movements well before they appear and offer it to the public. One of the youngest and the best, in my opinion, Kiyoshi Mismau, says a short prayer before going on stage. So it is not surprising that with such actors, so well integrated in their function, a mere glance is enough to make themselves understood, a gesture is enough to awaken the most complete and elevated dramatic action.

This perfection is due to the fact that all have studied the sacred

'Noh' and been influenced by this musical and choreographic art which is one of the purest expressions of the soul ever known.

This reverence which the Japanese actor professes before the majesty of the performance, before his own dignity, and the superiority of the act he accomplishes, appears in his least actions, not only on stage but also off, in the care which he takes in choosing his properties, his costume, his wig, his ornaments, in the ritual courtesy and respect towards his elders and the head of the company. Late that night, in Tsutsui's dressing room, while I was attempting to communicate by gestures my appreciation and respect, I saw how, one by one, all the actors came in before leaving the theatre to make a low bow before their master. [From 'Disciplina escénica', *La Nación*, 23 November 1930]

13 The public performance of the Vieux Colombier School's version of the Noh *Kantan* for which this programme note was preparatory, did not eventually take place since one of the leading actors, Aman Maistre, sprained his knee. The play, translated and adapted by Copeau and Suzanne Bing from Arthur Waley's English version, was given a dress-rehearsal in early March 1924, in the presence of Copeau, Gide and Granville Barker. The latter, who had first visited the school the previous year, was greatly moved by the performance: 'He told me and the students', Copeau noted in his Journal (18 March), 'that full of doubt up to now about the possibility of a drama school, today he was convinced that only on this foundation could a work of dramatic art emerge, and that if three years of work gave this result, in ten years we would be capable of any kind of production.'

Returning to his hotel, Granville Barker wrote to Copeau: 'I wanted to make it even clearer than enthusiastic words will, how impressed I was by that rehearsal. [...] Now what I saw on Tuesday has life in it – that's the first thing. [...] The Moscow people have it as well – that for second. And it leads me on to the third, which is, of course, that while the Noh was in itself as complete and beautiful thing of its kind as I have ever seen (Oh! falling short of perfect execution of course, but *right* always in intention), what stirred me was that I could see the future in it. And that, when one has seen so many successful vanishing "presents", is what cheers me. [...]

I hope that you will find things *native* for them to do. The Noh has the advantage of things strange – one can make it more objectively complete and detached – can isolate it from life as we see and interpret it. But there's a danger here, we need convention. But our own convention. This leads us though into deep waters.' [M-H D]

14 Prénat, a long-time admirer of the Vieux Colombier, collaborated with Henri Ghéon in 1924 to found the Compagnons de Notre Dame.

15 365 seats.

5   IDEAS IN COMMON: EMILE JACQUES DALCROZE

1 The son-in-law of the founder of the Théâtre des Arts, Jacques Rouché.
2 *The Eurhythmics of Jaques-Dalcroze*, introduced by Prof. M. E. Sadler, Boston, Small Maynard & Co., 1913, 66pp.
3 'Igor Stravinsky on the podium, making a horrible face, stops the musicians, mops away his perspiration, wipes his steamy glasses, and red-faced, eyes popping, leans towards the orchestra, menacingly polite: "Please, gentlemen... We cannot do as we please... It's constructed... do you understand? *It is con-structed!*" He repeats this complaint, this advice, this plea, at least twenty times during the rehearsal: It is constructed, gentlemen!... [...] Dramatic masterpieces worthy of the name are no less constructed than musical masterpieces.'
  [From 'El teatro moderno y la interpretacion de la obras maestras', *La Nación*, 21 July 1929]
4 'Realise' is used in rhythmic gymnastics in the technical sense of 'express by movements of the body'.
5 After his years of experience as a theatre critic, Copeau summed up his distaste for star performers in his 1913 manifesto: 'As for the Boulevard theatres, they belong to the great "stars" who force directors into ruinous expense, alter the balance of the interpretation, draw all the audience's attention to themselves rather than to the play, and force the authors to bend their talent by writing plays which show them off to best advantage.'
6 See 'Educating the Actor', note 8.
7 Translation of collection of Dalcroze's articles, published in New York, G. P. Putnam's Sons, 1921; reprinted, New York, Arno Press, 1976.

6   THE PROBLEM OF THE ACTOR

1 Lee Strasberg: *Strasberg at the Actors Studio*, ed. Robert H. Hethmon, New York, Viking Press, 1965 (quoted in Cole and Chinoy (eds.) *Actors on Acting*, New York, Crown, 1970, p.624).
2 See Part One, Chapter 4, 'The Vieux Colombier School in Burgundy'.
3 Denis Diderot (1713–1784) – his ideas on acting, formulated in his celebrated brochure, *Le Paradoxe sur le Comédien* – to which Copeau wrote his 1929 Preface – were part of his broader thinking on theatre. In a dogmatic manner he insisted that the actor must be devoid of sensibility. Not without influence on Diderot was his acquaintance with David Garrick when the latter visited Paris in the winter of 1764–5. Diderot greatly admired Garrick, impressed by the latter's ability to sit in a drawing room and entertain friends by letting his face run through the gamut of emotions without feeling anything himself. Diderot's *Paradoxe* became the source of a long-standing quarrel between the emotionalists and the anti-emotionalists, and the dispute was continued by the elder Coquelin, who ranged himself with Diderot.

Their debate precipitated William Archer's study of emotion in acting, *Masks or Faces?*.

4 Copeau reviewed a performance of Ibsen's *Ghosts* at the Theatre Royal in Copenhagen. In an interview with the leading actress playing Mrs Alving, he learned that she had a great antipathy to the play and difficulty in feeling her role:

> Thus she had to force her intellect and all that was most deep-seated in her nature. She had to struggle against her physical resources: her attitude, appearance, and voice. She had to lose all of her habits. This was precisely the opportunity for her to become a great artist. She did not succeed. She gives a certain coldness to the grandeur of the character, and vainly seeks the true emotion through arbitrary pantomime full of irrelevant manner-isms. I could perhaps sum up my criticism by saying that the actress lacked that certain *inner authority* which the character had achieved in solitary practice. [From *Revue d'Art Dramatique*, April 1903]

5 *Eckermann, Conversations with Goethe*, 'Feb. 26, 1824'.
6 'And it is about time, as in the old song,
To leave this century behind or to conquer it!'
[Alfred de Musset: *'Une soirée perdue'*, 1840]
7 Letter from Charles Dullin, 'At the front', 15 January 1917, published in *Registres III*, pp. 373–4]

7   SCENIC ARCHITECTURE

1 From 'La mise en scène', Encyclopédie Française, December 1935, 17/64, pp. 1–5; translated as 'Dramatic Economy', in *Directors on Directing*, Cole and Chinoy (eds), Indianapolis, Bobbs-Merrill, 1963.
2 Elisabeth S. Sergeant, 'A New French Theatre', *The New Republic*, New York, 21 April 1917, an interview with Copeau; almost the exact words he wrote in an unpublished notebook, 'L'Art du Théâtre', November 1916, M-H D.

8   IDEAS IN COMMON: ADOLPHE APPIA

1 Jaques-Dalcroze's theatre at Hellerau, where stage and auditorium formed a single continuous space, was designed by Appia and was the venue for two influential festivals in 1912 and 1913. Gluck's *Orpheus* was the most successful production in the 1913 Hellerau Festival. A showcase for Appia's ideas on design and lighting, it was acclaimed by, among others, Stanislavsky, Reinhardt, Claudel, Pitoëff, Granville Barker and Shaw.
2 See Part Three, Chapter 13 'Improvised Comedy'.
3 Michel Baron (1653–1729), Molière actor. Madame Marie Champmeslé (1642–98), tragedienne.
4 Diderot 'Second entretien sur *Le Fils Naturel*' (1757).

9 THE POET IN THE THEATRE

1 'Confidences d'auteurs: au Vieux Colombier', lecture, 3 February 1933, to Societé des Annales, published in *Conferencia*, 1 April 1933, op. cit.
2 'La scène libre au gré des fictions...', in Mallarmé's *Divagations*, Fasquelle, 1897, from a review of a performance by Loie Fuller.
3 Copeau discusses several other authors at this point: we have included only his comments on those likely to be familiar to the English reader.

10 THE DIRECTOR

1 Ermete Zacconi (1856–1948), outstanding Italian actor who founded his own company and, with Duse, was instrumental in bringing Ibsen's works to Italy. He was the leading actor in the 'verist' school, noted for his versatility, both in the classical repertoire and in contemporary roles.

11 THE PUBLIC

1 From 'An Attempt at Dramatic Renovation', op. cit. The quotation by Copeau is from Mr Archibald Henderson, *à propos* Granville Barker's Court Theatre in London (now the Royal Court).

12 MOLIERE

1 From 'Notice', vol. 1, Cité des Livres, 1926; reprinted in *Registres III*, p. 117–21.
2 At this point, Jouvet notes, Copeau read from the text (and, presumably, gave a physical illustration).
3 During his second term as director of the Odéon (1906–14), Antoine had put on three Molière plays.
4 Copeau is quoting from a lecture given by Antoine, published in the *Revue de Paris*, 1 April 1903.
5 'Stanislavky's *mise en scène* is unnecessarily realistic. In order to explain Scapin's sack, Stanislavsky puts a boat loaded with grain sacks at the back of the set, from which Scapin borrows the prop in the sack scene.' Remark noted by Louis Jouvet in his *Mise en scène des Fourberies de Scapin*, op. cit., p. 21.
6 A probable reference to Max Reinhardt.

13 IMPROVISED COMEDY

1 Giorgio Strehler and Paolo Grassi founded the 600-seat Piccolo Teatro in Milano in May 1947. Strehler's 1950 production of Goldoni's *A Servant of Two Masters*, with Marcello Moretti as Truffaldino and masks by Donato Sartori, was to be a watershed in terms of faithful reconstruction of the *commedia*. After an absence of five years, from

1968 to 1973, Strehler resumed direction of the theatre and Grassi left to direct La Scala. [See Appendix J]

2 'La Mort de Stanislavsky', *La Nación*, Buenos Aires, 6 November 1938.

3 From: *The Journals of André Gide, III*, New York, Knopf, 1949, p. 139, translated by Justin O'Brien: entry dated 15 January 1931. Gide, after twenty years of self-imposed exile from the stage, accepted Copeau's proposal to produce *Saul* (written in 1903) for the 1921/2 Vieux Colombier season.

4 A detailed account of these discussions can be found in *Registres III*, pp. 318–49, 424–45.

5 From 'In Wigs and Things', by Heywood Broun, in *New York Tribune*, 25 February 1917. *Canary Cottage* was the first production at the new Morosco Theatre, book by Oliver Morosco and Elmer Harris, music by Earl Carroll.

6 Max Dearly (1874–1943), was a popular Music Hall entertainer who perfected the character of a phlegmatic Englishman. In a letter to his wife (January 1916), Copeau wrote: 'This evening, went to the theatre with Gide, to see an English farce with Max Dearly. I believe that I really like nothing more in the theatre than farce.'

7 In the winter of 1846, a group of cultured people comprising the novelist George Sand and some of her family and friends decided to pass an evening acting charades. Over the next few years these divertissements grew and centred on rediscovery and re-animation of the Italian comedy, developing first into a little theatre, then a puppet show and finally into a book by her son Maurice (1862, translated into English as *The History of the Harlequinade*, London, Martin Secker, 1915).

8 Henri Ghéon (1875–1944), member of the *NRF* group, wrote two plays for the Vieux Colombier: *L'Eau de Vie* (1944) and *Le Pauvre sous l'escalier* (1920).

9 Roger Martin du Gard (1881–1958) had made a start with a farce entitled *Hollé-Ira!*, which he showed Copeau, instigating this detailed critique. The following year, the novelist abandoned the project and turned his efforts to the composition of his saga, *Les Thibault*.

10 A typical French rustic character, akin to the medieval English figure, Hodge.

11 No text of this scenario has been discovered.

12 A month later Copeau developed this idea in his *Journal*: 'In this new Comedy there will be, perhaps eventually emerging from myself, surely if I have time to think about it, a character who is never seen, who will become well known, of whom all the other characters will speak, each giving his own opinion. He will decide all ideas and actions. He will influence the dramatic events. When I say that he will never appear, I am mistaken. He will appear sometimes. It will be me. But no one will know, when I appear, that I am the character of whom everyone is speaking, and what I do and say will not in any way reveal the enormous psychological complexity created around my name by the character's remarks. No, I shall not show it. I will be called by name when spoken about, but as soon as I appear I shall no longer have a name. What is the use of a name for he who is present? To those who

ask my name, I shall reply: Have your little joke! But you know me well enough...'

13 This description of the illusion/reality dichotomy prefigures the enormous success of Pirandello on the French stage in the inter-war years. Two years later, some biographers state, Copeau was given first option on production in French of *Six Characters in Search of an Author*, which he declined as being insufficiently interesting. If so, though the present editors have found no evidence for the assertion, one might speculate that Pirandello's vision was in fact too close to Copeau's own not to interfere with it. His preoccupation later surfaced in the Copiaus' production of *L'Illusion* (1926). Claude Sicard, editor of the Copeau-Martin du Gard correspondence [op. cit., p. 319], gives the following gloss to this passage:

> In this lengthy analysis, we can observe that Copeau is delineating the image of an 'anti-theatre', comparable to Diderot's 'anti-novel', of an open theatre capable of questioning all the established 'truths', beginning with the very aesthetics of drama. A realism which doubts itself in order to reach a more general efficacy. One is reminded of Giraudoux's famous formula, for whom theatre 'is to be real in the unreal'. [*Impromptu de Paris*, 1937]

14   THE CHORUS

1 From the 5th lecture in the Little Theatre, New York, op. cit.
2 Interview with Mme Bresinhan for her thesis (1951), quoted by Clément Borgal, *Jacques Copeau*, L'Arche, 1960, pp. 283–4.
3 ibid., p. 282.
4 Suzanne Bing had played the role of Viola in *Twelfth Night*.
5 A deformation of the French word *besogne*, meaning hard work.
6 A character invented by Michel Saint-Denis, half peasant vine-grower, half god of wine, he gave prologues before performances by the Copiaus.
7 Friedrich Wilhelm Foerster, *L'Europe et la question allemande*, Paris, Plon, 1937 (in translation). From notes in JC's Journal dated 8 August 1938, ref. Foerster pp. 1, 5.

15   TOWARDS A POPULAR THEATRE

1 Leonard C. Pronko, *Theater East and West*, University of California, 1967, p. 137.
2 The post-war Socialist government of France, desirous of restoring the cultural eminence of the nation, revived the idea of breaking the monopoly of the Parisian elitist and commercialised theatre by a policy of providing support to the creation of provincial companies. In January 1947, under the inspired direction of Jeanne Laurent, Under-Secretary of Arts and Letters in the Ministry of Education, subsidies

were given to the first two Centres Dramatiques: the Comédie de l'Est in Strasbourg, founded by André Clavé the previous year (he was succeeded by Michel Saint-Denis, 1953–7), and the Comédie de Saint-Etienne, founded by Jean Dasté, who had moved to that city with his Comédiens de Grenoble, founded in April 1945. The year 1947 also saw the creation of the Festival d'Avignon by Jean Vilar, later the first director of the Théâtre Nationale Populaire. The policy of decentralisation continues today under the direction of the Ministry of Culture which subsidises some dozen Centres Dramatiques and, since 1963, about twenty Maisons de la Culture, and innumerable small touring companies throughout France.

3 Ghéon founded the Compagnons de Notre-Dame in 1925, for which he wrote several plays in the tradition of the medieval mysteries and miracles. Some of the companies he inspired include the Compagnons de Saint-Lambert in Brussels; the Compagnons de Saint-Laurent in Montreal; and the Vlaamische Volkstoonel in Amsterdam. Léon Chancerel (1886–1965), dramatist and director, sometime associate of Copeau from 1920–5, founded the Comédiens Routiers in 1930 in association with the Scout movement. In 1935, he founded the Théâtre de l'Oncle Sebastien for the production of plays for children, written or adapted by himself. In 1948 he founded the *Revue d'Histoire du Théâtre*. Two of his pupils, Jean-Pierre Grenier and Olivier Hussenot, founded their own company in 1941 and pursued a successful career until 1965.

4 The Roman amphitheatre in Orange was restored in 1888 for the presentation of revivals of French classic drama and operas during annual summer festivals.

16 SACRED DRAMA

1 Eric Bentley, 'Copeau and the Chimera', in *In Search of Theatre*, New York, Knopf, p. 245.

2 Introduction to *Port Royal and Other Plays*, New York, Hill & Wang, 1962.

3 From 'Lettres de jeunesse à Léon Bellé. 1894–1912', *Mercure de France* (November, December) 1954: pp. 414–44, 606–29. The quotation is from Alfred de Vigny's *Chatterton* (1835), III, vi.

4 Published in 1897; translated by Dorothy Bussy, *Fruits of the Earth*, London, Secker & Warburg, 1949.

5 Earlier in the same year, in the midst of a second and particularly hectic season in New York, beset by dissensions among his actors who were anxious to return to a France now at peace, Copeau had written in his Journal (29 January):

> Discipline – means: no answering back. Do not disturb the thought of the leader. You may voice an objection which he will consider fair in itself and momentarily obscure all his vision. The objection may be valid as pertains to discipline, but not to intention. You should support the will of the leader. Then you will be sharing the command.

Discussion, at rest, leisurely. Improvement through discussion, explanation, interpenetration. But while in action, no criticism, no arguments, no answering back.

One must not disturb the man who is thinking and developing his project. Try to see what he sees. But do not question him. Conrad's man at the helm: 'By Heavens, sir! I can steer for ever if nobody talks to me!' [*Typhoon*]

Destroy that brood of parliamentarians, not one of whom has the experience of command. Give them an occasional opportunity at command.

No collaborators, or counsellors; only assistants.

6 An adaptation of a fourteenth century Miracle play, *Pierre le Changeur, Marchand*, published in *Nos Spectacles*, nos 49–50 (May-August) 1956: pp. 84–135. Manuscript and programme in F.C.
7 Joseph Samson – Choirmaster of Dijon Cathedral.
8 Jean Dasté (born 1907) – see Appendix G.
9 André Barsacq (1909–73) – see Appendix F.
10 Louis-Noël Latour, wine-grower from Aloxe-Corton.
11 Agnès Thomsen Copeau (1872–1950).
12 Catherine Dasté (born 1929) – see Appendix L.
13 The town of San Miniato, not to be confused with the church in Florence.
14 Lamennais, quoted by Dom André Mocquerau. [JC's note]

17 AN APPEAL TO THE YOUNG

1 From an open letter to the Swiss press, op. cit.
2 Jules Delacre (1883–1945), founded the Théâtre du Marais in 1922, taking much of his repertoire from the Vieux Colombier, whose *tréteau* he reconstructed with the aid of Jouvet.

Also, unbeknown to Copeau at the time of writing, in Algiers, a fervent young communist writer, Albert Camus, had the previous year (1936) founded a small acting company, the Théâtre du Travail. The following year he broke with the Party and formed the Théâtre de l'Equipe, issuing a manifesto entitled 'A Young Theatre', in which he quoted Copeau: 'Of the theatres whose watchword is work, research and daring, one can say that they have not been formed to prosper, but to last without becoming enslaved.' The new company declared itself to be popular, non-political and non-religious, offering low-price subscriptions and a free programme. Its first season included plays by Gide, Vildrac, Synge and Copeau's adaptation of *Brothers Karamazov*. In the meanwhile Camus worked on his *Caligula*, which was not produced until 1942 (in Paris). Interviewed about the source of his interest in theatre, Camus replied: 'The story of the Vieux Colombier and Copeau's writings first gave me the urge and the passion for the theatre. I created the Théâtre de l'Equipe under the aegis of Copeau, and I borrowed a part of his repertoire. I still believe that we owe him the reform of

French theatre, and that that debt is inexhaustible.' [*Paris-Théâtre*, no. 125, 1938]

In a brochure for a Copeau exhibtion at the Théâtre de France, Camus wrote: 'In the history of French theatre, there are two periods: before Copeau and after Copeau.' [1959]

3 Jean-Louis Barrault began his career as a student of Charles Dullin at the Atelier, and was engaged by Copeau at the Comédie-Française, where he starred in Corneille's *Le Cid*. After the war, Barrault and his wife, Madeleine Renaud, formed their own company. On the death of Copeau, Barrault wrote: 'For those who, like myself, belong to the generation too young to have known the Vieux Colombier, Jacques Copeau's power is, above all, one of radiance, thus it is the most *alive*. Copeau was the *seed* from which we have all grown and it will remain alive as long as we live.' [*Combat*, 22, 23 October 1949]

APPENDIX A   ANDRE ANTOINE

1 Copeau had just turned sixteen.

APPENDIX C   CHARLES DULLIN

1 Arsène Durec (1880–1930) played the role of Ivan, the part that Copeau would later take as his own in hundreds of performances at the Vieux Colombier. Durec's proposal for founding a big theatre with Copeau in 1912 was not accepted by the latter.

2 Published in *CRB*, VI, (1954), and in Dullin's *Ce sont les dieux qu'il nous faut*, Paris, Gallimard, 1969.

3 See Part Three, Chapter 13, 'Improvised Comedy' and *Registres III*, pp. 323–49.

4 Firmin Gémier (1865–1933), director and theatre manager, had created the role of Ubu (1896), successively managed several theatres, later created the Théâtre National Ambulant (1911), the first touring company which foreshadowed the French national decentralisation project in 1947.

APPENDIX D   LOUIS JOUVET

1 Mme Louise Lara (1876–1952); Gustave Worms (1836–1910), actor of the Comédie-Française from 1877 to 1901; professor at the Conservatoire, 1901–10.

APPENDIX K   MARIE-HELENE DASTE

1 Jean-Paul Jouvet was not to be born until July 1917; he did not pursue a theatrical career.

SELECT BIBLIOGRAPHY

All works cited published in Paris unless otherwise indicated.

WORKS BY COPEAU

Plays

La Maison natale, 3 acts, Coll. 'Répertoire du Vieux Colombier', no. 19, Editions de la NRF, 1923. Première at Vieux Colombier, 18 December 1923.

Translation by Ralph Roeder, *The House into which we are born*, 3 acts, New York, Theatre Arts Inc., 1924. Première by Cornell Dramatic Club, Ithaca, N.Y., 1925.

Le Petit Pauvre, 6 acts, Gallimard, 1946. Radio adaptation, 1975; provincial tour by Compagnie Djamel Guesmi, 1988–9.

Translation by G. Manacorda, *Il poverello. Francesco d'Assisi*, 6 acts, Florence, Sansoni, 1950. Première by Istituto del Dramma Popolare, San Miniato, 15 August 1950.

Translation by Beverly Thurman, *The Little Poor Man*, 6 acts, New York, Hill & Wang, 1962. Unperformed.

Twelve unpublished plays; nine manuscripts (some incomplete), in Fonds Copeau, Bibliothèque de l'Arsenal.

Play translations and adaptations

Les Frères Karamazov, 5 acts, from Dostoevsky's novel, in collaboration with Jean Croué. Editions de la NRF, 1911. Première at Théâtre des Arts, 6 April 1911.

Translation by Rosalind Ivan, *The Brothers Karamazov*, 5 acts, New York, Doubleday Page, 1927 Première by Theatre Guild, 3 January 1927.

Impromptu du Vieux Colombier, 1 act, Paris–New York, Gallimard, 1917. Première at Vieux Colombier, New York, 27 November 1917.

Une Femme tuée par la douceur, 5 acts, from Thomas Heywood, *A Woman Killed with Kindness*, Coll. 'Répertoire du Vieux Colombier', no. 23, Editions de la NRF, 1924. Première at Vieux Colombier, 22 October 1913.

Le Conte d'hiver, 5 acts, in collaboration with Suzanne Bing, from Shakespeare's *Winter's Tale*. Coll. 'Répertoire du Vieux Colombier', no. 20, Editions de la NRF, 1924. Première at Vieux Colombier, 10 February 1920.

Les Tragédies, of Shakespeare, in collaboration with Suzanne Bing, 5 vols, Union Latine d'Editions, 1939.

Le Miracle du pain doré, 1 act, from fourteenth-century Miracle, *Pierre le Changeur*. *Marchand*, in *Nos Spectacles*, nos 49–50 (May–August) 1956: 84–135. Première at Hospices de Beaune, 21–2 July 1943.

Les Comédies, of Shakespeare, in collaboration with Suzanne Bing, 7 vols, Union Latine d'Editions, 1952.

Six unpublished plays for 'Les Copiaus', 1925–7; manuscripts in Fonds Copeau.

Prefaces and notices

Les Fratellini. Histoire de trois clowns, by Pierre Mariel, Société Anonyme d'Editions, 1923.

Oeuvres complètes, of Molière, 10 vols, La Cité des Livres, 1926–9.

Paradoxe sur le Comédien, by Diderot, Plon, 1929.

Comédies et proverbes, by Alfred de Musset, 2 vols, La Cité des Livres, 1931.

La Tempête, of Shakespeare, translated by P. L. Matthey, Correa, 1931.

Ma Vie dans l'art, by Constantin Stanislavsky, translated by Nina Gourfinkel and Léon Chancerel, Editions Albert, 1934.

Molière, 4 vols, Lyons, IAC 1943–4.

Théâtre complet, of André Obey (undated, unpublished).

Reviews and articles on theatre, art and literature (1901–40)

in: *La Revue d'Art Dramatique, L'Ermitage, Les Essais, Le Théâtre, La Grande Revue, La Nouvelle Revue Francaise, Les Nouvelles Littéraires, La Nación* (Buenos Aires), *Comedia, L'Art Décoratif, Art et Décoration, Le Figaro, Encyclopédie Française,* etc.

Books and brochures

Les Amis du Vieux Colombier, Cahier 1, Editions de la NRF, (November 1920).

L'Ecole du Vieux Colombier, Cahier 2, Editions de la NRF, (November 1921).

Critiques d'un autre temps, Editions de la NRF, 1923.

Souvenirs du Vieux Colombier, Nouvelles Editions Latines, 1931.

Le Théâtre Populaire, Presses Universitaires Françaises, 1941.

Notes sur le métier de comédien, Editions Michel Brient, 1955. Preface by Michel Saint-Denis.

Le Journal de bord des Copiaus, (1924–9), by Suzanne Bing, Copeau and Léon Chancerel, edited by Denis Gontard, Seghers, 1974.

Registres I. Appels, edited by Marie-Hélène Dasté and Suzanne Maistre Saint-Denis, Gallimard, 1974.

Registres II. Molière, edited by André Cabanis, Gallimard, 1976.

Registres III. Les Registres du Vieux Colombier I, edited by Marie-Hélène Dasté and Suzanne Maistre Saint-Denis, Gallimard, 1979.

Registres IV. Les Registres du Vieux Colombier II. America, edited by Marie-Hélène Dasté and Suzanne Maistre Saint-Denis, Gallimard, 1984.

Correspondence

Claudel homme de théâtre. Correspondance avec Copeau, Dullin, Jouvet, edited by H. Micciollo, J. Petit, Cahiers Paul Claudel, 6, Gallimard, 1966.

Correspondance Jacques Copeau–Roger Martin du Gard, edited by C. Sicard, 2 vols, Gallimard, 1972.

Correspondance Proust–Copeau, edited by M. Raimond, Cahiers d'inédits, 9, Editions de l'Université d'Ottawa, 1976.

Correspondance Jacques Copeau–Jules Romains, edited by O. Rony, Cahiers Jules Romains, 2, Flammarion, 1978.

Le Dialogue entre Jacques Rivière et Jacques Copeau, edited by H. T. Naughton, Bulletin des Amis de Jacques Rivière et d'Alain-Fournier, nos 26, 27, 29, 1982–3.

'Note e documenti sulla *Santa Uliva* di Jacques Copeau (1932–1933)', by Maria Ines Aliverti, in *Teatro Archivio*, 6, Rome (June) 1982: 12–103. Correspondence with Silvio d'Amico.

Correspondance André Gide–Jacques Copeau, edited by J. Claude, Cahiers André Gide, nos 12,13, 1987–8.

Unpublished letters with some 200 correspondents in the Fonds Copeau and Collection of Marie-Hélène Dasté, notably: Adolphe Appia, André Barsacq, Léon Chancerel, Edward Gordon Craig, Charles Dullin, Waldo Frank, Gaston Gallimard, Harley Granville Barker, Louis Jouvet, André Obey, Michel Saint-Denis, Jean Schlumberger, André Suarès, Valentine Tessier.

Unpublished writings

Journal (1890–1949)
'La Comédie improvisée' (1916), 80 typed pages
'Ecole du Vieux Colombier' (1915–20), 205 typed pages
'L'Art du théâtre' (1916), 78 typed pages.

Anthology

II luogo del teatro, edited by Maria Ines Aliverti, Florence, La Casa Usher, 1988.

WORKS ON COPEAU

Books

Anders, France, *Jacques Copeau et le Cartel des Quatre*, Nizet, 1959.

Borgal, Clément, *Jacques Copeau*, l'Arche, 1960.

Jacques Copeau et le Vieux Colombier, Catalogue for exhibition at Bibliothèque Nationale, 1963.

Doisy, Marcel, *Jacques Copeau ou l'Absolu dans l'art*, Le Cercle du Livre, 1954.

Frank, Waldo, *The Art of the Vieux Colombier*, Paris–New York, Editions de la NRF, 1918; reprinted in his *Salvos*, New York, Boni & Liveright, 1924.

Kurtz, Maurice, *Jacques Copeau. Biographie d'un théâtre*, Nagel, 1950.

Lerminier, Georges, *Jacques Copeau, le Réformateur* PLF, 1953.

Levaux, Léopold, *Jacques Copeau*, Louvain–Paris, Rex, 1933.

Mahn, Berthold, *Souvenirs du Vieux Colombier*, 55 sketches, text by Jules Romains, Aveline, 1926.

Paul, Norman H., *Bibliographie Jacques Copeau*, Société les Belles Lettres, 1979.

Rudlin, John, *Jacques Copeau*, Cambridge University Press, 1986.

Articles and parts of books

'Jacques Copeau. Notes biographiques et bibliographiques', *Revue d'Histoire du Théâtre*, I, 1950: 7–50.

'Hommage à Jacques Copeau', *Revue d'Histoire du Théâtre*, 4, 1963: 353–404.

'Jacques Copeau. 1879–1979', *Revue d'Histoire du Théâtre*, 1, 1983: 1–138.

'Jacques Copeau', *Théâtre en Europe*, 9 (January) 1986: 1–36.

d'Amico, Silvio, 'The Play of St Uliva', *Theatre Arts Monthly*, New York (September) 1983: 680–5.

Barsacq, André, 'L'Expérience de trois mises en scène de plein air', in *Architecture et Dramaturgie*, by André Villiers, Flammarion, 1950, pp. 169–86.

Bentley, Eric, 'Copeau and the Chimera', in his *In Search of Theatre*, New York, Knopf, 1953, pp. 242–9.

Bradby, David, *Modern French Drama. 1940–1980*, Cambridge University Press, 1984.

Cheney, Sheldon, 'At the Théâtre du Vieux Colombier', *Theatre Arts Magazine*, II, 2 (February) 1918: 2.

Chiari, Joseph, 'Jacques Copeau', in his *Contemporary French Theatre*, London, Rockliff, 1958, pp. 85–94.

Corbin, John, 'Molière Reborn', *New York Times*, 2 December 1917.

Corbin, John, 'The Vieux Colombier', *New York Times*, 23 December 1917.

Corbin, John, 'Another Year of the Vieux Colombier', *New York Times*, 10 March 1918.

Corbin, John, 'Does Society Shun High Art?', *The Theatre*, New York, (June) 1919: 334.

Dasté, Jean, *Voyage d'un comédien*, Stock, 1977.

Dasté, Jean, *Qui êtes-vous?* Lyons, La Manufacture, 1987.

Decroux, Etienne, *Paroles sur le mime*, Gallimard, 1963.

Defoe, Louis V., 'Plays That Die of Talk', *New York World*, 13 January 1918.

Dhomme, Sylvain, *La Mise en scène d'Antoine à Brecht*, F. Nathan, 1959.

Dorcy, Jean, *The Mime*, New York, R. Speller & Sons, 1961.

Dullin, Charles, *Souvenirs et notes de travail d'un acteur*, Odette Lieutier, 1946.

Eliot, Samuel A. Jr, 'Le Théâtre du Vieux Colombier', *Theatre Arts Magazine*, III, 1 (January) 1919: 25–30.

Frank, Waldo, 'Copeau Begins Again', *Theatre Arts Monthly*, IX, 9 (September) 1925: 584–90.

Frank, Waldo, *Our America*, New York, Boni & Liveright, 1919.

Ghéon, Henri, 'La Sincérité dans la mise en scène', *La Nouvelle Revue Française*, January 1920: 105–10.

Ghéon, Henri, *The Art of the Theatre*, Introduction by Michel Saint-Denis, New York, Hill & Wang, 1961.

Granville Barker, Harley, 'A Letter to M. Copeau', *The Observer*, London, 1 September 1929.

Guicharnaud, Jacques, *Modern French Theatre from Giraudoux to Beckett*, Yale University Press, 1961.

Hamilton, Clayton, *Seen on the Stage*, New York, Holt 1920.

Harrop, John, 'A Constructive Promise: Jacques Copeau in New York', *Theatre Survey*, XII, 2 November 1971: 104–18.

Katz, Alfred M., 'The Genesis of the Viéux Colombier', *Educational Theatre Journal*, XXIX December 1967: 433–46.

Katz, Alfred M., 'Jacques Copeau. The American Reaction', *Players' Magazine*, New York, 45, 3 (February–March) 1970: 133–43.

Katz, Alfred M., 'Copeau as *Régisseur*: An Analysis', *Educational Theatre Journal*, XXV May 1973: 160–72.

Kusler Leigh, Barbara, 'Jacques Copeau's School for Actors', *Mime Journal*, nos. 9–10, Allendale, Mich., 1979: 4–75.

Lefèvre, Frédéric, 'An Hour with Jacques Copeau', *The Living Age*, Boston, 15 April 1927.

MacGowan, Kenneth and R. E. Jones, *Continental Stagecraft*, New York, Harcourt Brace, 1922.

Mambrino, Jean, 'The Solitude of Jacques Copeau', *The Dublin Review*, 452, 1951: 83–112.

Moderwell, Hiram K., 'Jacques Copeau: Personality and Pioneer', *Boston Evening Transcript*, 24 February 1917.

Moderwell, Hiram K., 'At Last for America a Truly French Stage', *Boston Evening Transcript*, 28 November 1917.

Nathan, George Jean, *The Popular Theatre*, New York, Knopf, 1918, p. 67–79.

Parker, H. T., 'Copeau Departs', *Boston Evening Transcript*, 9 April 1919.

Paul, Norman H., 'Jacques Copeau Looks at the American Stage, 1917–1919', *Educational Theatre Journal*, XXIX, 1 (March) 1977: 61–9.

Paul, Norman H., 'Jacques Copeau, Drama Critic', *Theatre Research International*, II, 3 (May) 1977: 221–9.

Paul, Norman H., 'Paul Claudel et Jacques Copeau', *Claudel Studies*, University of Dallas, XIII, 1, 1986: 31–9.

Raymond, Antonin, 'The Théâtre du Vieux Colombier in New York', *Journal of the American Institute of Architects*, V, 8 (August) 1917: 384–7.

Raymond, Marcel, *Le Jeu retrouvé*, Montreal, l'Arbre, 1943.

Roché, Henri-Pierre. 'Arch-Rebel of French Theatre Coming Here', *New York Times*, 28 January 1917.

Roose-Evans, James, *Experimental Theatre*, New York, Universe Books, 1984.

Saint-Denis, Michel, *Theatre. The Rediscovery of Style*, New York, Theatre Arts Books, 1960.

Saint-Denis, Michel, *Training for the Theatre*, New York, Theatre Arts Books, 1982.

Saint-Denis, Michel, 'The Modern Theatre's Debt to Copeau', *The Listener*, London, 16 February 1950.

Schlumberger, Jean, *Eveils*, Gallimard, 1950.

Slaughter, Helena T., 'Jacques Copeau, Metteur en scène de Shakespeare et des Elisabéthains', *Etudes Anglaises*, XIII, 2 (April–June) 1960: 176–91.

Spiers, A. G. H., 'Modern Stage Settings', *The Nation*, New York 27 December 1917: 726–8.

Strehler, Giorgio, *Un Théatre pour la vie*, Fayard, 1980.

Veinstein, André, *Du Théâtre Libre au Théâtre Louis Jouvet*, Librairie Théâtrale, 1955.

Wardle, Irving, 'The Mystery of Jacques Copeau', *The Times Saturday Review*, London, 10 May 1969.

Whitton, David, *Stage Directors in Modern France*, Manchester University Press, 1987.

Index

INDEX